ENCYCLOPEDIA OF
FAMILY HEALTH

ENCYCLOPEDIA OF

FAMILY HEALTH

CONSULTANT

DAVID B. JACOBY, MD

JOHNS HOPKINS SCHOOL OF MEDICINE

VOLUME
14

SMOKING—SWELLINGS

MARSHALL CAVENDISH
NEW YORK · LONDON · TORONTO · SYDNEY

Marshall Cavendish Corporation

99 White Plains Road

Tarrytown, New York 10591-9001

© Marshall Cavendish Corporation, 1998

© Marshall Cavendish Limited 1998, 1991, 1988, 1986, 1983, 1982, 1971

Update by Brown Partworks

The material in this set was first published in the English language by

Marshall Cavendish Limited of 119 Wardour Street, London W1V 3TD, England.

Printed and bound in Italy

Library of Congress Cataloging-in-Publication Data

Encyclopedia of family health
17v. cm.
Includes index
1. Medicine, Popular-Encyclopedias. 2. Health-Encyclopedias. I. Marshall Cavendish Corporation.
RC81.A2M336 1998   96-49537
610'. 3-dc21   CIP
ISBN 0-7614-0625-5 (set)
ISBN 0-7614-0639-5 (v.14)

INTRODUCTION

We Americans live under a constant bombardment of information (and misinformation) about the latest supposed threats to our health. We are taught to believe that disease is the result of not taking care of ourselves. Death becomes optional. Preventive medicine becomes a moral crusade, illness the punishment for the foolish excesses of the American lifestyle. It is not the intent of the authors of this encyclopedia to contribute to this atmosphere. While it is undoubtedly true that Americans could improve their health by smoking less, exercising more, and controlling their weight, this is already widely understood.

As Mencken put it, "It is not the aim of medicine to make men virtuous. The physician should not preach salvation, he should offer absolution." The aims of this encyclopedia are to present a summary of human biology, anatomy, and physiology, to outline the more common diseases, and to discuss, in a general way, the diagnosis and treatment of these diseases. This is not a do-it-yourself book. It will not be possible to treat most conditions based on the information presented here. But it will be possible to understand most diseases and their treatments. Informed in this way, you will be able to discuss your condition and its treatment with your physician. It is also hoped that this will alleviate some of the fears associated with diseases, doctors, and hospitals.

The authors of this encyclopedia have also attempted to present, in an open-minded way, alternative therapies. There is undoubtedly value to some of these. However, when dealing with serious diseases, they should not be viewed as a substitute for conventional treatment. The reason that conventional treatment is accepted is that it has been systematically tested, and because scientific evidence backs it up. It would be a tragedy to miss the opportunity for effective treatment while pursuing an ineffective alternative therapy.

Finally, it should be remembered that the word *doctor* is originally from the Latin word for "teacher." Applied to medicine, this should remind us that the doctor's duty is not only to diagnose and treat disease, but to help the patient to understand. If this encyclopedia can aid in this process, its authors will be gratified.

DAVID B. JACOBY, MD
JOHNS HOPKINS SCHOOL OF MEDICINE

CONTENTS

Smoking

Q Are nicotine chewing gum or patches of any real help in trying to give up smoking?

A Yes. Reliable trials have shown that nicotine chewing gum or transdermal patches do reduce the craving for a cigarette, which in itself is distressing, and which is sometimes a cause of failure in the first weeks of trying to give up smoking. They are effective antismoking aids worth trying.

Q Despite many attempts, I have not been able to give up smoking. Can I do anything to reduce the risk of getting a smoking-related disease?

A Yes, there are several things that are worth doing. First, deliberately move down the scale of tar content step by step from high, to middle to high, to middle, and so on until you are smoking low-tar cigarettes. Second, use filter-tipped cigarettes, the benefit is not dramatic but it's enough to make some difference. Third, try not to inhale. Even though some of the nicotine is absorbed through the mouth and throat there are still substantial advantages. Try to smoke less by gradually increasing the interval between cigarettes, leaving very long stubs, taking the cigarette out of your mouth between puffs and increase the interval between each puff. However, if you really can't give up altogether you would be much better off smoking cigars or a pipe.

Q My five-year-old daughter has asthma. I smoked very heavily during pregnancy. Could this have caused her condition?

A There is no longer any doubt that the children of mothers who smoke during pregnancy do have substantial disadvantages. In particular, they have a generally lower level of resistance that makes them more likely to get infectious diseases, and they are usually slower to develop both physically and mentally. However, there is no evidence that the presence of asthma in young children can be attributed to the mother smoking when pregnant.

The phrase dying for a cigarette is brutally apt. Fatal smoking-related diseases constitute a genuine epidemic and, unusually, it is one that is solely in the hands of the potential victims to wipe out.

Smoking the dried leaves of the tobacco plant in the form of cigarettes, cigars, or in pipes was introduced into England around the middle of the 16th century by explorers and adventurers who had found the practice established in the New World. Consumption of tobacco in industrialized countries continued to increase until 1973, and then began to fall, but it remains among the most common habits in the Western world. Unfortunately it is an extremely dangerous habit with no less than lethal consequences for a very large proportion of those who indulge in it. And it is a very hard one to break.

Why do people smoke?

People smoke for a wide variety of reasons. Once they have smoked their first few experimental cigarettes, which can cause coughing, nausea, and sometimes vomiting, most smokers get pleasure from the taste and aroma of tobacco and tobacco smoke. They may also get pleasure from the whole ritual of lighting up: from handling cigarettes, a lighter or matches; from the action of inhaling; and from watching the smoke curl upward.

Smokers make two claims for their habit. First, that smoking sedates them, or settles their nerves, when they need sedating. Second, that it acts as a stimulant when they need to work. Evidence has shown that these effects are due to nicotine and that both these claims are true, depending on the dose, on what the smoker is doing, and on his or her particular psychological and physical makeup (see Sedatives, and Stimulants).

There may be a true physical addiction to nicotine so that when deprived of the drug the person concerned suffers from unpleasant physical withdrawal symptoms which are only relieved by a further dose (see Nicotine).

Dependence on smoking may be psychological as well as physical; the smoker misses whatever they get from smoking but does not really need it. Often, too, smoking has become such an ingrained habit that the smoker has a cigarette almost without knowing it.

Some people smoke because they associate smoking with being sociable. To offer and to take cigarettes establishes a bond between people. To the shy and introverted, it offers something for them to do with their hands and makes them appear self-confident. The smoker may smoke as much to be one of the company, as to get any pleasure from it. The pleasure comes from being with others and not from the cigarette.

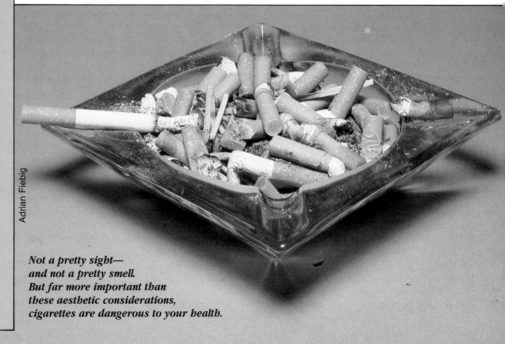

Adrian Fiebig

*Not a pretty sight—
and not a pretty smell.
But far more important than
these aesthetic considerations,
cigarettes are dangerous to your health.*

The glamorous image that smoking developed in film and fashion (above and above right) concealed the cost in health. Humphrey Bogart died from throat cancer.

The climate of opinion in which we live is an important factor in determining smoking, and over the last few years much has been done to try and discourage smokers. In more and more countries, smoking is now banned in public places such as movie theaters and subways. Many restaurants, bars, and places of work have taken a no-smoking policy and it is no longer assumed that we all wish to be in smoke-filled environments.

Some US states are now pressing, and winning, claims for damages against the tobacco industry (which is worth millions of dollars) in order to finance the growing costs of health care resulting from smoking-related diseases.

Factors in starting smoking

There are strong connections between children smoking and the smoking habits of their parents and older brothers and sisters. This is not surprising when the strength of family bonds and the desire of small children to be like their elders is taken into account. Children in the early years at school usually disapprove of the tobacco habit intensely. By the early teens, however, they are ready to try such things out, and this is because of the strong identification formed at an earlier stage between drinking and smoking and being and acting grown up.

What's wrong with smoking?

In Britain, shortly after the end of World War II, Professor A. Bradford Hill and Dr. Richard Doll published the first of a series of papers leading to the inescapable conclusion that cigarette smoking was the major factor in the rising incidence of lung cancer (see Cancer, and Lung and lung diseases). They began with a retrospective study, in which they investigated a large number of patients with cancer of the lung and compared them with a carefully matched control group that did not have this form of cancer. After comparing a number of factors that might have a bearing on the cause of this disease, the only great difference to emerge was that the smoking habits of the two groups varied.

Only one in 200 male lung cancer patients were nonsmokers, indicating smoking as the cause. The same type of statistics appeared among studies of women. Furthermore, there appeared to be a relationship between the risk of someone getting lung cancer and the number of cigarettes they smoked.

In the past, cigarette advertisers freely promoted the image of smoking as being sophisticated, and even, by associating it with the rigors of outdoor life, healthy. Now that there is cast-iron proof of the risks smokers run, and strict curbs have been placed on cigarette advertising, things are not so simple for the tobacco companies. They now have to advertise their products more obliquely, and with health warnings attached that sometimes loom larger than the advertisement itself. The sponsorship of sport is one of the principal means it employs to promote its product, although there are now moves to ban the practice.

Adrian Fiebig

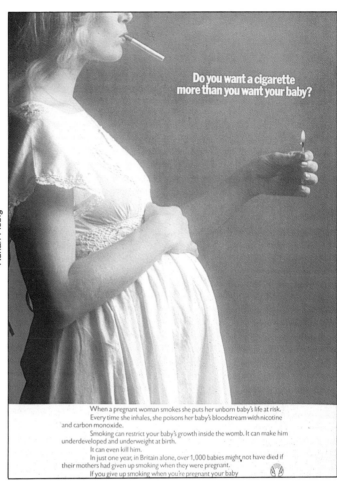

Do you want a cigarette
more than you want your baby?

When a pregnant woman smokes she puts her unborn baby's life at risk.
Every time she inhales, she poisons her baby's bloodstream with nicotine and carbon monoxide.
Smoking can restrict your baby's growth inside the womb. It can make him underdeveloped and underweight at birth.
It can even kill him.
In just one year, in Britain alone, over 1,000 babies might not have died if their mothers had given up smoking when they were pregnant.
If you give up smoking when you're pregnant your baby

Smoking is in part a social habit: the pleasure comes from relaxing in the company of others, and not just from smoking. Appealing, too, are the accoutrements of smoking found in the traditional tobacconist's. Peer groups also play a part: if your friends smoke and pressure you to, you may succumb. But as these posters clearly show, smoking is a lethal threat, not just to smokers, but also to their unborn children.

Zefa

The problem with this kind of retrospective investigation is that a person's memory, especially if they are sick, is inclined to be faulty. Bradford Hill and Doll therefore set up an investigation that would study the prospective health of smokers. They had 25,000 British doctors give details of their smoking habits as

No wonder smokers cough.

The tar and discharge that collects in the lungs of an average smoker.

The Health Education Council
Helping you to better health

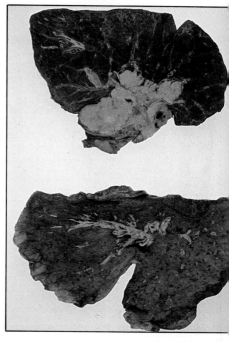

Q How efficient are filters in actually removing the harmful substances from cigarette smoke?

A Putting a filter on the cigarette certainly reduces the tar and nicotine levels your body absorbs. In addition, there is evidence that people who smoke filter-tipped cigarettes are at less risk of getting lung cancer. So there certainly is some advantage. However, the benefit is certainly not so great that it is safe to smoke filter cigarettes. Probably the best that can be said for them is that if you cannot give up altogether, they are a little less dangerous than nonfilter brands.

Q Why do doctors tell you that if you must smoke, smoke only the first half of the cigarette?

A For two reasons. The first is that the tar concentration in the bottom half of the cigarette, and particularly in the stub, is very much greater than in the top half. If you smoke only the top half of the cigarette, or at least leave a long stub, you are doing yourself a big favor. The second reason is that any change in your habit which has the effect of decreasing the total amount that you actually smoke will benefit you by a similar amount. That is why those who have not been able to give up are strongly encouraged to at least try to make do with only half a cigarette at a time.

Q I stopped smoking five years ago. Will my lungs have returned to a normally healthy state?

A That really depends on how long and how heavily you smoked before you gave up the habit. What is certain is that further damage to your lungs—and other parts of your body—stops from the time you give it up. It is clear that there is a definite improvement in lung capacity and your chances of getting either lung cancer or bronchitis drop dramatically. After 12 to 15 years of not smoking, the risk of contracting lung cancer is about the same as if you had never smoked at all.

well as a variety of other relevant information. All the doctors were apparently well and had no reason to lie, and gave details of present smoking habits rather than the sometimes faulty recollections of past smoking.

As the years passed, some of these doctors died; Doll and Bradford Hill investigated the cause of death in each case. Some of the deaths were from lung cancer and two facts emerged quite clearly. First, there was a very clear relationship between cigarette smoking and lung cancer. Second, the chances of dying from the disease increased with increasing cigarette consumption.

Since then a mass of evidence confirming these results has poured in from all over the world. It also soon became clear that cigarette smoking was an important factor in causing other diseases, of which the most important are chronic bronchitis (see Bronchitis) and coronary heart disease (see Heart disease). The end result was the demonstration of two important facts: first, cigarette smokers live, on average, shorter lives than nonsmokers, and second, that giving up smoking removes this excess risk in proportion to the amount of time that has elapsed since giving up.

In addition to the main diseases already mentioned above, there is evidence that

The large, visible mass of white tissue is a cancer in the lung of a smoker (top). The lung beneath it is healthy and free from this deadly disease. A survey carried out in the late 1960s revealed that the death rate from lung cancer had risen dramatically since the 1930s. The overriding factor causing the total number of deaths from cancer to be so high was the incidence of cancer of the lung.

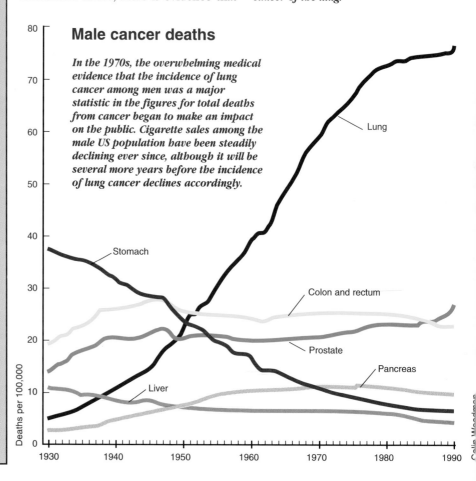

Male cancer deaths

In the 1970s, the overwhelming medical evidence that the incidence of lung cancer among men was a major statistic in the figures for total deaths from cancer began to make an impact on the public. Cigarette sales among the male US population have been steadily declining ever since, although it will be several more years before the incidence of lung cancer declines accordingly.

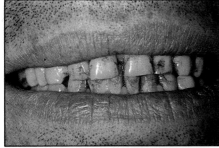
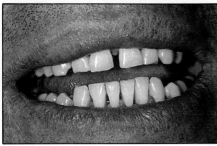
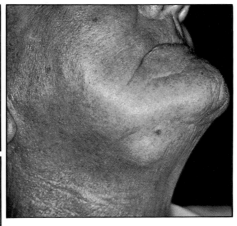

Nicotine badly stains the teeth, but if you stop smoking, your teeth can once again be sparkling clean (left). No such simple treatment is possible when you have a smoking-related cancer of the jaw (above).

cigarette smoking can cause other types of pulmonary disorders (see Pulmonary disorders), delays the healing of gastric ulcers (see Ulcers), plays a major role in the cause of various cancers of the mouth, voice box, esophagus, and bladder, and leads to a degree of skin wrinkling appropriate to nonsmokers who are 20 years older (see Wrinkles).

There are other factors about smoking that are worth knowing. Among nonsmokers, only about one in five will not reach retirement age; but for smokers of over 25 cigarettes a day, two in five will not reach retirement age. The death rate for smokers is much higher among those who inhale than among those who do not; the earlier you start smoking the greater the risk; and the more you smoke the greater the risk. According to findings in the US, the use of filter-tipped cigarettes does slightly reduce the risk of lung cancer. The risk of pipe (only) and cigar (only) smokers getting lung cancer is small, provided they don't inhale, although it is greater than for nonsmokers.

Effects on nonsmokers
There is an increasing amount of evidence that the smoke inhaled by nonsmokers is harmful to their health. It has been shown that the smoke drifting up from the burning end of the cigarette contains twice as much tar and nicotine as that inhaled by the smoker, and also that the carbon monoxide level in the blood of nonsmokers in a smoke-filled room also rises.

Concern about the effects of second-hand smoke and the rights of nonsmokers has led to changes in attitudes and even in the law in some cases. Nonsmoking areas are now common in public places and at work, and many theaters, restaurants, and public transport facilities ban smoking altogether.

There is also an increasing awareness about the risks to the unborn baby if women smoke during pregnancy (see Pregnancy). Smoking mothers have higher rates of miscarriages, stillbirths (see Stillbirth), and infant deaths than nonsmoking mothers.

How to stop smoking
Giving up isn't easy. There are no miracle cures, no magic methods, no shortcuts, and no foolproof formulas. Nevertheless it is a battle that can be won; several million people stop smoking every year.

Courage comes first. It is going to hurt. Giving up something that you enjoy and have come to rely on is painful. The temptation to have just one cigarette, especially if you are stressed, is extremely difficult to resist. But standing up to that cigarette is crucial. Many people have given up smoking time and again. It takes courage not to remain one of them.

Determination comes next. A half-hearted attempt, or a strategy based on gradual cutting down, is almost certain to fail. It is almost better not to make the attempt until you have firmly decided that you are finally going to kick the habit. Plan your campaign, and stick to it. Beware of the times and places when you most enjoyed smoking and break those routines if necessary.

The first day without is just the beginning; for many people it can take three or four weeks, or longer, before quitting is no longer a struggle.

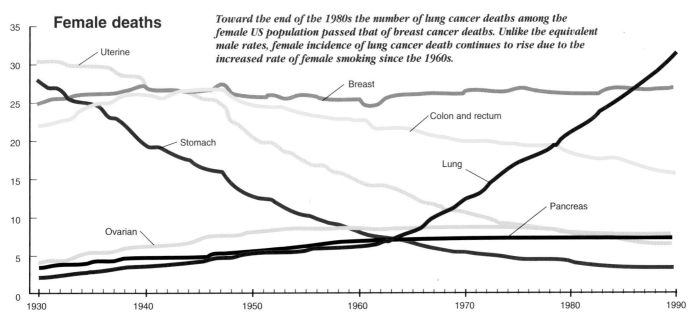

Female deaths

Toward the end of the 1980s the number of lung cancer deaths among the female US population passed that of breast cancer deaths. Unlike the equivalent male rates, female incidence of lung cancer death continues to rise due to the increased rate of female smoking since the 1960s.

Snakebite

Q What is the world's most dangerous venomous snake?

A If the toxicity of the venom was the only criterion, there is little doubt that the sea snake would have pride of place. But other factors have to be taken into account in conjunction with toxicity: the snake's efficiency in injecting venom, its willingness to attack, and its accessibility to man, for example. Thus sea snakes, which are dangerous only to barefooted fishermen, come far down the danger scale. Probably the most dangerous snake is the cobra, which is highly venomous, aggressive, and widespread across Africa and Asia.

Q Is it true that some snakes can spit venom?

A Yes, the Egyptian cobra and the spitting cobra are notorious for their habit of spitting venom when aroused. Venom can be forced out by the fangs to a distance of several feet. If it strikes an enemy in the eye, temporary or sometimes permanent blindness can result unless the area is washed promptly and thoroughly.

Q I've heard that if antisnakebite serum is not available, sucking at the wound and applying a tight tourniquet is effective. Is this true?

A This is the subject of much controversy. This form of treatment is often featured in adventure fiction, but current medical opinion suggests that it could actually be dangerous. It is better to put a firm bandage above the site of the bite: this may reduce the spread of the venom and enhance the effect of antivenin at a later stage.

Q Is antivenin widely available in the US?

A It is unlikely that there will be stocks of antivenin in every hospital, but each emergency room personnel will know where to obtain it and when necessary it can be supplied very speedily.

The prospect of being attacked by a venomous snake will send shivers down the bravest spine. However, antivenins have been developed to counteract the bite of even the most poisonous species.

Stephen Dalton/Oxford Scientific Films

The western diamondback rattlesnake, found in the United States from Texas to California, is extremely dangerous—not only because of the toxicity of its venom, but also because of its aggressiveness and speed. Fortunately, thanks to improved methods of treatment, fatalities are rare.

Snakes have always filled human beings with feelings of fear and revulsion. A misconception that dies hard is that all snakes are dangerous. In fact, species that are actually venomous form a very small part of the snake population.

In the United States deaths from snakebite are extremely rare. There are roughly 7,000 snakebites per year, leading to only fifteen deaths. Almost 3,000 of this total of snakebites occur in people handling the snakes. The chance of surviving a venomous snakebite is thus about 99.8 percent. Deaths are far more common, however, in less developed countries. It has been estimated that between 30,000 and 40,000 people die worldwide from snakebites each year, 75 percent of them in India. Myanmar (formerly Burma) has the highest mortality rate of 15.4 deaths per 100,000 population per annum (see Bites and stings).

Venomous snakes

Venomous snakes are characterized by the structure of their fangs. For example, the African boomslang has fangs at the back of the mouth, each bearing a groove down which venom flows. The cobra has fangs at the front of the mouth, again grooved. Rattlesnakes and vipers have the most sophisticated biting apparatus: their fangs are hinged, and, when not in use,

fold back along the roof of the mouth. The toxicity of snake venom varies considerably. The world's most venomous snakes are the sea snakes (*Hydrophidae*), which have a venom one hundred times as powerful as that of the king cobra, whose poison can kill an adult in minutes if it strikes at the face.

The amount of venom injected by a particular snake during an attack is also important. Thus cobra venom is five times more powerful than viper venom, but vipers have a far more efficient injection apparatus than cobras, notwithstanding the latter's awesome and well-deserved reputation. In addition, a lot depends on the habits of the snake and the vulnerability of its victim: for example, the cobra is very alert and is found in areas where many people go about barefoot, making the snake doubly dangerous. Vipers, on the other hand, are sluggish and thus easily trodden on, so the majority of attacks are the result of carelessness on the part of the walker.

Animals, particularly horses, are injected with venom, and their blood is then used to make antivenom serum. When a snake strikes, its fangs leave characteristic puncture marks in the skin (inset right). The process of extracting venom (inset far right) is called milking.

Symptoms

The action of snake venom depends on the species. Generally speaking, the venom may affect the body in one of three ways: it may cause hemorrhage (see Hemorrhage), clotting, or inhibition of clotting, or tissue damage; it may affect the central nervous system or the heart; or it may release histamine and bradykinin from the tissues, causing pain or swelling.

The main effect of viper venom is to disturb the action of the blood, often stopping it from clotting. There will be pain and swelling and in some cases tissue will be lost at the site of the bite.

Cobra venom, on the other hand, is neurotoxic; it attacks the nervous system, causing paralysis (see Paralysis), especially of the respiratory system, and failure of the swallowing mechanism.

Sea snakes inject an extremely powerful venom that actually breaks down the muscle tissues in the body, and causes the body's vital organs, such as the kidneys, to fail (see Kidneys and kidney diseases). Remember, however, that an attack by a snake is usually a defensive measure and that in roughly 50 percent of cases little or no venom is injected.

Treatment

The development of antisnakebite serum (antivenin), which can be injected intravenously or intramuscularly, has made treating snakebite much easier than it used to be, providing that the serum is administered in reasonable time.

Sera are made by injecting animals with small amounts of venom until they build up antibodies to the poison. The serum derived from the animals' blood will thus contain these antibodies, and can be used to combat the effects of the bite in human beings. However, since antivenins are blood from a foreign species, they are likely to cause a reaction in the host and other drugs need to be given to cover the injection (Epinephrine or steroids, for example). Because of this danger, doctors use antivenom serum only with discretion (see Steroids).

Almost inevitably, however, there will be a time lag between the snakebite and the administration of the necessary

The cobra (below left) is revered in some parts of the East and feared universally. The sea snake (below center) is the world's most venomous snake. However, it is limited to the seas in the Far East and Australasia. The deadly Pope's pit viper (below right) is found only in Asia: its venom acts on both the blood and the muscles.

antivenin. However, for the great majority of bites by poisonous snakes there are a number of first-aid measures that can be taken. Most important, the patient should be reassured: fright is often the major symptom. The bitten limb should be immobilized and a firm bandage applied, and the patient should be taken to the hospital, along with the body of the snake for identification, if possible.

Do not cut into the bite under any circumstances, or suck the wound to extract the venom: either practice may do more harm than good.

Sneezing

Q I used to sneeze a lot and have a permanently blocked nose, but I found that using a spray I bought from the drugstore helped. I now find I have to use it in increasing amounts to obtain relief. Is it safe to continue?

A You should see your doctor. Many people unwittingly cause permanent damage to the lining of the nose with these preparations, which tend gradually to lose their effectiveness. Your doctor will be able to give you a prescription for a medication which does not damage the nose, or send you to an ear, nose, and throat specialist.

Q I was told that your heart misses a beat when you sneeze. Is this true?

A Not entirely. When you breathe in your heart speeds up and when you breathe out it slows down. The more pronounced the inspiration and expiration, the more your heart speeds up or slows down. Sneezing involves deep inspiration and expiration, therefore, your heart rate may be markedly affected by it. This is of no consequence to your health and is a normal phenomenon called sinus arrhythmia.

Q I heard recently that a girl who couldn't stop sneezing was sent to Switzerland. What was the reason for this?

A Mountain air is free from allergens so that patients with allergic rhinitis may improve in this environment. Sea air may have a similar effect.

Q I have hay fever for which I take antihistamines. They relieve the condition but I have been told it is dangerous to drive at the same time as taking them. Is this so?

A No, unless these tablets make you sleepy. If this is the case you should reduce the dose or ask your doctor to prescribe a nonsedative preparation. Alcohol also enhances the sedative effects of antihistamines.

Like so many of our reflexes, sneezing is an important mechanism designed to protect the body. It may, however, sometimes be a sign of an abnormal state needing investigation and suitable treatment.

Ron Sutherland

The prime function of the nose is to clean up inspired air—the air we breathe in. The structure of the nose is dictated by this function (see Breathing).

There is a coarse sieve of hairs within the nostrils, called the nasal vibrissae, and a finer sieve, the nasal mucosa, which line the nostrils with mucus. Both these filter out dust and other particles from the incoming air. The sense of smell monitors inspired air, and a reflex action, the sneeze, totally clears the nasal and mouth passages when all else fails (see Nose).

The sneezing mechanism
Sneezing is triggered by irritation of the nasal mucosa and results in a sudden, violent expulsion of expiratory gases through the nose and mouth. This outburst carries with it the irritant in the form of droplets, which may be projected up to 30 ft (9 m). During the explosive phase the eyes close reflexly.

Causes
Sneezing can be a normal reaction to irritants of the nasal mucosa, such as smoke and sudden changes in temperature or humidity. It may even follow a knock on the nose. The common cold is probably the most frequent cause of sneezing (see

Always use a handkerchief when you sneeze. A virus can travel from person to person in the droplets, which are often carried a long way by the violence of a sneeze.

Common cold), the virus and secondary bacterial infection making the nasal mucosa hypersensitive to minor stimuli.

There are, however, conditions in which the nose is irritated abnormally, or where sneezing is induced by factors which do not affect the majority of people. These include the presence of foreign bodies, and cases where the nasal lining is abnormally sensitive.

Foreign bodies
Children are frequently admitted to the hospital when objects, such as beads or peanuts, have become lodged in the nasal passages. Within a few hours the child has begun to sneeze as the foreign body irritates the nasal mucosa, secretions are trapped and infection builds up. This results in a nasal discharge containing pus (see Pus), bad breath, and sometimes intermittent nosebleeds.

Removal of these objects often requires general anesthesia. The doctor will also check that no other foreign bodies are hidden in the ears, for instance.

Allergic rhinitis

Sneezing is also part of an abnormal reaction to an inhaled substance or allergen, so called because it is allergy-producing. The most common allergens are the grass and tree pollens that are responsible for hay fever, and the droppings of the house dust mite, which are found in most houses and may cause many allergic problems (see Hay fever).

In a sensitive person antibodies are already attached to certain cells in the nasal mucosa called mast cells. When the allergen enters, the antibodies fuse with them and in so doing upset the structure of the mast cells. These then fall apart and release histamine, which is highly irritant and produces the inflammatory response.

Patients are overcome by bouts of violent sneezing, and have a profuse watery discharge and nasal obstruction. Treatment involves identification of the particular allergen so that it can be avoided or at least reduced. This is done by skin testing (see Allergies).

Three types of drug are also in use which control the patient's nasal symptoms. Antihistamines act by blocking the effect of histamine on surrounding cells. Disodium cromoglycate, taken as a spray or in drops, prevents the release of histamine from the mast cells, but only if taken in advance of an attack. Topical steroids work by suppressing the inflammatory reaction triggered by histamine release. Their activity is confined solely to the nose, and they are therefore totally safe. Where no medicine is at all effective, desensitizing injections may be needed.

Vasomotor rhinitis

A condition that produces similar symptoms to allergic rhinitis, but where there is no obvious allergen, is called vasomotor rhinitis. There are two types, one of which involves a great deal of sneezing and a watery nasal discharge.

Most cases also respond to antihistamines and topical steroids, and some may be controlled by oral decongestant preparations, which shrink and soothe the nasal lining. Sneezing and nasal secretions are thereby reduced and airflow improved. A few patients may need minor surgery to reduce the amount of nasal lining without damaging the sense of smell. This is not painful, and results can be obvious in a few weeks.

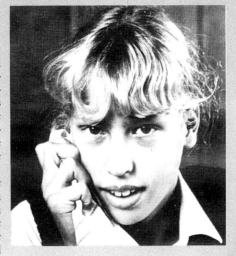

Rex Features

Peter Lea Productions

This adolescent girl was photographed while still suffering from a sneezing fit that had already lasted almost a year. She would sneeze at least once or twice every five minutes in the daytime, but was able to sleep without interruption at night. A similar case was cured at a clinic in Switzerland. The air in the Swiss mountains is virtually free from the allergens which, in a sensitive person, can cause bouts of sneezing. On the other hand, we are all likely to sneeze in an atmosphere that is heavily laden with irritants, as is likely to occur, for example, when a building is demolished.

Snoring

Q Does drinking alcohol at night make people snore?

A Alcohol does not actually trigger snoring, but what it does do, however, is make it easier to fall asleep in a position in which the sleeper breathes through his or her mouth, making snoring more likely. Alcohol (and sedatives) also cause very deep sleep: snoring may be continuous.

Q I've heard that a pregnant woman will snore, even if she has never snored before. Is this true?

A This isn't true of all pregnant women, but it does happen. One theory is that in pregnancy there is a tendency to fluid retention in the tissues, which affects the membranes in the breathing passages. They may become congested, forcing the woman to breathe through her mouth, making snoring likely.

Q When my husband starts snoring in bed I give him a push and he stops. Why is this?

A Perhaps he wakes up! More seriously, if he sleeps on his back or on his side with his head thrown back, it's possible that his position causes him to breathe through his mouth and snore. Your pushing forces him into a different position, one in which he breathes through his nose.

Q When I get hay fever I start snoring. Why is this?

A Hay fever is an allergy: a sensitivity to various kinds of pollen. It affects the mucous membranes of the nose and air passages, causing congestion and forcing you to breathe through your mouth. In sleep the muscles of your soft palate and uvula relax, and as you inhale through your mouth they vibrate noisily. The best way to stop snoring is to relieve the hay fever symptoms which are causing you to breathe through your mouth. Antihistamines will help. Sleep with your windows closed at the time you are most vulnerable to pollen.

Sleeping with your mouth open—whether it's because you have a cold or have simply fallen asleep in an uncomfortable position—may make you snore. It's a harmless phenomenon, but can be very irritating to others.

Ron Sutherland

Falling asleep in a chair is likely to cause someone to snore. The head is thrown back and the mouth opened. This makes breathing through the mouth all too easy.

Snoring, breathing heavily through the mouth with a vibrating or snorting noise when asleep, is chronic in as many as one in eight sleepers. It is a medically innocent occurrence, but at the same time few things can be quite as irritating as lying awake, listening to someone snore loudly. It's been suggested that this can cause marital disharmony, and it's no wonder, since the noise generated by the snoring partner may rival somebody speaking, and can at its worst put a pneumatic drill to shame!

What causes snoring?

Snoring is an involuntary act. The characteristic noise is created when, for some reason, the sleeper begins to breathe through his or her mouth, and the muscles of the soft palate and the uvula are allowed to relax. Thus the passage through which air passes is narrowed, and, as the sleeper inhales the air drawn into the lungs, causes the soft palate and the uvula to vibrate (see Muscles).

The quality and the intensity of the snoring will be governed by the shape of the mouth, the elasticity of the tissues, and the vigor with which the snorer inhales. Occasionally people snore so vigorously that they wake themselves up, but generally a snorer is oblivious to the noise he or she is making.

Because snoring occurs when a person sleeps with their mouth open, a blocked nose or anything obstructing the nasal airways which forces breath out through the mouth will make it far more likely. A stuffy nose because of a cold, or enlarged tonsils or adenoids may make someone likely to breathe through their mouth (see Adenoids, and Tonsils).

If the muscles of the lower jaw and palate relax in sleep, snoring may start. A person who is sitting up and falls asleep loses control over these muscles and they relax. This is why so many people snore when they fall asleep sitting up on trains or in armchairs. Similarly, people who lie on their backs when they are asleep may also be prone to snoring because the lower jaw drops and the muscles of the palate relax (see Palate).

There have been suggestions that people who are overweight are more likely to snore than their normal counterparts, though it is hard to see why this should be the case. After all, no fat is laid down in the nasal passages to cause obstruction. But it has been shown that if a snorer who is overweight loses a few pounds, there is likely to be a reduction of noise, if not a complete cessation of snoring.

Atmosphere may also have an effect. A very dry, centrally heated room can lead to snoring in a susceptible individual, as can a humid environment.

Stopping snoring

Since snoring involves breathing through the mouth in sleep, most forms of treatment to alleviate the condition aim at trying to reestablish breathing through the nose. So if someone who does not normally snore contracts a cold and is told, presumably with some irritation, that he has started snoring, all he needs to do is relieve the symptoms of the cold so that he can breathe through his nose again. In the same way, treating obstructions like enlarged adenoids in the nasal airways will relieve, if not cure, the snoring.

Unfortunately, colds and nasal obstructions account for only part of the snoring problem, and other forms of treatment have to be tried in more indeterminate cases. Some are commonsense, for example, if people snore when they are sleeping on their backs, they can be persuaded to sleep on their side, or their stomachs. There are also exercises designed to keep the mouth closed while the snorer is asleep, for example clenching the teeth for 10 minutes or so before retiring, and these have often proved successful.

A more modern suggestion for helping persistent snorers involves using a cervical collar—the same type that is used for treating a sprained neck—when going to bed. The rationale is justifiable: snoring is often at its worst when the sufferer is lying on his or her back with the head sagging on the chest. The cervical collar will keep the chin and the lower jaw elevated, and so, hopefully, prevent snoring from beginning.

Tony Stone Associates

Living with a snorer
The irritation that can be engendered by a persistent snorer, who is blissfully ignorant of the noise he or she is making, can be almost unbearable. However, there is usually a physical reason for the condition, and it should be possible to relieve it. But if snoring continues, earplugs may be the only solution.

If your child has adenoid problems, he or she is quite likely to start snoring because the blocked nose, caused by the adenoids, forces him or her to breathe through the mouth. The peace of a public park can be shattered by a snorer dozing in a deckchair. For some reason, people who are overweight are more prone to snoring. Often, losing a few pounds lowers the likelihood of snoring.

Sally and Richard Greenhill

Solvent abuse

Q Is it really possible to die from sniffing a bottle of correction fluid?

A Yes. Correction fluid is made from the same poisonous chemicals as paint strippers, bleach, and pesticides. These toxic vapors replace the oxygen in your body, and can permanently damage your brain, destroy your kidneys and liver, collapse your lungs, and stop your heart. Any anxiety, sudden scare, or stress—such as might be caused by a frantic parent—can also provoke a cardiac arrest. People can die the first time they try inhalants.

Q Isn't it unlikely that my six-year-old sister is sniffing the chemicals in our garage?

A Unfortunately inhalant abuse is more common than many would like to believe. In a 1996 Texas Commission on alcohol and Drug Abuse survey of 176,000 students, one out of every eleven 4th graders admitted to having tried inhalants. These poisons are dangerous precisely because they are so wide-spread, and because their dangers are so unrecognized.

Q How can I tell if my teenage son is using inhalants?

A There are several telltale signs. Drunken behavior, a glazed look, and loss of appetite can all occur. You may smell the characteristic chemical odor on his breath or clothing, or notice red rashes, spots, or sores around his mouth due to chemical contact. Other clues include paint or other stains on the body and clothing, or hidden stashes of solvents.

Q Isn't telling people about solvent abuse the same thing as suggesting they do it?

A No. Extensive, state-wide prevention campaigns held in Texas from 1992 to 1994 reduced elementary school inhalant use by more than 30 percent, and high-school use by 20 percent. In other words, education convinced 100,000 students who may otherwise have used inhalants to avoid them.

Called "The Silent Epidemic," solvent abuse is becoming one of the most common—and preventable—forms of substance abuse that kills both children and adolescents alike. But what is solvent abuse, and how can it be prevented?

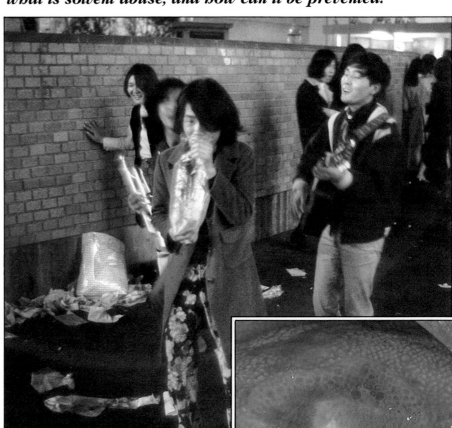

Colorific!

Young people aged eight to 17 are the main abusers of solvents; those involved often inhale glue vapor by pouring the adhesive into a plastic bag and breathing in and out (above). Apart from the obvious dangers of suffocation, prolonged abuse can cause appalling sores in and around the mouth, such as those shown on the right.

Solvents are just one of the many harmful poisons that growing numbers of children and adolescents are intentionally abusing to get high. Unfortunately, inhalant abuse is akin to playing Russian roulette, and for many people their first experience will also be their last. Out of every 10 deaths caused by inhalant abuse, three of the victims will be first-time users.

Where are solvents found?
Solvents are easily available to everyone. Ammonia, bleach, lighter fluid, and disinfectants can be found in most kitchens; antifreeze, turpentine, and kerosene can be found in the garage; while aerosol sprays, felt-tip markers, glues, paints, and rust removers can be found in workshops.

School supplies that contain dangerous chemicals include cements and glues, type-writer correction fluid, and permanent markers; wood shops may have varnishes and paint remover; graphic arts classes might stock printing inks and computer cleaners; culinary arts students have access to whipping cream cartridges and cans; while beauticians are exposed to hair sprays, and nail polish remover.

Who does it?

According to medical examiners' reports, inhalant victims come from either sex and all ethnic backgrounds and economic classes. However, chronic use is most common among young white males. Young people aged eight to 17 are the main abusers; the peak age is 13. Some sniff the solvents, some huff the inhalants directly into their mouths. According to a 1994 National Institute on Drug Abuse survey, 14 percent, or one in six of all US eighth graders, had tried some form of inhalant. In 1995, that number increased to 22 percent, or one in five. For preteenage children, solvent abuse is more popular than marijuana.

Where are the effects?

When inhaled, most solvents produce effects similar to anesthetics. The user can experience slight stimulation, feelings of less inhibition, an intoxication similar to that produced by alcohol, or loss of consciousness. Some people may become nauseated, forgetful, and unable to see things clearly. Spray paint and butane damage the peripheral nerves, causing numbness or tingling sensations (see Nervous system). Others may lose control of their body, including the use of arms and legs. Because inhalants are fat soluble, they stay in the

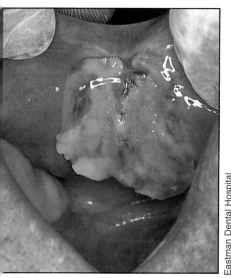

Eastman Dental Hospital

body for a long time, and can severely damage many vital organs, including the heart, liver, and kidneys. Repeated use of spray paints can permanently damage the brain and lungs, or cause death by asphyxiation.

Sudden Sniffing Death (SSD) syndrome can happen the first time or any time an inhalant is abused. The heart begins to overwork, beating rapidly but unevenly, which can lead to cardiac arrest (see Heart attack). Toluene (spray paint) and butane (lighter fluid) are the top causes of SSD.

Because preteens are still growing, the toxic effects of solvents have long-term repercussions on a child's physical, mental,

Substances abused and their hazards		
Product	**Principal constituents**	**Main hazards**
Aerosols	Propellants Particles (depending on type of spray)	Damage to lungs Suffocation during direct inhalation
Fire extinguishers	Extinguishant	Accidental death. Heart toxicity
Impact adhesives and other glues	Solvents Additives	Suffocation. Accidental death Brain damage, liver, and kidney damage
Lighter fuel	Fuel gases	Accidental death
Gasoline	Petroleum compounds Additives (including tetraethyl lead)	Accidental death Possible lead poisoning
Typewriter correcting fluid	Solvent	Accidental death. Heart toxicity

and emotional development. The most vulnerable organ to toxic buildup is the brain (see Brain). Cellular death in the cerebral cortex causes permanent personality changes, memory impairment, hallucinations, and learning disabilities.

Detection, action, and prevention

Solvent abuse may become apparent in a number of ways. Children may behave as if drunk. Their breath may smell of solvents, and the chemicals may burn their skin to leave red nostrils or sores around their mouths. They may appear dreamy and moody, and may lose their appetite. Finding hidden piles of rags, paper or plastic bags, and tubes or cans of glue or other potentially abused products, may also help confirm a child has been sniffing solvents.

If you catch someone in the act, keep calm. Excitement may cause the user to hallucinate or become violent. The stress might also overstimulate their heart, causing palpitations or cardiac arrest. If the person is conscious, keep them calm and in a well-ventilated room. If they are unconscious or not breathing, call for an ambulance immediately. If you've been trained to give CPR or artificial respiration, do it. If you haven't, don't; you might cause unnecessary damage. Once the person has recovered, urge them to seek professional help.

Treatment facilities for inhalant users are rare. Even if an adequate treatment facility is found, there is still much work to be done. Chronic users tend to suffer a high rate of relapse, and usually require 30 to 40 days or more of intensive detoxification. In addition, withdrawal symptoms can be as severe as those experienced by alcoholics or heroin addicts. Physical detoxification is followed by individual or group therapy. For all these reasons, prevention is obviously of paramount importance.

Rex Features

Some manufacturers have changed the chemical composition of their products to reduce the likelihood of solvent abuse. In addition, retailers can display prominent signs warning of the dangers of the practice and back them up by refusing to sell glue to children under the age of 16.

The most effective method of prevention is frank discussion of the facts. Parents and teachers, as well as medical professionals, retailers, elected officials, and law enforcement officers, need to be informed of the problem and its dangers. Fortunately it is the students themselves who often make the best educators, alerting their peers to the dangers of solvent abuse.

Sore throat

Q I always seem to get sore throats. What should I do about them?

A People have persistent or chronic sore throats for many different reasons. Smoking is one of the most common, and quitting may be all that's necessary. However, it is often difficult to pinpoint the trouble, and it may be advisable for your doctor to send you to an otolaryngologist for investigation. It is important to have your complaint properly treated: so don't merely rely on gargling or sucking lozenges.

Q What is the best type of lozenge to suck?

A The most lozenges can do is to ease or soothe the soreness. They have no curative effect on the condition itself because most of the germs that are responsible for the sore throat are not on the surface of the throat but in the tissues below, where the chemicals in the lozenge simply cannot reach. In fact, these strong antiseptic chemicals may actually make matters worse by causing a chemical inflammation on top of the inflammation from the infection that is already present. In addition, by killing off many of the normal organisms of the throat, lozenges may disturb the natural balance so drastically that other troubles (such as the growth of fungi) are actually encouraged. It is for these reasons that many doctors advise against using lozenges. If you do want to suck them, opt for something very simple rather than for the so-called antiseptic lozenges. If your sore throat persists, see your doctor.

Q What is the difference between sore throat and tonsillitis?

A Sore throat is a symptom that can have many causes and can result from inflammation in any of the tissues that surround the throat. The tonsils are part of these tissues, and *tonsillitis* is a medical term which refers specifically to inflammation of the tonsils. Thus tonsillitis is only one possible cause of sore throats.

This common symptom results from inflammation of the throat or the surrounding tissues. In most cases very simple treatment is all that is warranted.

The throat is one of the major passages of the body (see Throat). Air constantly passes up and down from the nose and mouth to the lungs. Food and drink pass through the throat on their way from the mouth to the stomach. Obviously the throat is the only entry into the lungs or the stomach, so that all the air that we breathe and all the food and drink that we take have to pass through it. The throat is exposed to any material coughed up from the lungs and bronchial passage or vomited up from the stomach.

The tissues that make up and surround the throat (the back of the tongue, the tonsils, the pharynx, and the space at the back of the nose) are constantly exposed to the risk of infection (see Infection and infectious diseases), making a sore throat a most common human ailment.

Three different views of the throat. Inflammation of many of the tissues shown here may result in a sore throat.

Causes

Sore throat is not a disease in itself. The basic feeling of soreness in the throat may be the result of inflammation of any of the surrounding tissues (see Inflammation). In addition, a sore throat is not necessarily caused by one particular germ, since there is a wide range of bacteria, viruses, and other microorganisms (such as fungi in the case of sore throat due to oral thrush; see Thrush) that can attack the throat.

In some cases the soreness is due not to infection, but to damage from other sources: swallowing foods and drinks that are too hot (see Burns), discharge running down from the back of the nose (see Nose), excessive smoking (see Smoking), or sucking too many strong sweets.

In some diseases (for example, influenza, scarlet fever, measles, and diphtheria), a sore throat is only the first, and relatively unimportant, stage of a disease that develops into something much more

The throat and surrounding tissue

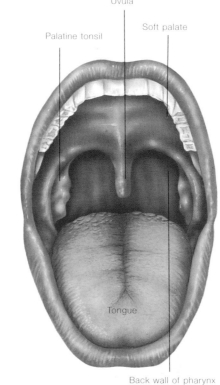

Uvula

Palatine tonsil

Soft palate

Tongue

Back wall of pharynx

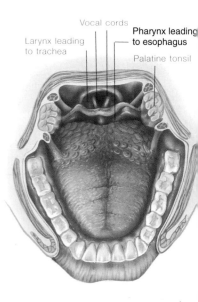

Vocal cords

Larynx leading to trachea

Pharynx leading to esophagus

Palatine tonsil

Cross section through the mouth

Mike Saunders

Gargling, even with something as mundane as ordinary salt and water or a mixture of aspirin and water, is an effective way of soothing the symptoms of a sore throat. In a streptococcal throat (inset) the tissues of the throat and neighboring organs have been infected with streptococcus bacteria. This is what the infected area would look like to the doctor examining the patient's throat.

Biophoto Associates

Ron Sutherland

widespread and serious. In most cases of sore throat, however, the trouble is confined to the throat.

The most common cause of sore throat is acute inflammation of the pharynx (see Pharynx), or pharyngitis. Inflammation of the pharynx usually occurs suddenly, with a feeling of dryness, irritation, and soreness. There is a constant desire to clear the throat, pain on swallowing, a persistent dry cough, and often headache and fever. Pharyngitis is usually due to infection by a virus rather than by bacteria, and taking antibiotics is not only useless (viruses are unaffected by them) but may actually make things worse because of unwanted side effects. Like most viral conditions, the infection clears up of its

own accord in a few days, and the only worthwhile treatment is to try to relieve the symptoms by means of hot drinks or the appropriate gargles.

Chronic pharyngitis may be the result of repeated attacks of acute pharyngitis, heavy smoking, working in dust or fumes, infected adenoids or tonsils, or discharge from the back of the nose or sinuses. It is important to find out exactly what is causing the chronic pharyngitis in order to resolve it.

Tonsillitis

Infections which start with a sore throat or pharyngitis often spread to nearby tissues and involve them too. The most commonly affected neighboring organ is the tonsil (see Tonsils). This is likely to be affected if the sore throat is due to infection with streptococcus bacteria: the septic, or strep, throat. In sore throat associated with tonsillitis the pain becomes more severe and swallowing is almost impossible. The affected tonsil is enlarged and red, the glands are swollen and tender, and the patient develops a high temperature (see Fevers). If the tonsillitis is not treated, quinsy (a peritonsillar abscess) may develop.

Another serious complication of an ordinary sore throat is when infection spreads from the pharynx upward to the eustachian tube, which leads to the inside

of the ear. This causes otitis media, which is characterized by earache as well as a sore throat (see Otitis). Infection may also spread downward from the pharynx into the voice box, or larynx, leading to laryngitis (see Larynx and laryngitis).

Diphtheria (thankfully much less common than it used to be) is yet another infection that involves a sore throat (see Diphtheria). This is characterized by the development of a membrane which is dirty gray in color and a sweetish smell to the breath, as well as the sore throat. Diphtheria was once a common cause of death in children and was the terror of parents. The germs that cause it secrete a powerful poison, an exotoxin that gets into the bloodstream and is carried to all parts of the body, damaging the heart and other organs. Many children who survived the infection were left with severely damaged hearts and nervous systems.

The sharp decline in the prevalence of diphtheria has nothing to do with antibiotics; it was the result of almost universal immunization against the disease (see Immunization). Public health authorities in countries in which this is not mandatory are constantly concerned that parents who have never known the disease may become casual about immunization. US regulations for schoolchildren make it unlikely that vaccination levels will drop,

Mounth

Soft palate

Pharynx

Epiglottis

Larynx

Vocal cords

Tongue

Trachea

Esophagus

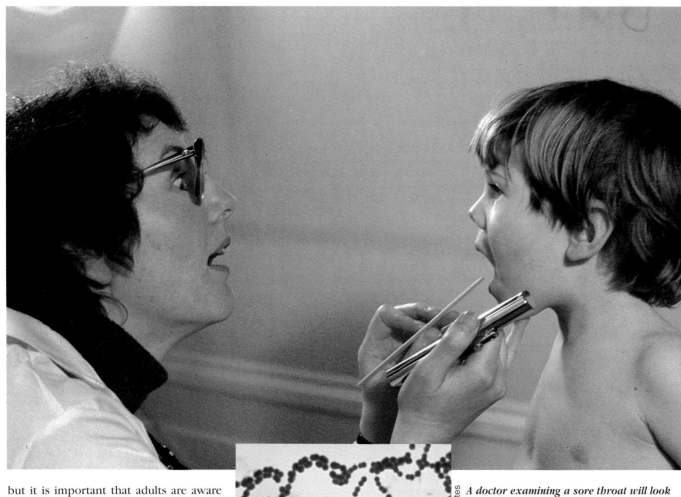

but it is important that adults are aware of the danger.

Throat abscess

One of the most acute and alarming complications of tonsillitis is peritonsillar abscess, or quinsy. This starts with a simple sore throat with tonsillitis, which seems to settle down. However, after a few days of comfort the affected person begins to suffer increasing difficulty in swallowing. Pain now recurs and usually spreads to the ear on one side. It becomes difficult to open the mouth because of spasm of the chewing muscles, and the speech becomes thick and indistinct.

Pain rapidly increases to a level that prevents eating. There is strong pressure in the neck and the head is tilted to the affected side. Rapid head movements are avoided. There is excessive salivation and bad breath. The temperature rises to 101°F (38°C) and the person becomes obviously ill. There may be partial obstruction to the airway by obstruction to the inlet of the voice box (larynx). This will produce difficulty in breathing.

Peritonsillar abscess is caused by a spread of infection from the tonsil to the tissues around and behind it. Occasionally it may arise from an infect-

A doctor examining a sore throat will look down the patient's throat, often with the help of a flashlight, to identify any inflammation that may be present. He or she may also take a throat swab to be sent to a laboratory for identification of the germ involved. The micrograph (left) shows streptococcus bacteria which, by inflaming the tissues of the throat and surrounding organs, often cause sore throats. Corynebacterium diphtheriae (below) is the organism that causes diphtheria—a potentially fatal infectious disease that is, fortunately, rare today.

ed and impacted wisdom tooth (third molar). If the inside of the mouth is inspected (which may be difficult because of the difficulty in opening the mouth widely) a distinct, red swelling will be seen, with marked protrusion of the tonsil, on one side.

The uvula (the soft, floppy flap of mucous membrane hanging from the center of the soft palate) is pushed across to the healthy side. The tongue is usually coated and the lymph nodes behind the angle of the jaw on the affected side will be enlarged and tender. Rarely, there may be an abscess on both sides.

Biophoto Associates

Biophoto Associates

Once any abscess, here or elsewhere, is fully developed, antibiotics are useless. This is because the center of an abscess is cut off from the general blood supply and no antibiotics can get to the germs. If severe tonsillitis is treated at an early stage with antibiotics, quinsy will be avoided; and if high dosage antibiotics are given at an early stage of abscess formation, it may be prevented from becoming established. Painkiller drugs (see Painkillers) are given, an ice pack is applied to the neck, mouthwashes are prescribed, and a cold liquid or semisolid diet is taken. Gargling is useless and, in the presence of partial airway obstruction, dangerous.

An established abscess is full of pus (see Pus), and the only effective treatment is to drain the pus through an incision. This is done under local anesthesia and produces an almost immediate and profound relief of pain and other symptoms. In addition to surgery, antibiotics are normally given to cope with the infection that caused the problem.

The surgeon has two options. The first is to open and drain the abscess at the site of maximum protrusion, using a long scalpel which is wrapped in sterile tape so that only the tip is exposed. This is to prevent the danger of injury to the large blood vessels of the neck by too deep penetration. This procedure is followed by removal of the tonsils under general anesthesia (tonsillectomy) three or four days later. Alternatively, tonsillectomy may be done under general anesthesia as the initial procedure. Once the tonsils have been removed there is no longer any danger of developing further quinsies.

Tonsillectomy is almost always done under general anesthesia. The head is tilted back and the mouth is propped open by a ratchet instrument called a gag. Each tonsil in turn is grasped with toothed forceps and is separated from its bed with minimal cutting. This is called blunt dissection. Bleeding from the raw areas left is sometimes brisk, and it is occasionally necessary to secure and close a small bleeding artery by tying it off. In rare cases, severe bleeding occurs some hours after the operation. This will require a return to the operating room for control of the hemorrhage. After tonsillectomy there is severe local discomfort, especially on swallowing, for about two weeks (see Surgery).

Consulting your doctor

Most sore throats are more of a nuisance than an illness, clear up quickly on their own, and require neither medical advice nor treatment. Nevertheless, some do not, and you should know when it is necessary to consult your doctor. If you have ever had rheumatic fever (see Rheumatic fever) or nephritis, or you develop a rash, or are running a fever of 102°F (38.9°C), or if your throat has a gray or yellow coating, you may need medical help. You should also see your doctor if your sore throat shows no signs of improving by the third day.

Your doctor will probably look down your throat with a flashlight. He or she may wipe the back of your throat with a swab and send it to a laboratory for testing, so that the germ that causes your sore throat can be identified and appropriate treatment given. He or she may also feel your neck for enlarged glands, and examine your nose, ears, and chest to see if they are involved too. If you have had a lot of sore throats your doctor may consider it necessary to refer you to an otolaryngologist for more conclusive diagnosis.

Self-help

Sore throat is one of those conditions for which you can do a great deal to help yourself. Hot drinks are soothing for a painful throat, and it is worth putting yourself on a semisolid food diet so that swallowing is as free from pain as possible. Gargling is also helpful, though probably the relief is due more to the effect of the heat of the gargle than to what you choose to use as the gargle. Ordinary salt and water or a mixture of aspirin and water are effective. Make up a salt gargle by putting two teaspoonsful of ordinary household salt in a cup of hot, but not too hot, water and stirring until it is completely dissolved.

Similarly, the aspirin gargle is made by dissolving two soluble aspirin in a cup of hot water. It should be swallowed rather than discarded when you have finished gargling so that the aspirin can do you good internally as well by its painkilling and fever-reducing action.

In between gargling you may find it helpful to suck a soothing lozenge; fruit pastilles or mentholated lozenges are traditional and effective. If the soreness and irritation in your throat causes you to cough, old-fashioned lozenges, sucked as far back in your throat as you can manage, are safe and soothing. It should be pointed out, however, that the most lozenges will do is soothe your sore throat. Not even the so-called antiseptic lozenges have a specific medicinal property apart from their soothing effect.

We may not all use our voices like Axel Rose, from the band Guns and Roses, but sometimes excessive use of the voice can irritate the laryngitis to such an extent that we lose our voice and suffer a painful sore throat. When this happens, rest your voice completely (even whispering will aggravate the condition) and keep your throat moist.

Rex Features

Sores

Q Should a sore be covered with a bandage or is it best left to heal uncovered?

A It depends on the type of sore. Small, clean open sores should be left uncovered if possible. But it may be more sensible to cover a child's wounded knee so that he or she doesn't get it dirty or knock off the protective scab that will form. The dressing or bandage will keep the sore moist, and to a certain extent will slow down healing, so it should not be left on for too long. If there is no obvious infection in the sore do not apply ointment as a protection against infection: it is better to allow a scab to form.

Q What is the difference between a sore and an ulcer?

A Generally speaking, the two are very similar: many sores are ulcers, and many ulcers are also sores. However, most sores are usually painful, whereas many ulcers may be entirely painless. Sores form only on the skin, whereas ulcers are breaches of any of the membranes of the body as well as of the skin.

Q Why do I keep getting cold sores?

A You were originally infected with the *Herpes simplex* virus from another person. Cold sores around the lips and mouth usually take a little time to heal, and no treatment is necessary other than petroleum jelly to prevent cracking. However, they do tend to recur in people who are run down and whose resistance to colds is low. Perhaps this is the reason you seem to be prone to them.

Q Can eating acidic foods cause mouth sores?

A No. Mouth sores, or mouth ulcers, occur singly or in crops of a few at a time, and have no known cause. They are very painful, and eating sharp citrus fruits will cause a sore in the mouth to smart. It's worth noting that frequent mouth sores may be caused by dental trouble, and it would be wise to consult a dentist about the problem.

This is a general term that describes breaks in the skin resulting from external or internal injury. Treatment may be unnecessary unless a sore persists.

The skin is the body's principal protective covering and it is extremely tough, although it can be injured externally by abrasions, heat and cold, chemicals, and sunlight, and internally by allergic substances, infections, and certain diseases. Any of these agents can produce different injuries or breaks in the skin. The popular term for a painful, irritating break in the skin is a sore (see Skin and skin diseases).

Sores develop from many skin conditions. For example, if blisters are broken, the raw patch would be called a sore. Scratching the skin when it is itchy due can cause small breaks in the skin which may bleed or become infected.

Cold sores and bedsores

The cold sore is a very common painful and irritating condition, usually found around the mouth or nose. It is caused by a virus called Herpes simplex (see Herpes). The virus remains in the skin and the cold sore is caused when the sufferer has a cold or resistance is low. No treatment is necessary since it normally disappears in a few days. Applying petroleum jelly may give some relief.

Bedsores are caused by constant, lengthy pressure on the same area of skin. They develop extremely quickly in unconscious patients, especially those who have taken an overdose of barbiturates, and in people who have had strokes or are immobile because of physical weakness. The most common site of bedsores is over the sacrum at the base

A patient who is bedridden and unable to move for any length of time may develop bedsores. The computerized "active pressure relieving mattress overlay system" can help to alleviate this painful condition.

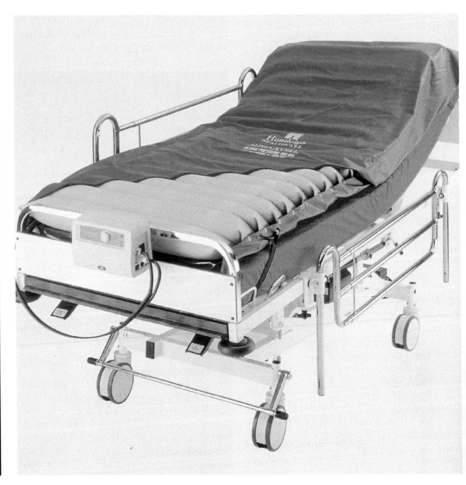

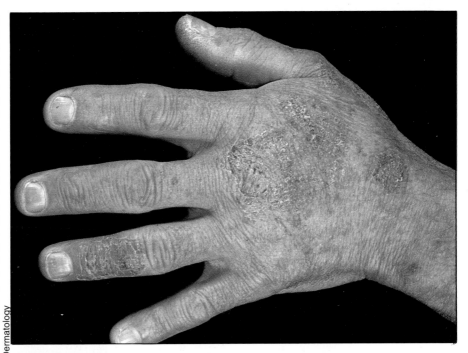

of the spine. Blisters develop which break, and the underlying sore can take a long time to heal. The patient must be turned often and the pressure areas rubbed with a zinc and castor oil cream or surgical spirit to prevent sores. If bedsores do appear, dressings and antibiotics will be necessary for the young, while elderly people will need careful nursing.

Genital sores

These have many causes. The sore, which is occasionally caused by intercourse, is painful, irregular in shape, and may become infected. A fungal infection candidosis (see Thrush) causes sore patches in the vagina and small sores on the foreskin and glans of the penis. The herpes virus causes numerous small blisters which are itchy and painful. These blisters burst and leave many small sores. An attack may last for one or two weeks, and often recurs. Herpes genitalis is usually transmitted by sexual contact (see Sexually transmitted diseases).

Industrial sores

Industrial sores are caused by dust, liquids or vapor, or any other skin irritant in the working environment. About 70 percent of industrial dermatitis is caused by direct damage to the skin by friction from abrasive dust such as coal, stone, brick, or steel wool. Acids and other chemicals such as paraffin, petroleum, and turpentine can all cause skin damage. After many years of exposure of the skin to irritating dusts or liquids, thickening and scaling of the skin often develops. This is seen most commonly in the elderly coal miner or building laborer. Small minor injuries to the skin are often slower to heal if the sore is in constant contact with an irritant. In people

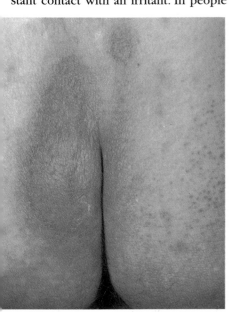

Those who work with chrome become sensitive after constant exposure to chromic acid and chromates, and risk developing chrome sores (above). Those in daily contact with rubber may develop rubber dermatitis (far left). Bedridden patients risk developing bedsores (below left).

who work with chrome and are thus exposed to chromic acid and chromates, ulcers called chrome sores often develop around trivial cuts and abrasions. These are usually seen on the skin of the fingers and the midline septum of the nose.

Another hazard is exposure to radioactive material and X rays that can cause acute burns (see Burns). The burns often develop into sores that are slow to heal. Sometimes a skin cancer may form in the sore (see Cancer).

Tropical sores

Tropical sores are common throughout the tropics and subtropics and can affect both immigrants and visitors from these areas. They may also develop in people who have been on vacation in tropical countries. The infection that causes tropical sores is caused by parasites called leishmania. The infection spreads through sandfly bites, which may persist for several weeks. A tropical sore is characterized by a shallow break in the center and the formation of a scab; after several months a scar will be left. This scar can be unsightly, and some forms of tropical sore may actually destroy the skin and tissues underneath (see Scars).

Implications of sores

Any sore which persists for several weeks should be examined by a doctor. There may be infection delaying the healing and treatment may be required.

All serious skin conditions benefit from early treatment. As a general rule, the skin should be kept dry, so it is best not to apply anything to a sore. Ointments (see Ointments) may delay healing by keeping it moist. Do not prick or squeeze sores, as this will delay healing and cause a scar to form.

Specimens

Q What is so characteristic about a urine sample taken during pregnancy?

A During pregnancy, the placenta produces a substance called human chorionic gonadotropin (HCG), which is detectable from about six weeks. This substance is produced in increasing amounts throughout pregnancy and is excreted into the urine. Its presence in the urine almost always means that the patient is pregnant.

Q Are specimens of skin tissue ever taken to diagnose skin disease?

A Yes. This may be done to diagnose skin cancer, which can often be completely cured by removing the abnormal skin and a thin rim of normal skin around it or by radiotherapy. A skin sample may also be taken to rule out the possibility of skin cancer since it mimics many other conditions, and to identify the exact disease because this will affect treatment. Taking a specimen of skin is usually a simple procedure which can be carried out under local anesthesia.

Q Why does every patient in a hospital have a blood test?

A Sometimes blood tests are done to look for a specific disease such as anemia during pregnancy. Often, however, blood is taken as part of a screening procedure, and is subjected to those tests that are most likely to give clues to diagnosis. Similarly, every patient has a urine test for sugar, blood, and protein, which may show unsuspected diabetes or kidney disease.

Q Can specimens be taken from a baby in the womb?

A Yes. The amniotic fluid in the womb can be tested for chemicals which may reveal deformities or important blood group incompatibilities between mother and baby. The baby is also constantly shedding cells into this fluid. These can be cultured and then tested.

Taking a specimen from the body is usually a simple, painless procedure, but the information it provides is invaluable in the diagnosis and treatment of disease.

Daily Telegraph Colour Library

Most people have had a blood or urine test at some time. These are the most common of a wide range of samples which may be taken from the body's tissues or fluids in the course of diagnosing a disease. A huge number of specimens is sent daily to pathology laboratories where all detailed analysis is carried out. Thus the physician's skill in piecing together his or her patient's symptoms is supported by extensive laboratory data (see Diagnosis, and Pathology).

The variety of specimens that can be taken is almost endless. Blood and urine are the most common because they are easy to obtain, relatively cheap to test, and very useful in diagnosis. On even a routine examination they can reveal seri-ous diseases, such as anemia, leukemia, and diabetes. A very wide range of more detailed tests of the blood and urine is routinely involved in clinical medicine.

Blood tests

In addition to the assessment of the number and appearance of the red blood cells and of their hemoglobin content, blood is commonly examined for the presence of some of the large number of specific enzymes and antibodies it may contain (see Blood). When heart muscle is damaged in a heart attack, particular enzymes are released into the blood from the affected cells. A measurement of the levels of such enzymes can give an accurate assessment of the amount of heart mus-

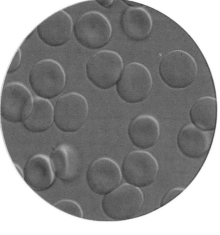

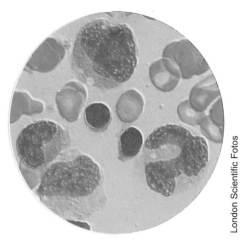

Blood, urine, and tissue testing is done in the pathology laboratory (far left). In cases of infertility, a sperm sample (above left) is examined for abnormalities. Blood analysis (center) is a routine but invaluable aid in diagnosis. A bone marrow smear (right) can reveal the presence of leukemia and rare types of anemia.

cle affected and hence of the severity of the heart attack and the probable outcome (see Heart attack). The process is similar when the liver is damaged by infection or poisoning.

Blood antibody levels are among the most important of the many tests that can be performed on blood specimens. Modern techniques of identification of antibodies and of their quantity allow very precise diagnosis of previous infection. Many hundreds of different conditions can be identified in this way.

For most blood tests, a specimen of blood may be taken from a vein in the arm using a syringe and fine needle. In some cases it is sufficient to prick a finger and obtain a drop of blood. There are conditions, however, in which it is essential that the specimen should be taken from the bloodstream in the heart or in the large vessels running to or from the lungs. In this case, a fine sterile tube called a catheter is passed in through a vein or an artery and threaded along to the required point. Analysis of blood gases (oxygen and carbon dioxide) from these sites can provide vital information about the condition of the lungs and heart.

Urine and stool tests

Urine tests are also capable of detecting many more diseases than the diabetes that is indicated when the specimen is found to contain sugar. While many of the urine tests indicate disease of the kidneys, one or more of a wide range of abnormal constituents may be present, indicating disease of other organs or parts of the body.

Samples of stool (see Feces) are commonly taken to help in the diagnosis of a wide range of intestinal disorders. Stool samples can be tested, by sensitive chemical analysis, for blood that is present in such small quantities as to be otherwise inapparent. This is called occult blood and its presence can be highly important in various conditions such as cancer of the large intestine or amebic dysentery.

Chemical analysis of the stools is commonly performed to assess the fat content in conditions in which dietary fat is not being properly absorbed. Such malabsorption diseases produce characteristic fatty stools. Similarly, failure of protein digestion can be detected by stool analysis.

Another commonly performed test on stool specimens is the search for the eggs of intestinal worms. A small quantity of the specimen is shaken up in salt water and a drop of the suspension placed on a microscope slide and covered with a layer of very thin glass. The eggs of each parasite differ in subtle details from those of the others. This characteristic appearance can be detected by an expert so that a precise identification of the type of parasite can be determined (see Parasites).

Sputum tests

In cases of chest infection, sputum specimens can be cultured to identify the infecting organisms present, and the sensitivity of these to various antibiotics can be determined. In suspected tuberculosis,

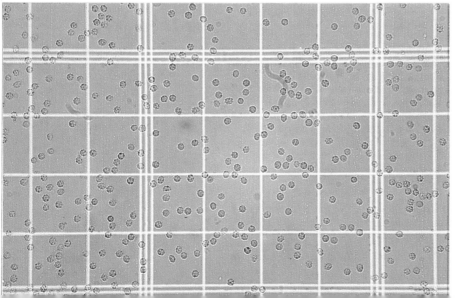

Specific types of anemia may be diagnosed by means of a hemocytometer, which is used to count the red cells in a blood sample.

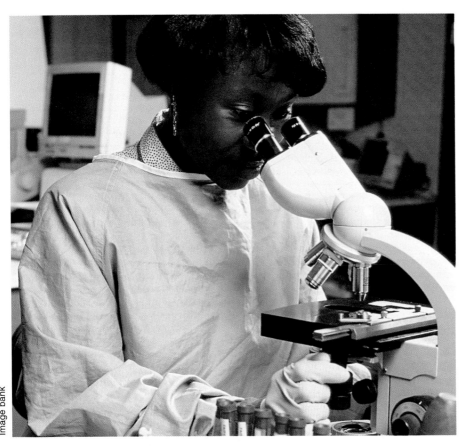

Image bank

A laboratory technician can tell a great deal by carefully examining blood samples for the presence of enzymes and antibodies.

Finally, specimens may be taken as part of a screening program to detect latent disease. No disease is suspected in any individual, but if enough people are examined some cases will be found. The aim must also be to detect the condition at an early enough stage for effective treatment. The best example of this is the cervical smear which is designed to detect early cancer of the cervix (see Pap smear). Cells from the cervix are removed and spread on a glass slide for examination under a microscope. Many cases of cancer discovered in this way are still at an early stage and can be completely cured.

Processing specimens

Often the simplest test gives the most information. Probably more can be learned from examining blood film than from any other laboratory test, yet the specimen is easily obtained and prepared. The routine testing of urine is also straightforward but unexpected diseases may be diagnosed in this way.

It is vital to insure that specimens do not get mixed up, so each department takes the utmost precautions to guard against this possibility. All labeling is checked at every stage and errors virtually never occur.

Routine analysis is carried out by specially trained laboratory staff. Results are sent directly to the patient's doctor. Abnormal results are usually shown to the relevant pathologist, who advises the clinicians about the significance of the abnormality and the best procedure to follow can then be discussed. The pathologist reports on all tissue samples.

sputum can be stained and examined under the microscope, and various other tests can be done to identify the causal organism. In lung cancer, sputum will often contain cast-off cancer cells and these can be identified by a skilled pathologist.

In a case of suspected meningitis the fluid that circulates around the brain is examined, while fluid from a swollen joint might be analyzed for clues as to its cause (see Meningitis). Sputum can provide evidence of infection of cancer.

Biopsies

It is possible to take tissue samples from organs without using surgery, in a process that is known as biopsy (see Biopsy). Flexible tubes, or endoscopes, can be inserted into the stomach and along the rectum and colon. Small pieces of tissue may then be removed for examination under the microscope. Similarly, pieces of the liver, kidneys, and bone marrow can be obtained using fine, rigid tubes or special probes and needles. Even such vital organs as the heart and brain can have tiny pieces removed and examined. Obviously this method of sampling is not without risk, but most of these procedures are now routine and the hazards are minimal.

Biopsies are the most reliable way of making a diagnosis and will usually be required if a serious condition, such as cancer, is in question (see Cancer). Histopathology is the subdivision of general pathology concerned with the microscopic examination of specimens obtained by biopsy. Such specimens are cut into thin slices, placed on glass slides, stained, and examined. Histopathologists are familiar with the subtle changes that occur in cells and tissues as a result of disease and can determine with a high degree of reliability the presence of many different diseases.

Why a specimen is taken

The main reason for taking a specimen is to confirm a diagnosis. A doctor will seldom feel happy about making a diagnosis without the evidence supplied from an examination of blood, urine, or biopsy material. Blood and urine are particularly useful in monitoring the progress and treatment of disease. For instance, there are some kinds of cancer that secrete substances into the blood. As the cancer responds to treatment these substances will disappear, so in such cases regular blood tests are an accurate means of charting the course of the disease.

Biochemical analysis of urine is used in the diagnosis of such conditions as diabetes and for the detection of illicit drugs.

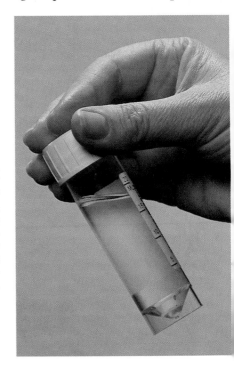

Speculum

Q I would like to have contraceptive advice from the family planning clinic before I have sexual intercourse for the first time. Will I have to have a pelvic examination, and if so, will it be painful?

A Pelvic and vaginal speculum examinations are performed at family planning clinics to establish that the reproductive organs are normal and healthy. It is very unlikely that a virgin will have any abnormality of the cervix. Because of this, and because an internal examination may be uncomfortable if you have an intact hymen (the membranous fold which partly covers the entrance to the vagina), most gynecologists would be prepared to delay the internal examination until you have experienced sexual intercourse.

Q I had a miscarriage shortly after an internal examination, during which a speculum was used. I am now pregnant again and am worried that this might happen again. Is this examination necessary?

A There is no evidence that a gentle internal examination will cause a miscarriage although your anxiety is understandable. You should explain this to your obstetrician. Much useful information is gained by a pelvic examination early in pregnancy and a speculum is used to check for infection in the vagina and to examine the cervix. Your obstetrician may, however, be prepared to avoid doing this if he or she feels that it will cause you great anxiety.

Q My gynecologist says he has difficulty inserting the speculum into my vagina. Why is this?

A If you are tense the muscles surrounding the vagina go into spasm and narrow the vagina instead of allowing it to expand as when it is relaxed. Perhaps you could learn to relax more when being examined by concentrating on deep breathing exercises.

Doctors use a speculum to examine the body's various passages. It helps them to make a diagnosis without causing the patient any undue discomfort.

To make an accurate diagnosis of some conditions it is necessary for the doctor to look into various passages of the body, for example, the ear, nostrils, vagina, or rectum. Those instruments designed to help the doctor to do this are called specula (singular, speculum). They vary in shape and size depending on what they are used for. Most of them are made of highly polished metal which will reflect light well. Recently, however, a disposable plastic one has been developed.

A speculum is gently inserted into the passage which is to be examined. The doctor initially separates the walls at the entrance of the body passage with his or her fingers to facilitate this.

The vaginal speculum

Some vaginal specula are only used during surgical procedures (see Vagina). The most commonly used of the others is the duckbill shaped Cusco's speculum. When the blades of this are separated they divide and completely cover the opposing sides of the vaginal walls. This speculum therefore exposes the cervix to view.

It is possible to take swabs of vaginal and cervical secretions so that the doctor can check for genital infection. It also makes it possible to check that the thread of an intrauterine contraceptive device is in place (see Contraception), and to take Pap tests. The cervix can be examined in the same way (see Cervix and cervical smear, and Pap smear).

The Sim's speculum is another commonly used vaginal speculum. It enables the doctor to examine the vaginal walls for prolapse, ulcers, or atrophic (thinned) mucous membranes. The speculum is used to depress the front or back vaginal walls and reflect light, which enables the opposite wall to be examined easily.

Other types of speculum

A nasal speculum is used to help the doctor look for such things as foreign bodies, polyps, or very fragile blood vessels which may cause the patient to have frequent nosebleeds. Much more frequently used is the speculum for examining the eardrum and external canal of the ear.

The three vaginal specula often used are Grave's, Sim's, and Cusco's, shown top to bottom on the left of the picture. Those on the right are for nose, ears, and rectum.

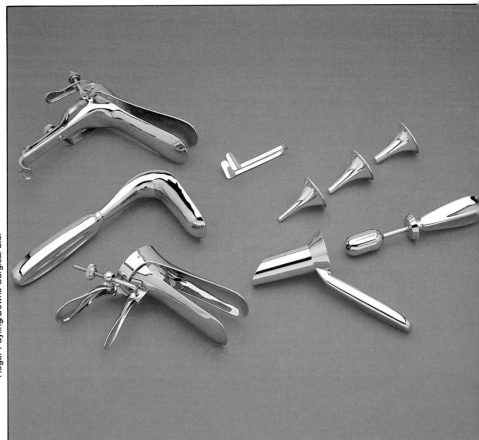

Roger Payling/Downs Surgical Ltd.

Speech

Q My son does not speak very clearly, and sometimes we cannot even make out what he is saying. Is he just going through a lazy phase or should we worry about it?

A If you think your child has some sort of speech problem, take him to your doctor immediately. He or she may not be able to find out the exact nature of the problem but will be able to refer him to a specialist for further tests and diagnosis if necessary. It is unlikely that laziness is a factor in your child's poor speech, particularly if the defect is bad enough to make him hard to understand. A child may grow out of a genuine speech problem but as time goes on the problem could get worse, so it is essential that he sees a doctor.

Q My son is two years old and has not made any attempts at speech. All my friends' children of a similar age started speaking some time ago; is there any real need for me to be concerned?

A It is not unusual for children, especially boys, not to attempt speech until around the age of three. After this time they usually make excellent progress and catch up very quickly. As a precaution, take your son to your doctor. He or she will be able to assess him and might send him, for further examinations, to a speech therapist. If there is some genuine reason for his slow speech development, the cause can be any number of things, from the purely physical (some abnormality of the voice box) to a more deep-seated psychological problem. Whatever the cause, early diagnosis is very important, because it becomes harder for a child to pick up language as he or she gets older. If the delay in developing language is marked, there can often be an associated problem in learning the rules of syntax and grammar. Dyslexia or word blindness, for instance, is associated to some degree with problems of development of speech and some people maintain that dyslexia is a lot more common than was previously thought.

If you've ever lost your voice for some reason, you will know how extremely frustrating it can be not to be able to communicate. Speech, one of man's most essential and flexible abilities, is indeed a precious faculty.

Speech is one of the most complex and delicate operations that the body is asked to undertake. Ultimately all speech, talking, and comprehension are controlled and coordinated by the brain, and it is in the cerebral cortex that there are areas called the speech centers where words are deciphered and signals and instructions are sent out to the hundreds of muscles in the lungs, throat, and mouth that are involved in producing speech. All this complex control is something that we are born with the ability to do, but the actual way we speak and the sounds we make are learned from our parents and the people around us as we grow up.

Speech production

Messages from the motor cortex in the brain, control with nerve impulses all the complicated actions involved in speech

production. The sound produced by the vocal cords is turned into words by the lips, tongue, soft palate, and shape of the mouth.

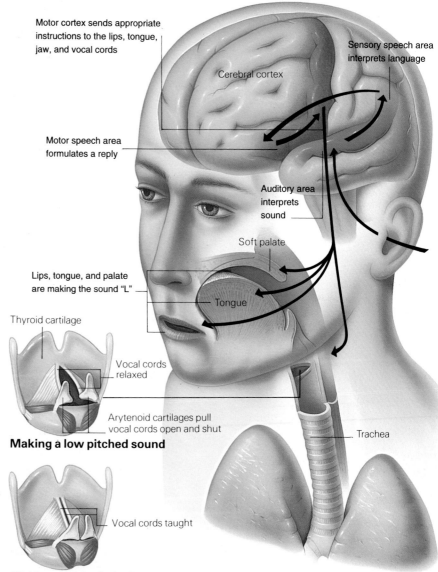

Motor cortex sends appropriate instructions to the lips, tongue, jaw, and vocal cords

Cerebral cortex

Sensory speech area interprets language

Motor speech area formulates a reply

Auditory area interprets sound

Soft palate

Lips, tongue, and palate are making the sound "L"

Tongue

Thyroid cartilage

Vocal cords relaxed

Arytenoid cartilages pull vocal cords open and shut

Making a low pitched sound

Trachea

Vocal cords taught

Making a high pitched sound

Mike Courteney

reply has been thought up, the motor speech center and another part of the brain, called the brain stem, come into operation. The brain stem controls both the intercostal muscles, between the ribs, which inflate the lungs, and the abdominal muscles, which determine the pressure of the incoming and outgoing air. As air is expelled from the lungs, the motor speech area signals the vocal cords simultaneously to move into the stream of air in the throat, causing the cords to vibrate and produce a simple sound (see Vocal cords). This is called phonation.

The amount of pressure applied to the lungs during exhalation governs the speed with which the air passes over the vocal cords, and the faster the air, the louder the sound produced. During whispering the vocal cords are set wide apart so that they do not actually vibrate as the air passes between them, they merely act as friction surfaces. But for the most part, the shaping of words is performed by movements of the lips, tongue, and soft palate—controlled by the cortex.

Babies, who all have the potential of speech, learn to talk by imitating those around them, especially their mothers. Control of the mouth, lips, and tongue can be hard and many children lisp for a time.

Thinking and speaking

The cerebral cortex of the brain is divided into left and right sections called hemispheres (see Brain); speech and its associated functions are usually concentrated in one hemisphere. In a right-handed person this is usually in the left hemisphere and in a left-handed person it is usually in the right hemisphere. This area of the brain is divided into the motor speech center, which controls the muscles of the mouth and throat, and the sensory speech center, which interprets the incoming sound signals coming along the nerve from the ears. Also nearby are the parts of the brain which coordinate hearing (by which we comprehend what others around us are saying), vision (by which we decipher the written word), and the complex hand movements used in writing, playing an instrument, and so on.

Conversation is a very complicated procedure, and the first thing that happens when we hear a person speaking is that the hearing centers, in the cerebral cortex, recognize the jumble of incoming auditory signals from the ears. The sensory speech center decodes the words so that the other parts of the brain involved in the process can then recognize the words and formulate an answer. Once a

Steve Bielschowsky

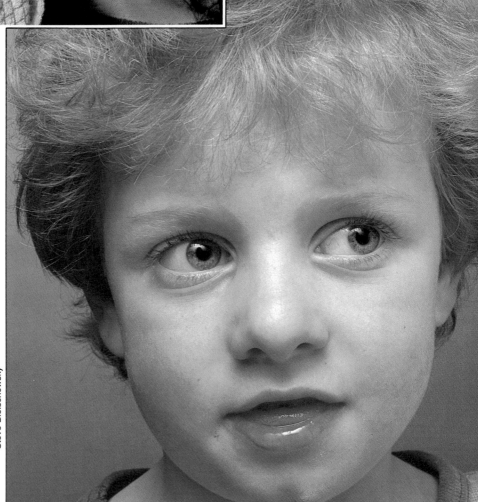

Q My husband suffered a heart attack some time ago which left him partially paralyzed. This also made him lose his powers of speech. What can be done to overcome his problem?

A The total loss of the powers of speech, including memory (aphasia), means that the patient must be totally reeducated and in effect learn language from scratch. Luckily the brain has the remarkable talent of being able to swap the faculties of one area of the brain to another when the need arises. The method that might be used to retrain your husband would involve laboriously repeating words and phrases and the rules of grammar, just as a child would when initially learning the language. This would be supervised by a speech therapist.

Q I have been told that the only way to cure my child of his speech problem is by sending him to a special school. Is this really necessary?

A Treatment of some speech defects can be a long and subtle process and is often most effective under confined and controlled conditions available at a special school. Treatment at a special school could last around three years, after which time the child may be able to return to a regular school. Obviously the length of time that the treatment lasts is variable and depends on the cause of the child's problem.

Q What can be done for someone with a cleft palate, and is treatment effective?

A A cleft palate is a gap or a cleft in the roof of the mouth or upper jaw. This condition is usually treated in babies immediately, or quite soon, after birth. The fissure is closed by surgery. If the cleft palate was not treated until after the person began speaking, speech therapy is used to clear up any language defects that may have developed. Today, a cleft palate does not have any real effect on the way a person speaks since the surgery available mends the damage completely.

Vision International

Producing speech sounds

To turn the simple sounds produced by the vocal cords into intelligible words, the lips, the tongue, the soft palate, and the chambers which give resonance to the voice all play a part. The resonating chambers include the whole mouth chamber, the nose, the pharynx (the part of the throat between the mouth and the esophagus), and to a lesser degree the chest cavity.

The control of these structures is achieved by hundreds of tiny muscles

The mobile phone, a device that gives more scope for talk, is eagerly exploited by humans—compulsive communicators all.

which work very closely together and at incredible speed. Put simply, speech is made up of vowels and consonants; vowels are all phonated sounds.

The resonant qualities of the various chambers of the mouth and respiratory system provide us with the individuality of our voices. For instance, the so-called nasal sounds like m, n, and ng depend for their correct vocalization on free resonance in the nose; try pinching your nose when you speak—the comic effect shows how the air space of the nose gives our speech roundness and clarity. Everyone has a differently shaped nose, chest, and mouth, hence different people have different sounding voices.

The skull also resonates when we speak, and we hear part of what we say transmitted through the bones of the skull, as well as what is picked up by the ears. This not only provides us with vital feedback about what we are saying, but also explains why our voices sound so strange when played back through a tape recorder—the sounds we then hear being only those transmitted through air.

Gesture, facial expression, and body language are important accompaniments of speech—they aid understanding of all the fine points in an exchange of ideas.

Learning to speak

The rate at which children acquire the power of speech varies from one individual to another, but the same landmarks in speech development normally occur in all growing children. For up to three or four months after birth, most of the sounds a baby makes are those used in crying. After this the baby starts to make speechlike sounds when gurgling and babbling. These noises are thought to be common to babies of all different nationalities, and are even found in babies who are deaf (see Deafness). This has led many people to conclude that the capability for language is inherent in all people.

At around four months of age the baby starts to coo and chuckle, and toward 10 months sounds heard around the infant may be repeated. From 10 to 12 months the first audible words are usually produced. These words are often nouns naming the things that the infant sees around him or her or mean that the baby is asking for something with one word.

From 12 to 18 months the child jabbers tunefully while at play and uses between 6 and 20 recognizable words; the child also understands many more words. From the age of two the structuring of language begins and more than two or so words are strung together at one time. Also, the child starts to pick up the idiomatic meaning of groups of words. From three to five years, sentences become longer and convey a more exact meaning, and basic grammar is gradually mastered. From school age, development of speech becomes more structured as vocabulary and grammar are learned in a more systematic manner.

One great asset that we possess is inquisitiveness, and this is nowhere more evident than in a child who is learning new words and phrases every day.

Speech defects

Because of the great complexity of the whole speech process, involving as it does many areas of the brain, the control of breathing, and all the many muscles that manipulate the sound-producing and modifying apparatus, speech problems can be very complicated.

The disorders can be divided into six types: problems of the voice (disorders of the larynx and its parts; see Larynx and laryngitis); problems of voice development; problems caused by damage to the various speech areas of the brain; abnormalities of the mouth; and problems brought on by or associated with deafness.

Basically, anything that gets in the way of the ability either to formulate speech (in the brain), communicate the commands to the bodily parts (along the nerve network), or execute the commands (in the muscles) can cause some kind of speech disorder.

Some disorders caused by problems with the nervous system are called dysarthria (see Nervous system). In this category are diseases such as cerebral palsy, shaking palsy, and chorea. Deafness can cause mutism because a deaf child will not be able to pick up the language being spoken around him. If the patient is deaf at birth, concentrated speech therapy must be undertaken using visual means to stimulate the correct vocalization of words.

These are some of the areas where there are problems with speech, and treatment depends on the actual cause of the disturbance. The determination of the cause can involve consultation with neurologists, psychologists, or any of the other specialists that have some involvement with any of the speech-producing mechanisms. Any eventual treatment may involve doctors and therapists from many specialties (see Speech therapy).

Speech is our most instantaneous and powerful method of getting through to others, and it can literally make the difference between life and death. The impact of a shouted warning is immediate and it demands attention and quick action.

Speech therapy

Q My child has a stutter that seems to be getting worse. What can be done to stop it?

A A speech therapist will be able to decide whether your child is just going through a phase of poor speech, often called disfluency, or whether the stuttering is permanent. If your child is showing real stuttering behavior, the therapist will decide whether it is appropriate to intervene with treatment. If so, the therapist will teach your child how to speak more easily and assist you, through parent counseling, on how to help your child at home between visits to the therapist.

Q What training does a speech therapist have and where do they practice?

A A speech therapist has at least a master's degree. Subjects covered include child development, phonetics, linguistics, psychology, anatomy and physiology, neurology, and speech pathology. Many work in schools, while others work in hospitals, rehabilitation centers, speech and hearing centers, and speech clinics.

Q My three-year-old son can certainly hear perfectly well, but is not speaking yet. Should I take him to see a speech therapist?

A Children, especially boys, often do not speak until quite late. But if you are worried, go to your doctor who might then refer you to a speech therapist who is trained to teach all kinds of speech and correct language difficulties including delayed speech and language development.

Q My father has developed Parkinson's disease. His speech is very faint and he speaks too quickly for me to understand what he says. Where can I get help for him?

A Contact the speech therapy department of your local hospital. A speech therapist will be able to treat your father's speech difficulty by training him to speak more slowly and distinctly.

From stroke victims to children with a lisp, speech therapy plays a vital role in helping people to communicate clearly and thus live as normal and happy a life as possible.

John Walmsley

1808

Many people confuse speech therapy with elocution or teaching people to pronounce English clearly. But a speech therapist is not someone who changes accents or dialects. He or she helps children and adults who have speech or language difficulties that make it hard for them to understand or be understood by other people. A speech therapist is responsible for assessment, diagnosis, and treatment of any speech or language difficulty, usually after the patient has been referred by a doctor.

Speech difficulty

The main areas in which people need speech therapy are where they have difficulty in understanding speech or language, difficulty in articulation (pronunciation of sounds), difficulty in expressing ideas through spoken, written, or sign language—perhaps following a stroke or an accident (see Stroke).

Speech therapy employs many techniques in the effort to restore lost speech or aid late development. Children who have been in accidents often have to be helped to try even the most basic of speech-related exercises. Having to stretch the mouth to accommodate a banana will exercise the muscles, while blowing out candles will help the child to control breathing and form the lips into one of the basic shapes used in the production of speech. A child with delayed speech development could be asked to point at pictures of items mentioned by the therapist. In all cases the therapist aims to make the session fun.

Causes of speech or language difficulty in children include delayed development or disorder of articulation (pronunciation of sounds), delayed or disordered development of language, physical or intellectual impairments, autism, cleft palate, deafness, voice disorder, and stammering. Adults can suffer from speech or language problems, caused by stroke, Parkinson's disease, multiple sclerosis, or cancer of the larynx (see Multiple sclerosis, Parkinson's disease).

Difficulties in understanding and expression of speech and language vary enormously. In children, problems usually result from damage to the brain, hearing, or speaking apparatus from birth, or delayed and sometimes abnormal development in childhood. Adults usually lose the ability to speak as a result of brain damage, or damage to nerves supplying the speech muscles, or the deterioration of the muscles of speech through disease. In some cases of cancer of the larynx the whole voice box is removed, and the patient has to learn to speak using the esophagus (see Esophagus).

Therapy for children

Unless the child's difficulty is purely in speaking, or the speech problems are very severe, the first area of treatment is language comprehension. In young children between the ages of three and six years this is usually done through play. The parents also take a major role in continuing therapy in between sessions with the therapist. Typically, language is taught by playing with a doll's house, items of furniture, and miniature people. Keeping language short and simple, the child is asked to select items—this teaches nouns. The child is then asked to do things with them, which teaches verbs.

Where children have difficulty in articulating, it is usually because they either do not know how to make particular sounds, or they do not recognize that certain sounds are different from other similar ones (see Speech).

Sounds develop until the age of six or seven, so a speech therapist would not treat a four-year-old who had difficulty with only *s* or *r* as these are difficult sounds to say. In therapy a child is first shown how to make the sound. He or she then says the sound by itself before going on to practice it as the first sound in short words. Then he or she says the sound at the end of words and finally in the middle of words before trying to use it in continuous speech.

Therapy for adults

Where speech or language is lost through brain damage as a result of stroke, the patient often recovers some or all of his speech spontaneously, usually between six months and two years after the stroke. The speech therapist's role is to guide and stimulate recovery with speech and language exercises. These range from pointing to pictures by name to reconstructing complex, abstract sentences in which written words have been jumbled.

The extent of recovery depends on the extent of brain damage (see Brain damage and disease). Some patients never recover speech and language. In these cases other forms of communication are taught. These may include simple gesture or sign language, or the patient pointing at pictures of what they need.

Slurred articulation, called dysarthria, is often caused by a stroke or multiple sclerosis, and occurs because the tongue cannot move rapidly enough from one sound to another. Patients are told to slow down their speech, allowing time to make the sounds accurately. Tongue and lip exercises are practiced in order to strengthen the muscles of speech.

This stroke victim is at an advanced stage of recovery (below). She is being asked to rearrange word cards into relatively complicated sentences. Often stroke victims have to learn language anew.

Sperm

Venner Artists

Q I have been told that it is possible for a man to become infertile through wearing tight trousers. Is this true?

A Yes, to a degree. Tight trousers and nylon underwear may increase the temperature inside the testicles to an unacceptable point where sperm production simply stops. Thankfully this is only a temporary condition.

Q At what age does a young man start to produce sperm, and for how long does this continue?

A Sperm is first produced at puberty, at about age 12, and continues throughout the life of a healthy male. Even a man of 90 is able to father a child.

Q If the sperm is of poor quality, could the child be unhealthy or deformed?

A Approximately 20 percent of sperm in the typical ejaculate are thought to be abnormal. Such sperm are, however, normally unable to fertilize an egg. If fertilization occurs, the result is often spontaneous abortion—nature's way of coping. Recently, substances such as lead have been implicated in cases of fetal abnormality where damaged sperm are thought to be the cause.

Q A test showed that I have a low sperm count. What does this mean and will it improve?

A The sperm count is the number of sperm in each milliliter of seminal fluid. Between two and five milliliters are normally ejaculated at each orgasm. Sperm counts vary, and may depend on the body temperature when the sperm is formed or the frequency of intercourse. However, if your sperm count is consistently low in tests, and there is no treatable cause, then it is unlikely that it will improve. This doesn't mean that you are unable to father a child; it may be possible to artificially inseminate your sperm. A sub-fertility clinic can advise on this.

The human male is an amazingly prolific producer of sperm: up to 350 million are released in one ejaculation. But only one single sperm may actually complete the journey to the female's egg and achieve fertilization.

Sperm is the name given to the male reproductive cell. Its only purpose is to achieve fertilization by union with the female cell, the ovum.

Each sperm is about 0.05 mm in length and is shaped like a tadpole. It has three main sections, which consist of a head, a midsection, and a tail. The front of the head—the acrosome—contains special enzymes which enable the sperm to penetrate into the ovum and so achieve fertilization. The midsection contains structures called mitochondria. These structures hold the vital source of

How sperm mature

From puberty, sperm are constantly produced in the seminiferous tubules. To become sperm, the basic sperm cells go through three stages of cell division

(bottom) before passing through the tubules and into the epididymis, where they are stored (below left). A mature normal sperm has a head, midsection, and tail (below).

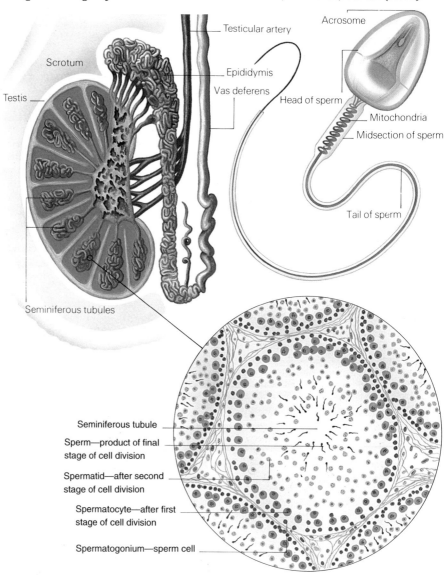

Testicular artery
Scrotum
Epididymis
Testis
Vas deferens
Seminiferous tubules

Acrosome
Head of sperm
Mitochondria
Midsection of sperm
Tail of sperm

Seminiferous tubule
Sperm—product of final stage of cell division
Spermatid—after second stage of cell division
Spermatocyte—after first stage of cell division
Spermatogonium—sperm cell

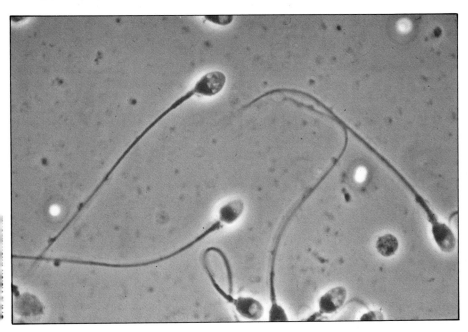

In order to reach and fertilize the female egg in the fallopian tube, the sperm must swim. Lashing their long tails is their sole method of propulsion.

energy needed by the sperm to fuel it on its journey to the ovum.

The tail's only function is to propel the sperm, which it does by moving in a whiplike fashion, generating a speed of about 3-3.5 mm per minute.

The sperm is made up of a number of essential chemicals and genetic material. These are the chromosomes which carry the genetic blueprint of the father, and which determine the paternally inherited characteristics of the child. It is also the sperm which carries the genetic message that determines the sex of the child (see Genetics).

The manufacture of sperm
The successful manufacture of sperm necessitates a temperature of about three degrees Centigrade lower than the rest of the body. Consequently, manufacture takes place outside the body, within the scrotum. Surrounding tissue helps to regulate the temperature of the testicles inside the scrotum by pulling them upward to the body in cold conditions, and by a rich supply of blood vessels which dissipate the heat when the temperature gets too high.

Sperm production—at the rate of 10 to 30 billion a month—takes place in the seminiferous tubules in the testicles. The newly formed sperm then pass through the seminiferous tubules into the epididymis, which is located behind the testicles. This serves as a storage and development area, the sperm taking between 60-72 hours to achieve full maturity. In fact, the epididymis can be emptied by three or four ejaculations in 12 hours; it takes about two days to be refilled. If ejaculation does not take

place, the sperm disintegrate and are absorbed back into the testicles.

Ejaculation
Before ejaculation occurs, the sperm move along the vas deferens, two tubes connecting the testicles to the prostate gland, and into a further storage area, the ampulla. Here, the sperm receive a secretion from the seminal vesicles, two coiled tubes adjoining the ampulla. This secretion, called seminal fluid, stimulates the motility—the ability to move—of the sperm, and helps them survive in the vaginal secretion. The prostate gland, through which the sperm pass during ejaculation, produces a small amount of a similar fluid, giving the sperm full motility (see Prostate gland).

At the moment of ejaculation the sperm and seminal fluid are forced out of the ampullae, and epididymis, into the urethra by a series of muscular contractions. If the sperm have been ejaculated into the vagina of a woman, they move as fast as they can through the cervix and into the uterus, where they make their way into the fallopian tubes. It is in these tubes that fertilization may occur if an egg is present (see Intercourse).

What can go wrong?
Fertilization is unlikely to take place if the concentration of the sperm is too low, if the sperm are abnormal in form, or if the sperm are unable to move or stop moving too soon. The condition of the seminal fluid is another vital factor, since it both nourishes and protects the sperm. Blocked tubes, infection, even stress and ill health can be the cause of infertility (see Infertility).

The number of normal, healthy sperm in one ejaculate varies widely—anything from 20-350 million in the semen (the seminal fluid and the sperm together). A sperm count lower than 20 million healthy sperm may well be responsible for infertility. Where infertility is suspected, a sperm specimen will be tested in a pathology lab (see Specimens), and treatment and advice will depend on the cause. A man with a low sperm count may be advised to save up his sperm for a few days so as to produce the optimum number of sperm in his ejaculate. In other cases, artificial insemination is recommended. Several ejaculations are placed in a centrifuge, and the resultant sperm concentrate placed on the woman's cervix at her most fertile time.

However, doctors are unlikely to think that investigation is needed until the couple have been trying to conceive for a year or more.

The moment of conception: chemicals in the tip of the sperm strip away the outer layer of the egg until one sperm can penetrate its smooth shell. Chemical changes in the outer layer of the egg then insure that no further sperm can enter.

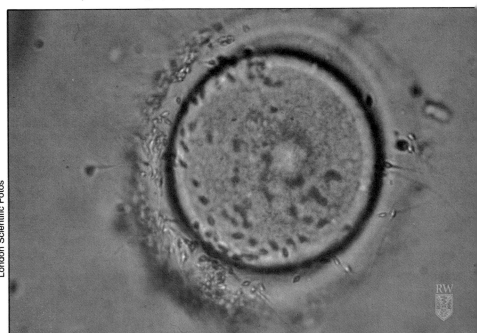

London Scientific Fotos

RW

Sphygmomanometer

Q Does it hurt to have your blood pressure taken?

A No, not at all. The most that you will feel is a tightness on your arm when the cuff is fully inflated; but this only lasts for a few seconds and amounts to mild discomfort rather than pain.

Q When my blood pressure is taken I get a thumping feeling in my arm. Why?

A This is the equivalent to what the doctor hears with a stethoscope and represents the moment at which the pressure in the cuff is dropped to a point at which blood can flow into the lower arm again. Since it can only do so at the peak of the heart's pumping action, called systole, you feel a thump in your arm each time your heart beats. When the pressure in the cuff is lowered again, and the blood flows freely again, the thumping dies away. At this point the reading on the scale represents the diastolic blood pressure.

Q I understand that having your blood pressure taken involves cutting off the blood supply to one arm. Isn't this rather dangerous?

A No, there is no risk of damage to the arm. The blood supply is only cut off for a matter of seconds; it needs to be interrupted for at least 10 minutes for there to be any danger of damaging the tissues of the arm.

Q One doctor I see always takes my blood pressure on the left arm, but others use the other arm. Which is right?

A Both are! Except in people with a very rare disease, the blood pressure is the same throughout the body, so it doesn't matter which arm is measured. The difference is probably in the arrangement of each doctors' office furniture. It is obviously more convenient to measure it in whichever arm is nearer to the desk with the sphygmomanometer on it, rather than having to ask the patient to move.

Our circulatory system needs a consistent pressure if it is to function efficiently. The machine used to measure this pressure is called a sphygmomanometer.

The pressure of blood in the arteries fluctuates, about 80 times each minute, between a maximum which occurs at the height of the heart's contraction (the systolic pressure) and a minimum which occurs when the heart muscle relaxes between beats (the diastolic pressure). The sphygmomanometer works by comparing the pressure in your arteries with that required to support a standard column of mercury at a certain height. Thus the familiar figures of normal blood pressure of 120/80 mean that your systolic pressure is equivalent to the force required to support a column of mercury 120 mm (4.75 in) high, while your diastolic pressure would support a column of mercury 80 mm (3.15 in) high.

The apparatus

An upright glass tube (a manometer), which is graduated in millimeters and closed at the top, is connected at the bottom to a glass bulb containing mercury. It is fixed on to a backboard for support. There is an armlet or cuff for compressing the upper arm; and the rubber bulb for pumping it up is fitted with a screw valve to enable air to be released from the cuff at the right time. The three parts of the apparatus are connected by short lengths of rubber tubing.

Measuring the blood pressure

The armlet is wrapped firmly around the arm just above the elbow. The doctor pumps air into it until the pressure is sufficient to stop the blood flowing into the lower arm. He or she then listens with a stethoscope over the brachial artery where it passes across the elbow. At this point the doctor will hear nothing.

Continuing to listen, the doctor slightly unscrews the valve on the bulb so that air is released from the cuff and the pressure in it slowly falls. When the pressure in the cuff and in the artery are the same, the blood can flow again, but only at the systolic part of the heart's action since the diastolic pressure is insufficient to get past the inflated cuff. The doctor will hear a series of thuds each time the heart beats and squeezes blood past the cuff. The reading on the scale when these thuds are first heard represents the systolic blood pressure (see Blood pressure).

Once he or she has recorded the systolic level, the doctor loosens the valve further. When the thumping finally dies away, the reading on the scale represents the diastolic blood pressure.

Measuring a patient's blood pressure is a simple and painless procedure that is done at all routine medical checkups.

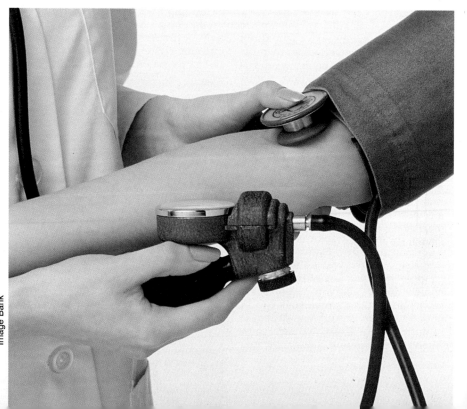

Image Bank

Spina bifida

Q My sister had a spina bifida baby. Does this mean I am more likely to have one?

A Possibly, but the risks are quite small. Before you conceive, you should ask your doctor whether or not you need to take extra vitamins. It has been found in recent research that some mothers of babies with spina bifida may have been lacking in certain vitamins, and that taking extra vitamins before conception may substantially reduce the chances of an affected baby being born. It is worthwhile consulting your doctor about this if you are considering becoming pregnant. As soon as you are pregnant, ask your gynecologist for a blood test to find out if the baby is healthy. In addition, be sure to look after yourself properly during pregnancy. Eat a varied diet, get plenty of fresh air and suitable exercise, do not smoke or take drugs, and drink very little alcohol. A healthy mother is far more likely to have a healthy baby.

Q Is it possible for a baby with spina bifida to grow into a perfectly healthy adult and to have healthy children?

A Yes. It depends entirely on the type of spina bifida with which the baby is born. If the baby is only mildly affected, then the important nerves to the legs and bladder will be undamaged. In such a case the child will develop normally and be able to have perfectly healthy children. However, adults with spina bifida do have a slightly increased risk of having a baby with spina bifida. On the other hand, if the baby is born with a severe form of the condition, he or she may have paralyzed legs and be unable to walk and will therefore have to use a wheelchair. In addition, the majority of badly affected children have poor bladder control and need to wear a special appliance to collect their urine. Owing to their numerous disabilities, severely affected adults are likely to have sexual difficulties. Nevertheless, it is possible for them to have completely healthy children.

This serious congenital condition is often severely disabling and can be fatal. Many people do not realize, however, that some spina bifida babies may be nearly normal or may be treated successfully after birth.

Many people are confused about spina bifida because the degree of disability can vary so broadly. This is because there are different types of spina bifida: the name simply means that some of the bones in the spine have not joined properly. In fact, many people have such an abnormality without realizing it, because it can cause no disabilities whatsoever.

Possible causes

Spina bifida occurs more commonly in some families than in others. The reasons for this are not fully understood, but once an affected baby has been born, the parents, brothers, and sisters, and even cousins are more likely to have an affected child than people from a family that has no history of spina bifida (see Genetics).

It has also been discovered that some mothers who have given birth to babies with spina bifida may have been lacking in certain vitamins, and there is now some evidence to suggest that taking extra vitamins before conception may substantially reduce the chances of an affected baby being born. Such vitamins, however, must only be prescribed by a doctor in the correct dosage (see Vitamins).

Types of spina bifida

Sometimes a baby is born with a soft cyst on the back, which is called a meningocele (see Cyst). It is usually on the neck or the bottom of the spine, but can occur at any point, and is an outward bulging of the fluid that surrounds the nerves and

This little boy with spina bifida can move himself along on his tricycle just like any other child: he simply uses his hands, not his feet.

Q I am 40 and pregnant. Do I have a greater risk of having a baby with spina bifida?

A No, not unless you have already had a baby with an abnormal brain or spine, or unless you have had several miscarriages. Statistically, however, a baby with some congenital abnormality, such as Down's syndrome, is more likely to be born to a woman over 35. Both Down's syndrome and spina bifida can be detected by amniocentesis, the test where some of the amniotic fluid (the fluid surrounding the fetus) is extracted from the womb and examined. In the case of spina bifida, the amniotic fluid will contain certain chemicals in abnormal amounts.

Q I had an abortion after the baby was diagnosed as having spina bifida in an amniocentesis test. Does this mean that my future pregnancies will not be normal?

A Not necessarily, but you do run a greater than average risk of conceiving another baby with a deformity of the brain or spine. However, the risk is still fairly small. To be precise, if you were to have another 25 babies, it is likely that one would have spina bifida. The problem is that you have no way of telling whether it will be the next one or the 25th. The only way to be sure is to have an amniocentesis with each pregnancy. In addition, your obstetrician will probably recommend an ultrasound examination of the developing baby or even an examination of the fetus using a special viewing instrument inserted into the womb. This is called a fetoscope and enables the doctor to view the fetus directly. However, it would be pointless to have these tests unless you were prepared to have another termination if an abnormality were to be discovered. Before you get pregnant again, visit your doctor because you may be lacking in certain vitamins. He or she will then be able to give you the correct dose on prescription, since they must be taken in exactly the right amounts, if other problems are not to be created.

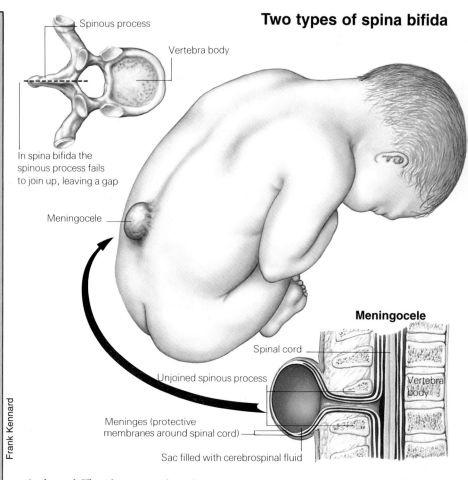

Frank Kennard

Spinous process

Vertebra body

In spina bifida the spinous process fails to join up, leaving a gap

Two types of spina bifida

Meningocele

Meningocele

Spinal cord

Unjoined spinous process

Vertebra body

Meninges (protective membranes around spinal cord)

Sac filled with cerebrospinal fluid

spinal cord. The danger is that the skin covering it may be very thin, and may become damaged and prone to infection. Early surgery is very successful in this type of spina bifida, and the baby usually grows into a perfectly normal adult.

Unfortunately most cases of spina bifida are more serious. In these types of open spina bifida, the baby is born with part of the backbone, some nerves, and the spinal cord lying exposed at the bottom of the cyst, which often bursts even before birth. Most of these babies will have disabilities, the severity of which depends on the part of the back affected and the amount of damage to nerves.

Since the extent of nerve damage varies greatly, the baby may have little or no disability or, at the other extreme, may be severely disabled. If the neck is affected, then the nerves used for breathing are usually damaged, and nearly all these babies die soon after birth. If the very bottom of the spine is involved, only a few nerves going to the feet may be abnormal and the baby can be born with nothing more serious than clubfoot (see Clubfoot). This can be cured by physical therapy (see Physical therapy) which the mother can be taught so that she can treat the baby herself at home, or by orthopedic surgery. Sometimes a few of

the nerves that control the bladder are slightly damaged so that the child may be incontinent (see Incontinence).

If the middle of the back is affected, the results are more serious. Generally the higher the opening in the back, the worse the outlook. All these children will have at least some deformity or weakness of the legs; some will never be able to walk and will always have to use a wheelchair. Others will be able to walk but only after repeated surgery on their bones and tendons, and provided they wear braces for support (see Orthopedics).

Many of these children are incontinent of bowel and bladder and may need some form of incontinence control such as a catheter to drain the urine. A severely affected child may also develop curvature of the spine at puberty, but which can, however, be rectified by major surgery (see Scoliosis). Hydrocephalus (excessive water in the brain) often accompanies this kind of spina bifida (see Hydrocephalus). It has to be drained out into the chest or abdomen through special tubes and valves.

In another form of spina bifida the baby is born apparently healthy except for a fatty lump at the bottom of the back. The danger of this is that it may be ignored because the baby can move his or her legs when newly born. However,

Myelomeningocele

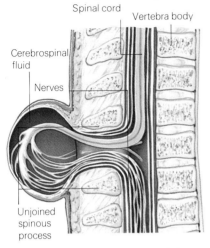

Spinal cord
Vertebra body
Cerebrospinal fluid
Nerves
Unjoined spinous process

In spina bifida, the two halves of the spinous process (which normally forms the vertebral arch) fail to join up. A baby may then be born with a meningocele, a cyst over the gap in the spine that contains spinal fluid. This can be treated by surgery on the newborn baby. A more serious form is the myelomeningocele, in which some nerves and the spinal cord are exposed, and bones may even be missing. This always causes a degree of paralysis.

this condition may deteriorate as the child gets older, so it is very important that a specialist sees him or her for regular checkups. Surgery may be undertaken to free the nerves at the first sign of trouble, though this is not always successful.

asbah

Possible treatments

An expert should examine a baby born with spina bifida immediately, even though this may mean that the baby has to be separated from his or her mother and sent to a special facility, where he or she will be in the care of a pediatric surgeon (see Pediatrics).

A whole team of specialists can then decide whether or not the baby will benefit from surgery, which is often carried out before the baby is 24 hours old in order to achieve the best results and to reduce the risk of serious infection. Many surgeons will not recommend surgery if it is thought that the baby will grow up with severe deformities, lack of bladder control, and hydrocephalus.

If the baby cannot be helped by urgent surgery, then doctors differ in their advice to parents. Some doctors recommend that the parents take the baby home as soon as they feel able to cope.

Even if spina bifida means that you have to use a wheelchair, this need not stop you doing everyday activities like shopping.

Many of these babies die from meningitis within a few weeks (see Meningitis). However, the others feed well and the spina bifida heals by itself in about six to eight weeks, although it frequently forms a big cyst, which has to be removed several months later.

Many of these babies develop fluid on the brain, which has to be treated surgically when they are three to six months old. Alternatively, some doctors think that they are best kept in a hospital to be given regular painkillers. Sadly, severely affected babies do not feed well and most die within six months.

It rests with the parents to decide the kind of treatment they want their baby to have. Parents who keep their baby at home may find it helpful to contact any one of the spina bifida associations which can give support.

Prevention

If a pregnant woman comes from a family where spina bifida has already occurred, she should tell her obstetrician who will arrange for her to have a special blood test (see Specimens). If this is not absolutely normal, the woman is usually advised to have an amniocentesis test (see Amniocentesis) and an ultrasound examination of the fetus. The purpose of these tests is to find out if the baby is affected, and, if so, to offer the mother a termination (see Abortion).

Recent evidence suggests that taking extra folic acid may reduce the likelihood of a baby being born with spina bifida. A woman should see her doctor before she conceives, who will recommend the correct dosage of folic acid.

Children with disabilities and those without disabilities are happy to play and learn together without any inhibitions.

1815

Spinal cord

Q Is the spinal column always damaged when an accident causes a broken neck?

A Not always, but quite often. But the spinal cord can be injured without there being a fracture of the spinal bones. This usually happens when the cord is suddenly stretched or twisted in an accident. So more important than the actual fracture is whether there is any displacement of the bones causing them to press onto the cord in the spinal canal which runs through the bones of the spine.

Q Is it true that ordinary viruses, such as those that cause flu, can cause an infection of the spinal cord?

A This type of myelitis can occur, but it is very rare. It's probable that those who are attacked by a virus in this way have some subtle abnormality of their immunity defenses at the time of exposure to the virus. The virus invades the body, after which there appears to be some form of reaction between the immune system and the virus, with the result that nervous tissue in the spine is damaged. Poliomyelitis is rather different since it is caused by one of three related viruses. The virus invades the motor cells of the spinal cord and parts of the brain, and disrupts the motor signals from the brain to the muscles.

Q A friend of mine who has multiple sclerosis has a lot of trouble controlling her bladder. Why should this be?

A The urge to urinate is controlled by the brain. Under normal conditions the bladder is controlled by reflex action; when the bladder is full, sensations pass to the brain telling us that the bladder desperately needs to be emptied. In multiple sclerosis, nerve damage impairs the passage of information. In some cases, sensations of a full bladder do not reach the brain, and in others the messages from the brain telling the bladder sphincter to remain shut do not reach the sphincter. Unfortunately, the outcome is usually a period of incontinence.

A vital link in the nervous system, the spinal cord gathers and analyzes information from the body and channels it to and from the brain. But when this link is damaged or broken, permanent disability may result.

The spinal cord runs down most of the length of the bony part of the spine. It forms a vital link between the brain and the nerves connected to the rest of the body. But the spinal cord is far more than simply a bundle of nerve fibers that go to and from the brain (see Brain). It acts as an important initial analyzer for incoming sensations, and as a programming station for organizing some of the basic movements of the limbs (see Nervous system).

A number of conditions can affect the spinal cord and injuries to this delicate structure can be devastating. The physical effects of any injury depend on which part of the cord is damaged, or which parts of it take the brunt of the injury.

The spinal cord

The spinal cord is protected by cerebrospinal fluid and membranes (bottom), and runs from the brain to the second lumbar vertebra before tapering into the filum terminale.

A cross section of the cord shows sensory and motor pathways carrying messages to and from the brain. Reflex action occurs when messages cross the connector nerve (below).

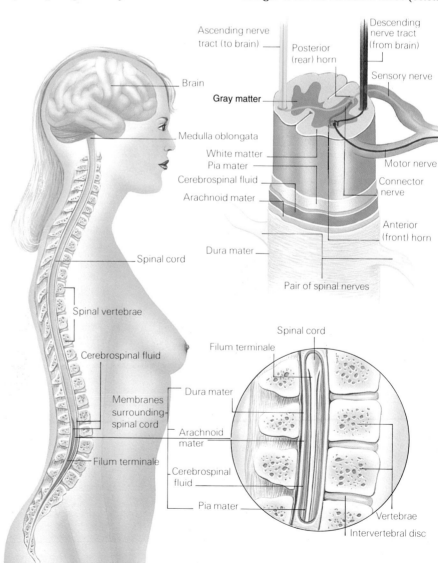

Ascending nerve tract (to brain)
Descending nerve tract (from brain)
Posterior (rear) horn
Sensory nerve
Brain
Gray matter
Medulla oblongata
White matter
Pia mater
Cerebrospinal fluid
Arachnoid mater
Motor nerve
Connector nerve
Anterior (front) horn
Dura mater
Spinal cord
Pair of spinal nerves
Spinal vertebrae
Spinal cord
Filum terminale
Cerebrospinal fluid
Dura mater
Membranes surrounding spinal cord
Arachnoid mater
Filum terminale
Cerebrospinal fluid
Pia mater
Vertebrae
Intervertebral disc

Elaine Keenan

Structure of the spinal cord

The spinal cord runs from the medulla oblongata in the brain down to the first or second lumbar vertebra.

The cord is well protected as it passes through the arches of the spinal vertebrae. Sensory and motor nerves of the peripheral nervous system leave the spinal cord separately just below the vertebrae and then join to form 31 pairs of spinal nerves (8 cervical, 12 thoracic, 5 lumbar, 5 sacral, and 1 coccygeal), each nerve corresponding to the vertebra that it leaves. These nerves branch out from the spinal cord, spreading to the surface of the body and to all the skeletal muscles.

The spinal cord is composed of collections of nerve cell bodies of neurons and bundles of nerve fibers. The gray matter, or the nerve cell collections, is H-shaped in cross section, with a posterior (rear) and anterior (front) horn (protuberance) in each half. The anterior is composed of motor neurons, while the posterior horn contains cell bodies of connector neurons and sensory neurons.

The gray matter is surrounded by the white matter. The white matter is divided into three columns and contains ascending and descending nerve tracts which connect the brain and the spinal cord in both directions. The descending tracts send motor impulses from the brain to the peripheral nervous system, while the ascending tracts channel sensory impulses to the brain.

Surrounding these nerves and fibers is a series of tough membranes which are extensions of those membranes that surround the brain. Between the outer two of these three membrane layers is a small gap which contains cerebrospinal fluid. This circulates around the spinal cord and the brain, providing nutrients to the nerves and acting as a protective buffer.

Functions of the spinal cord

The spinal cord has two main functions: to act as a two-way conduction system between the brain and the peripheral nervous system, and to control simple reflex actions (see Reflexes).

The spinal cord and the brain make up the central nervous system. Messages, in the form of electrical impulses created by the firing of interconnected neurons, from the surface of the body connect with the spinal cord via the sensory nerve fibers in the peripheral nervous system. The gray matter in the spinal cord rapidly processes the messages, and then relays some of them up the ascending tract of the spinal cord for more detailed analysis in the brain.

If some action is required, the brain sends messages of action, in the form of motor impulses, down the descending

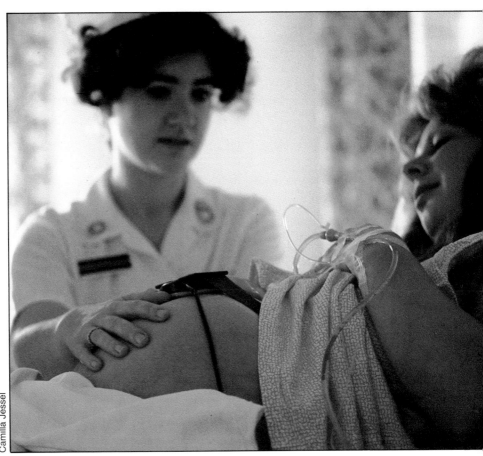

tract that result in coordinated muscular action involving many different muscles in the body. For example, when an itch is felt in the hand, initial analysis takes place at the spinal cord. Further analysis then takes place in the brain, which may then send messages in response, instructing the appropriate muscles of the body to move accordingly (see Muscles).

In controlling the simple reflex action the usual pattern of message transmission to the brain is drastically curtailed. If the skin touches something hot, streams of impulses are passed via the sensory neurons to the posterior horn in the gray matter of the spinal cord. Instead of then ascending to the brain, the messages are immediately processed, and then cross to the anterior horn of the gray matter via connector neurons. These allow messages to be transmitted from sensory neurons to motor neurons, giving an immediate physical response—the hand is rapidly and automatically withdrawn. This is known as the reflex arc. At the same time, information will be passed on to the brain, which will determine further action, if any.

Many of the body's important functions are controlled through reflex action and these occur at all levels of the spinal cord. Some movements involved in respiration, digestion, and especially excretion, for example, are reflex actions controlled in part by the spinal cord (see Autonomic nervous system).

The pain of childbirth can be eased through the use of epidural anesthesia. A drip fed into the space around the spinal cord anesthetizes the nerves carrying messages to and from the uterus and cervix.

Spinal cord problems

A variety of conditions can seriously affect the spinal cord, from those that are acquired before birth, such as spina bifida, to others that can appear later on in life, like multiple sclerosis (see Multiple sclerosis).

Spina bifida: In this fairly common type of birth defect, the spine and the spinal cord fail to develop normally in the womb. A flat plate of cells on the embryo's back normally folds itself into a tube, which then develops into the spine and spinal cord. In spina bifida, however, this process is disrupted, leaving the spinal cord malformed and exposed at the back.

The condition may leave the child with complete paralysis of the legs and no control over either urination or defecation. In some severe cases, brain damage may also occur. The type of treatment that may be possible will depend on how badly deformed the spinal cord is (see Spina bifida).

Injuries to the spinal cord: This is the most common cause of problems with the spinal cord, displaced vertebrae and whiplash injuries being the most frequent types of injury.

Q In a spinal tap, is the fluid taken off through the needle from the spinal cord itself? If so, isn't there a risk of damage to the cord?

A The spinal cord ends about three-quarters of the way down the spine. The spinal canal (the space enclosed by the bones of the spine), which is below that, is only partly filled by the nerves which go down to the legs. So there is room for a needle to remove fluid without damaging the nerves. The fluid is the same as that which circulates around the brain and through the center of the cord, so it is useful to examine it when diagnosing conditions affecting the nervous system.

Q Are the cells of the spinal cord like the cells of the brain or are they a special sort?

A The nerve cells, or neurons, of the spinal cord are the same pattern as those of the brain, and although some are specialized for their particular job—as are some in the brain—the cells of the spinal cord are essentially the same.

Q I have heard that the spinal cord is one of the parts of the body commonly affected by syphilis. Is this true?

A This is now uncommon, but one of the delayed effects of syphilis can be to attack the sensory nerves just as they are entering the spinal cord. This causes the rear part of the cord, which is made up of the sensory fibers on their way to the brain, to wither. The main symptom from the loss of these nerves is a poor sense of where the joints are, making walking difficult.

Q Is the spinal cord always seriously deformed when a baby is born with spina bifida?

A No, the spinal cord is not always deformed. There are degrees of severity. It is only in the most severe type that the spinal cord is involved and fails to fold over as it should as the baby develops in the womb. Sometimes spina bifida involves only the bones of the spine, and there is seldom any spinal cord trouble.

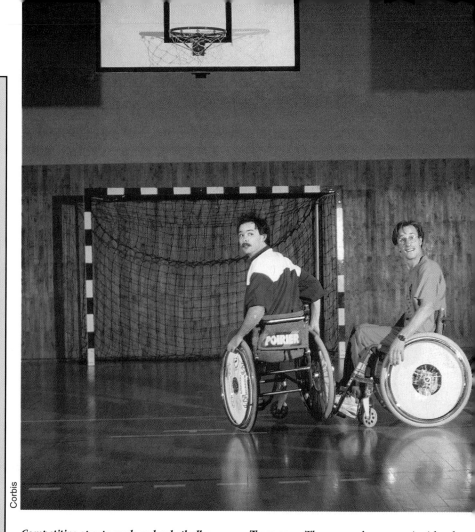

Competitive sports such as basketball are actively pursued and enjoyed by many people with severe spinal injuries (above). Differing degrees of mobility can be achieved and high standards of expertise obtained.

Exactly what functions are lost is determined by which part of the spinal cord is actually damaged. If the cord is damaged high in the neck, all the limbs will be paralyzed, and there may even be difficulty in breathing. Immediately after the injury all the limbs become limp, with all feeling being lost below the level of the injury. In addition, bladder control is considerably affected.

After a period of weeks or months, various changes appear in the paralyzed legs and arms, as the spinal cord below the injury recovers a little. The limbs become stiff and may respond briskly with reflex movements. In some cases, there may be more improvement, and the injured person may even achieve a stiff-legged walk.

If the injury is in the middle of the back, then only the legs are affected. The bladder's function is usually affected in any spinal cord injury, since the nerves to the bladder leave the cord at its lower end. Sexual function is lost, too, because the nerves involved are also located at the lower end.

Tumors: These rarely occur inside the spinal cord itself, but the cord can be pressed on by tumors from the outside. The effects of this type of complaint on the cord, and what symptoms are produced, depend on where the tumor is located. Occasional pains around the trunk, or down an arm or leg are common symptoms of a tumor pressing on the nerves emerging from the cord. Sensation may also be lost from either side of the body below the site of the trouble. As with spinal injuries, the person may also become incontinent.

Treatment depends on where the tumor is located, but it usually involves either surgical removal of the tumor or drainage of the abscess. In the case of a cancerous tumor, radiotherapy may be used (see Tumors).

Multiple sclerosis: The cause of this type of inflammation is still unknown. It attacks nerve tissue anywhere in the body, particularly the main nerves to the eye, the optic nerve, and nerves in the brain stem and the spinal cord, especially in the neck area. Spinal cord damage from multiple sclerosis can cause progressive loss of sensation and occasional tingling feelings in the hands and feet.

Myelitis: This term means inflammation of the spinal cord, and so includes multiple sclerosis. However, myelitis can be

Areas of the body controlled by the spinal nerves

The majority of signals that control the body's sensations and movement are fed to and from the brain via the 31 pairs of nerves joining the spinal column. These nerves control different areas of the body. If the cord is damaged, all areas fed by the nerves below the site of the injury will be affected.

caused by some common viruses, where there is only one attack, unlike the repetitive attacks which characterize multiple sclerosis. The cord becomes acutely inflamed at a particular spot; below this, all function may be lost. This form of myelitis may follow an attack of flu, or some other trivial form of viral infection.

Vitamin deficiency: A lack of the vitamin B_{12} can produce a particular pattern of damage to the spinal cord (as well as to the peripheral nerves). The parts of the spinal cord affected include the muscle running down the side of the cord and the sensory nerves which convey sensations of touch and a sense of where the joints are.

The affected person may suffer from a mild weakness in the limbs and have an odd, high-stepping walk because the person has difficulty in establishing where the feet are in relation to his or her body. Some recovery from this condition can be brought about when the vitamin deficiency is treated (see Vitamins).

Many conditions affecting the spinal cord are long-term problems; recovery, if any, is slow and painstaking, and the patient will require devoted nursing. Recovery from a spinal cord injury may never be complete, especially if the damage is severe. But considerable movement and control can be regained through regular exercise.

Mick Saunders

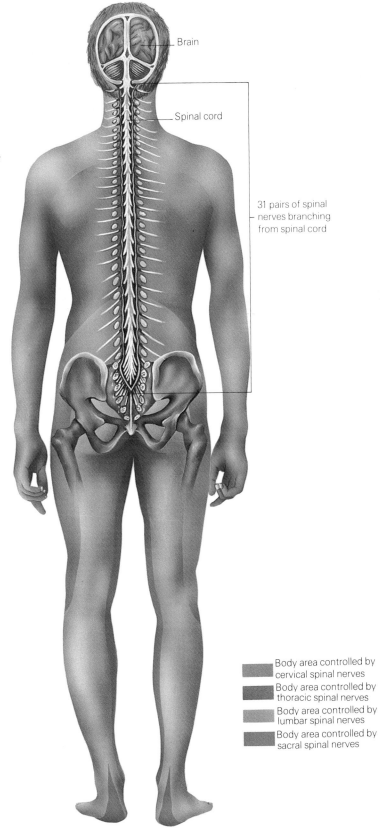

Brain

Spinal cord

31 pairs of spinal nerves branching from spinal cord

Body area controlled by cervical spinal nerves

Body area controlled by thoracic spinal nerves

Body area controlled by lumbar spinal nerves

Body area controlled by sacral spinal nerves

Spleen

Q I've heard of cases where the spleen burst during an attack of glandular fever. Is this true, and is it dangerous?

A It is possible that it may burst in this disease, but it is a very rare occurrence. If the spleen does burst as a result of the glandular fever virus, then its contents will be released into the abdomen where they may inflame the peritoneum, the membrane lining the abdomen, giving rise to peritonitis. A burst spleen can be dangerous, but it should be emphasized that it happens very infrequently.

Q My brother insists that he has two spleens. Can this be true?

A Yes. There is usually only one big spleen to be found in the abdomen, normally in the top left-hand corner, but occasionally there may be one or two accessory spleens in the same general area.

Q A friend of mine had to have his spleen removed after a traffic accident. Does this mean that his blood will be affected?

A Since the spleen plays a major part in ridding the body of harmful bacteria, and is instrumental in making antibodies, removal of the spleen makes a person susceptible to serious bacterial infections. This is particularly true in children, and some physicians recommend prophylactic antibiotic treatment for all postsplenectomy patients.

Q I read that the spleen influences a person's emotional state. Is this true?

A No. It was once thought that the spleen was the seat of anger, and morose or bad-tempered individuals were referred to as having a splenic personality. We still talk of venting your spleen on people, which means to get angry with them. But there is no scientific basis for this at all. It's hard to see why this innocent blood-forming and filtering organ should have acquired such an unsavory reputation.

Situated in the top left-hand corner of the abdomen, the spleen plays a major role in blood formation and influences the development of immunity. In addition, it may signal disease elsewhere in the body.

The spleen is an important organ of the body. Its main function is to act as a filter for the blood and to make antibodies. In addition, an enlarged spleen, which can be felt through the walls of the abdomen, is often an indication of disease somewhere in the body.

The spleen is also an integral part of the lymphatic system—the basis of the body's defense against infection.

Location

The spleen lies just below the diaphragm at the top of the left-hand side of the abdomen. It is normally about 5 in (13 cm) long, and it lies along the line of the tenth rib. The spleen usually weighs about .5 lb (about 200 g) in adults, but, in cases where it is enlarged, it can weigh up to 4.5 lb (2 kg) or more.

If a spleen is examined with the naked eye, it will look like a fibrous capsule surrounding a mass of featureless red pulp. It may just be possible to make out little granulations called Malpighian corpuscles. The organ is supplied with blood via the splenic artery, which, like any other artery, splits first into smaller arteries and then into tiny arterioles. However, the arterioles of the spleen are unusual in that they are wrapped in lymphatic tissue as they pass through the pulp of the spleen. The arterioles are unique in one other way: instead of being connected to

Position of the spleen

The spleen is situated in the top left-hand corner of the abdomen, just below the diaphragm. It is in a relatively exposed position, which is why it is frequently damaged in accidents and has to be removed, generally without any ill effects.

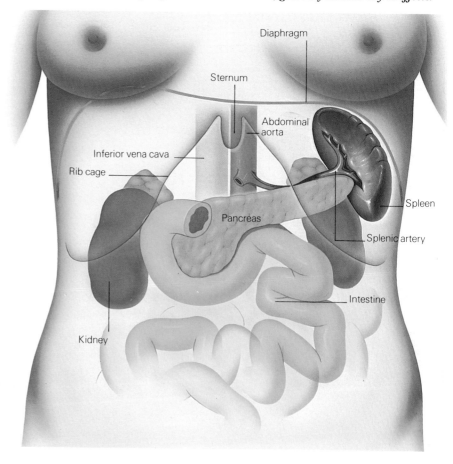

Diaphragm

Sternum

Abdominal aorta

Inferior vena cava

Rib cage

Pancreas

Spleen

Splenic artery

Intestine

Kidney

a network of capillaries, they seem to empty out into the substance of the spleen itself.

The odd way in which the spleen is supplied with blood is what enables it to perform two of its basic functions. First, the fact that the arterioles are wrapped with lymphatic tissue means that the lymphatic system comes into immediate contact with any abnormal protein in the blood and forms antibodies to it. Second, the way that the blood empties directly into the pulp of the spleen also allows the reticular cells of the organ to come into direct contact with the blood, filtering it of any old or worn-out cells.

Functions of the spleen

The spleen is one of the main filters of the blood. Not only do the reticular cells remove the old and worn-out blood cells, but they will also remove any abnormal cells. This applies, in particular, to red blood cells, but white cells and platelets are also filtered selectively when necessary by the spleen (see Blood).

The spleen will also remove abnormal particles floating in the bloodstream. This means that it plays a major part in ridding the body of harmful bacteria, to give just

A child with an enlarged spleen may be suffering from one of a wide range of diseases. Here the doctor is palpating the abdomen to determine the exact position and size of the spleen.

The healthy spleen: an almost featureless organ that usually weighs about 0.5 lb (200 g) in adults and is 5 in (13 cm) long.

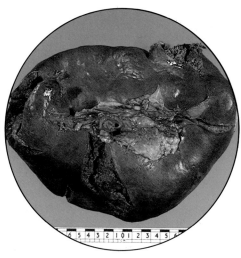

A diseased spleen: this spleen is greatly enlarged because of the presence of a lymphoma or lymphatic tumor.

one example. It is also instrumental in making antibodies—proteins circulating in the blood that bind onto and immobilize a foreign protein so that white blood cells called phagocytes can destroy it. The Malpighian corpuscles, which are collections of lymphocytes, make the antibody.

In some circumstances, the spleen has a very important role in the manufacture of new blood cells. This does not happen in the normal adult, but in people who have a bone marrow disease the spleen and the liver are major sites of red blood cell

production. In addition, the spleen makes much of the blood of a baby in the womb.

Feeling the spleen

The spleen cannot be felt in normal healthy people, but there is a large range of diseases that cause enlargement of the spleen, which can then be felt through the walls of the abdomen. The procedure is simple: with the patient lying on his or her back, the doctor starts to feel (or palpate) the bottom of the abdomen, and then works up toward the top left-hand

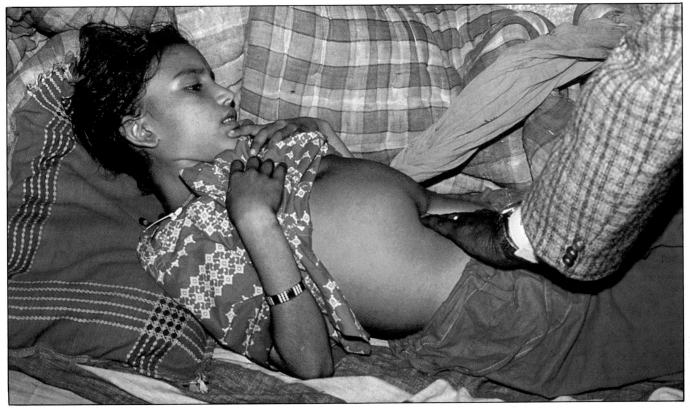

Geographical distribution of kala-azar

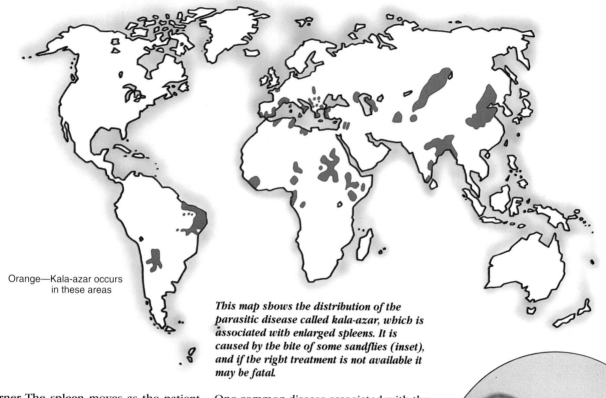

Orange—Kala-azar occurs
in these areas

This map shows the distribution of the parasitic disease called kala-azar, which is associated with enlarged spleens. It is caused by the bite of some sandflies (inset), and if the right treatment is not available it may be fatal.

John Hutchinson

corner. The spleen moves as the patient breathes, so he or she is asked to take deep breaths so that this movement can be felt. Enlargement of the spleen can also be detected on X rays or by using a radioactive isotope scan.

Enlargement of the spleen
The spleen may enlarge for many reasons. Since one of its main functions is to break down old and worn-out blood cells, those conditions where blood is broken down faster than normal are associated with an enlarged spleen. These diseases are called hemolytic anemias, and many of them, such as sickle-cell anemia or thalassemia, are inherited (see Sickle-cell anemia, and Thalassemia). Hemolytic problems can also have other causes; for example, some drugs like the anti-blood pressure drug methyldopa may cause hemolysis and thus a large spleen. Other blood diseases also cause the spleen to become enlarged. In some cases of leukemia, for example, the spleen grows so much that it stretches from the top left-hand corner of the abdomen to the bottom right-hand corner (see Leukemia).

There are two other diseases that are associated with enlarged spleens: malaria (see Malaria) and the parasitic disease called kala-azar, in which the parasites actually inhabit the spleen. Many other infections can cause an enlarged spleen. After all, it is involved in the body's immune mechanisms against infection.

One common disease associated with the enlargement of the spleen is glandular fever. Occasionally the big spleen in this illness can rupture as a result of a comparatively minor injury to the abdomen, and an operation will be needed (see Infectious mononucleosis).

The veins of the spleen drain into what is known as the portal system of veins. These are actually the veins that drain food-rich blood from the intestines into the liver. Thus, when liver disease is present, the pressure on the system tends to rise, and this in turn puts pressure on the spleen, causing it to enlarge. In this way an enlarged spleen can actually indicate that there is trouble in the liver.

The spleen is therefore a useful indicator of health, since it may become enlarged as a result of problems in other systems of the body. There is little that can go wrong with the spleen itself: cysts and benign tumors may form rarely.

Removal of the spleen
There are, however, a number of reasons why the spleen may have to be removed. Despite the fact that it is an important filter of the blood, very few ill effects seem to result from its removal, although it is possible to see changes in blood cells.

If the spleen is injured as the result of an accident it may bleed profusely, and this means that it will have to be removed. The spleen may also have to be removed during laparotomies (investigative operations during which the abdomen is opened) in order to investigate the extent of lymphomas (lymphatic tumors; see Lymphoma).

Occasionally the spleen becomes overactive in its function of breaking down blood cells, and this leads to excessive destruction of cells. This is likely to happen only when the spleen is already enlarged for some reason, such as a lymphoma or portal hypertension due to liver disease. In these cases, too, the spleen may be removed.

The spleen is therefore an unusual organ, for while it has straightforward functions, the body seems to be able to manage well without it. It is also unusual because, although it rarely malfunctions itself, it is often involved in other defects arising elsewhere.

Splinters

Q How should splinters or fragments that you get in the eye be dealt with?

A Splinters in the eye must be treated with great care because the danger of causing further damage is considerable and could have very serious results. First, stop the patient from rubbing his or her eye. Second, flood the eye with a steady flow of water, at the same time getting the patient to blink rapidly. If the object is on the center of the eye and does not come away with washing, make no further attempt to remove it. Take the patient to the hospital as soon as possible. If the splinter is not visible, sit down facing the patient and slowly draw the lower eyelid outward and downward while he or she looks up. If you still do not see it, repeat with the upper eyelid. When you see the object, try removing it using the corner of a clean handkerchief. If it does not come away easily, do not persist, and never use tweezers to dislodge the splinter. Again, take the patient to the hospital so that a doctor can deal with the problem.

Q How should fishhooks that have got embedded in the skin be removed?

A First, clean the area with soap and water, and, if possible, apply disinfectant. Never try to drag the hook, which is almost certain to be barbed, back through the skin. In fact, push it further forward until the point and the barb come out through the skin again. Then, using pliers or wire-cutters cut through the shaft of the hook. Remove the eye and the attached line. Finally, grip the hook firmly and pull that out of the second hole you have made in the skin.

Q What should you put on a splinter wound, and should it be covered?

A Most wounds are best left uncovered, and a splinter wound is unlikely to be very large. A clean dressing or adhesive bandage is all that is necessary if you do wish to cover the wound, to stop it getting dirty, for example.

Getting a splinter is a very common experience and often trivial. However, since it can cause infection or damage to tissues, it should be dealt with promptly.

Although we tend to think of splinters as pieces of wood, they can consist of some other material, such as glass or metal.

Why splinters can be harmful

Splinters may damage some underlying structure such as an artery or nerve by puncturing it. This is much more likely to happen with large metal splinters which enter the body with considerable force and penetrate deeply.

A splinter may also form a focus for infection. An inevitable result of a splinter is that germs are instantly transported through the body's defensive covering of skin and deposited into underlying tissue where conditions are ideal for infection.

Treatment

Large splinters, or splinters that have gone deep into the flesh, should be left undisturbed until they have been seen by a doctor. Even if there is a huge piece of glass sticking right out of a wound, leave it alone. It has done all the damage it is going to do for the time being.

If it has penetrated the wall of a major artery it may be effectively plugging the wound. Attempting to pull it out may cause a massive hemorrhage. In addition,

if it is very jagged, you may do far more damage dragging it out than the splinter did going in.

When a splinter can be seen clearly and safely removed without risk of causing further damage, you can remove it yourself. If it is sticking out from under the skin or a nail, hold the affected part firmly with one hand, grip the splinter as close to the site of entry as possible with tweezers, and pull it out in one firm movement. Never pull on the end; the splinter is likely to break or the tweezers may slip.

To deal with a splinter that is completely embedded, first sterilize a long, fine needle by holding the sharp end in a flame for 10 seconds. Then use the point to open up the track of the splinter from the tail toward the point of entry, and lift the splinter out with tweezers. Opening the track from the point of entry downward may drive it further in. Also, trying to lift it from the side is likely to break it. After removal, sterilize the wound with antiseptic and cover it with a dressing, or leave antiseptic cream on it for 24 hours.

Removing a splinter that is small and visible is a simple and safe procedure. If the splinter is sticking out of the skin, hold it firmly and, using tweezers, grip the splinter as close as possible to the site of entry. Pull the splinter out with a single firm movement. Never attempt to pull the splinter out by the tip since there is the likelihood that the splinter will break, or the tweezers may slip, causing further damage to the skin. Most splinter wounds are best left uncovered.

Phil Babb

Splints

Q I've been told that applying a splint to a broken leg does more harm than good. Is this true?

A If a splint is incorrectly fitted, it can be very dangerous. If applied too tightly to the limb, circulation may be impaired. Since a broken leg swells rapidly after injury, a splint which was initially safe may become too tight. Also, any sharp edges of the splint may dig into the flesh and cause a blister or sore. So if you must put a splint on someone's broken leg, make sure you know what you're doing. Better still, if possible, wait for someone who is qualified to do it.

Q Are splints used for all types of fractures, even hairline ones?

A Splints are used mainly where the fracture is actually unstable, that is, able to move around. Hairline fractures are usually stable, since they are held firm by the surrounding tissues. Splinting these isn't necessary and can even be harmful. Rib fractures, for example, are no longer splinted, since this has been found to make breathing difficult.

Q What is the difference between a splint and a brace?

A A brace is a type of splint. It is more sophisticated in that it often has hinges or springs to allow certain joints to move while preventing others from moving. Braces are used for long-term problems and are therefore made of very strong, durable materials.

Q I recently saw a paramedic applying what looked like a plastic bag to a broken leg. What was this?

A This must have been an inflatable splint: a clear, heavy plastic bag shaped roughly like a leg that opens along the top with a zipper. The injured leg is placed in the bag, which is inflated, giving good all around support. Such splints are only temporary.

Although most often used on limbs, splints can act as external supports for any injured part of the body. They range from simple wooden strips to highly sophisticated devices such as braces.

A splint is an external support for an injured or wounded part of the body. Splints can be used for various injuries, but are most commonly employed on the limbs. They can vary from simple wooden strips bandaged to a fractured bone to complicated devices with hinges, springs, and buckles. Casts, supports, and braces are all different types of splint.

Uses

Fractures and sprains: Splints have several functions in the treatment of these injuries. First, the splint protects an injured limb from further damage by providing a hard casing in the form of a cast and by stopping movement. Second, the splint holds the limb rigid in a particular position. This is important because once the fracture has begun to heal it is essential that the bone knits together without deformity. Third, the splint may allow the fractured limb to be used while the injury is healing (see Fractures, Skeleton, and Sprains).

Childhood disorders: In some childhood conditions certain parts of the body do not grow or develop properly because

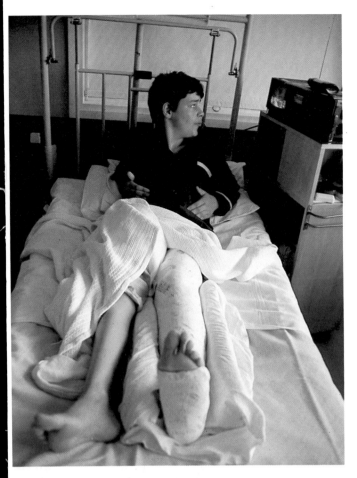

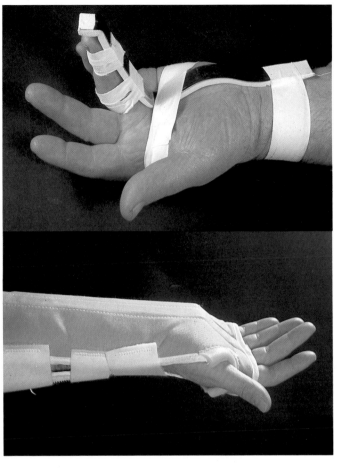

Wearing braces (left) may restrict this little girl's movement, but will not deny her the simple childhood pleasure of zooming down a slide. The traditional cast (above) is a type of splint. A finger splint (top right) will prevent deformity. An arm splint and brace (above right) will hold the limb rigid until the fracture heals.

they are in the wrong position. The best example is congenital dislocation of the hip. A splint may be used to keep the hip joint in position while it undergoes a period of growth, and at the same time allow the infant some freedom of movement and the parent access for diaper changing and washing (see Hip).

Paralytic conditions: In these conditions, splints are used either to take over the function of paralyzed muscles, or to prevent joints becoming deformed by the abnormal pull of the muscles on them. These splints are more complicated since they often need to be jointed to allow easy movement, and should be easily removable. They may also incorporate springs to take over from weak or paralyzed muscles.

Arthritis: Temporary splints may be useful in resting joints afflicted with acute arthritis. They may also be used to correct severe deformity (see Arthritis).

What are splints made of?

The simplest and most widely used splinting material is plaster of paris. Most common fractures that require splints are set in a cast made of bandage material coated with plaster. When the roll of plaster bandage is dipped in water it becomes soft, and it can then be molded closely to the injured limb in the few minutes that it takes for the cast to dry. Once dry the cast is strong and durable. However, it is heavy and breaks easily if it becomes wet.

Newer plastic materials have been developed to overcome the disadvantages of plaster. Simple plastic sheets, which become pliable when they are heated, can be molded to fit a limb. These tend to be softer than plaster and are particularly useful when a splint has to be replaced frequently.

However, splints needed for longer-term use continue to be made of leather and metal. Leg braces, for example, need to fit snugly and comfortably, and yet need to be strong and resilient enough to withstand the repeated stresses of walking. Leather braces have not yet been surpassed by synthetic versions: leather is strong and soft and, unlike plastic, it breathes, which prevents the skin from becoming soggy.

Splints may be used temporarily or permanently. A splint may be employed as an interim first-aid measure for transporting an injured person to the hospital. Casts for treating fractures will have to be worn for two weeks to several months. Some people may have to wear a splint permanently to stabilize a weak limb.

Dangers

Any rigid device fixed to the body involves certain risks. The most obvious is that the device may rub and chafe on the skin and cause a blister or sore (see Blisters, and Sores). A splint that encircles the limb is potentially more dangerous. If, for example, a limb swells when it is encased in a cast, the cast will compress the limb and may eventually damage its blood and nerve supply. For this reason, most hospitals will require you to return the day after the fracture has been set to make sure that the cast is safe and comfortable. In addition, the first cast put on a fracture may be split so that if the limb swells the cast will expand.

Another danger is that joints immobilized by a splint may become stiff. When the splint is removed they will need time to loosen up, and exercises or physical therapy may be necessary (see Exercise, and Physical therapy).

Sports medicine

Q Should my daughter, who is a sprinter, continue training during her period?

A The effects of menstruation vary considerably from one woman to another. Some women are virtually incapacitated during this time while others experience little or no discomfort. But it seems apparent that exercise can improve a woman's capacity to cope with the changes that occur during menstruation. So if your daughter is comfortable training during her period, there is every reason for her to continue doing so. Many women athletes find that their sporting performance varies over the menstrual cycle, usually deteriorating in the days preceding their period and picking up in midcycle, though some find that they actually perform best during their periods.

Q What is the value of high altitude training?

A The air at high altitudes is much thinner or more rarified than at sea level, so the body compensates by increasing the concentration of hemoglobin in the blood. This allows the body to use what available oxygen there is more efficiently. In theory, this increased oxygen-carrying capacity should also help an athlete's performance when he or she returns to sea level.

Q My son insists on wearing low-cut cleats when playing football. Wouldn't it be safer for him to wear cleats with a better ankle protection?

A Ankle injuries are more common with the low-cut type of show. Heavier show do generally provide more protection, but their use may lead to some loss of speed and agility, and may also be tiring. If your son plays in midfield, where the chances of the ankle being kicked are much higher, then a heavier shoe would certainly be advisable. But if he plays in one of the rear positions, where speed and agility may be more important, a lighter weight shoe would be more suitable.

Virtually every sport involves some risk of injury, from the trivial to the disastrous. Sports medicine investigates the causes, determines the treatment, and recommends methods of preventing sports injuries.

Corbis

Injuries in highly competitive sports such as baseball are widespread. Protective clothing and equipment are vital to help prevent serious physical damage. Baseball players wear shin guards, padded gloves, thigh pads, and helmets to protect them from the very hard ball and from other players! A football coach (right) helps an injured player.

One of the most important applications of sports medicine is to research the factors that can affect fitness including strength, speed, skill, stamina, agility, and personality. And also to suggest ways in which performance can be improved through diet, training, and lifestyle. Medical research and opinion may also make a valuable contribution to the design of sports equipment and protective clothing, and sporting authorities may turn to doctors for advice about the drugs that athletes can use without side effects. Generally, however, sports medicine is concerned with the causes, treatment, and prevention of sports injuries at all levels of participation.

Types of sports injury

Virtually every sport involves some risk of injury, although the pattern of injury varies considerably from one sport to another. Perhaps the most hazardous sports are those involving high speed, such as motor racing and skiing, or those that involve special environmental hazards, such as scuba diving, or mountaineering.

Body-contact sports, such as football, basketball, and boxing, can also pose significant dangers. Thus, with football, there is the chance of an injury to virtually any part of the legs, as well as the head and collarbone, as a result of the collisions that are so commonplace.

With basketball there are also risks, such as breaking an arm or leg, or being injured in a heavy tackle. Continuous heavy blows to the head in boxing may cause serious lasting damage to the brain as it is knocked around inside the skull (see Brain damage and disease). Cut eyes, mouths, broken noses, damaged hands, and cauliflower ears are also commonplace injuries in contact sports.

In noncontact sports, the main physical danger may come from the equipment

used in the sport. Being hit on the head by a baseball, or spiked by a fellow athlete's track shoes, are common examples. More often, injury is self-inflicted or it follows the overuse of some part of the body. Examples are strained elbows and damaged knee joints of tennis players, pulled muscles of sprinters or throwers who have failed to warm up properly before a competition, and stress fractures that sometimes affect long-distance runners in training.

Fractures

Sports fractures may occur as the result of a direct blow, and common types of fractures include the broken legs of footballers and skiers, broken collarbones among many ballplayers, and broken finger bones, ribs, and arms in baseball players.

Small finger and foot bones usually heal up completely after four or five weeks, but leg fractures may require immobilization for a much longer period (see Fractures).

Stress fractures are overuse injuries caused by repetitive loading of a bone during training or playing. Athletes who train over very long distances each week are the most prone to this type of injury, particularly if they run mainly on roads or other hard surfaces and wear shoes without sufficient cushioned support. The bones most

Thrills and spills of speed and power; racetrack driving is made safer by the use of helmets and leather suits; the country sport of point-to-point racing has its share of falls, which are usually more dramatic than dangerous. The bone-crushing sport of ice hockey makes extensive protective gear essential (below right).

Muscle stiffness is very common the morning after some unaccustomed effort, but it gradually disappears over a day or two. The stiffness is probably due to the combined effects of a number of very small tears in the muscle.

Tendons are the fibrous cords that join muscles to bone. They can be ruptured or torn by a direct blow or by excessive strain, or they may become inflamed through overuse. Oarsmen, tennis players, and hockey players often develop an inflammation of the tendons in their wrist due to a persistent tight grip on oar, racket, stick, or bat. A few days' rest usually relieves the condition (see Tendons).

Joint ligament injuries

Joint injury may involve damage to the bone ends that make up the joint; to the cartilage that coats each bone end; to the ligaments that determine the range of movement of the joint; or to a variety of other structures around and within the many different joints (see Ligaments).

Sprains can arise when a joint is forcibly moved beyond its normal range (see Joints) and may involve the tearing or rupturing of a ligament; knee and ankle sprains are the most common (see Knee, and Sprains).

Dislocations occur when one of the bone ends is completely displaced from its normal position, thus damaging the ligaments and rendering the joint either immobile or unstable. A doctor, or other qualified person, must quickly reposition the bone before the tissues swell (see Dislocation, and Osteopathy).

Following a sprain or a dislocation, a joint may need to be immobilized for several weeks so that the damaged ligaments can heal and regain their full strength (see Bandages, Healing, and Splints).

Apart from sprains and dislocations, one of the most common injuries to the knee joint is a torn cartilage, which is both painful and may considerably limit any

1

The Weisenfeld warm-up exercises loosen muscles and prevent injuries. Wall pushups (1) stretch calf and soleus muscles. The three-level leg lift (2) builds up abdominal and thigh muscles. The foot press exercise (3) strengthens the thigh muscles and can be used for the treatment and prevention of "runner's knee." Knee-press exercises stretch both hamstrings and lower-back muscles, preventing pulled hamstrings and lower back pain (4). By tensing the thigh muscles, turning the feet in or out, and holding for 10 seconds (5), the thigh muscles can be strengthened.

commonly affected are those in the middle part of the foot and the lower leg bones. Symptoms usually begin with pain in the affected area that occurs regularly during training and increases in severity with each training session.

At this point, the fracture may consist of a crack or a weakness in the bone structure. If the athlete rests from the activity for around four to six weeks, the injury will gradually start to heal, but to continue training in defiance of the pain could cause the bone to shatter suddenly with much more serious consequences (see Bones).

Muscle and tendon injuries

Muscle injuries are very common in sports and usually involve a rupture of some of the muscle's fibers, variously described as a pull, a tear, or a strain. The thigh and calf muscles are the most commonly injured among footballers and the hamstrings at the back of the thigh among sprinters.

The usual cause of muscle strain is an excessive demand made on the muscle before it has been warmed up properly. Cold muscles contract in a jerky fashion, which can produce too great a load on some of the fibers. When they tear, the usual symptom is a sudden stabbing ache. Such pain may continue for a week or more, but it is a good idea to continue exercising gently during this time to speed the return to full activity (see Muscles).

3

2

Ron Sutherland

knee movement. It is quite common for a damaged cartilage to require surgical removal (see Cartilage).

Rehabilitation

Initial treatment of most sports injuries consists of measures aimed at reducing pain and swelling in the area affected, together with the resetting of fractured bones and dislocated joints, and any other first-aid measures (see Rehabilitation). Although the injured part of the body

4

often has to be immobilized for some weeks to allow damaged tissues to heal, in many cases an early return to light exercise is encouraged to prevent muscle wasting or the formation of scar tissue that might delay full recovery (see Exercise).

A graded exercise program is worked out by doctor and physical therapist (see Physical therapy) with the aim of rebuilding muscle, tendon, and bone strength or joint stability, and restoring a full range of movement. The temptation to return to full participation in a sport before obtaining the doctor's permission should be resisted. This is likely to lead to a recurrence of the injury, followed by a further, and usually longer, spell on the sidelines.

Avoiding injury

Most sports injuries could be avoided through a mixture of common sense, fitness training, expert supervision, and adequate preparation for the particular activity in question, which includes selecting and using the right equipment.

5

If you have not had any exercise for several months, strenuous activities should be avoided until you have built up an appropriate level of fitness by taking part in a more moderate activity. Thorough stretching and warming up before a game will help to protect the muscles and joints from injury when the game begins.

Protective clothing, such as helmets, pads, gloves, and boxes to safeguard the genitals for ice hockey and football players, shin pads for baseball players, and gum shields for boxers, should be worn wherever possible.

Wearing the correct footwear is also particularly important for all types of sport. Training shoes should be comfortable and well padded with shock-absorbent material, and should have treads that provide an adequate grip on the training surface. For sports that involve rapid changes in direction, the shoe must provide adequate support to the side of the foot in order to prevent the ankle turning.

Any persistent pain that occurs in any part of the body during training sessions should be dealt with by refraining from the activity for a few days. Even better, you should pay a visit to the doctor. Ignoring the discomfort of a sports injury is likely to aggravate any persistent problem further, and also invites disaster, so always take note and act on what your body is telling you (see Pain).

Sprains

Q **What is the best type of bandage to use in treating a sprain?**

A The aim is to give the joint firm support while it heals, but it should not be completely immobilized as a fracture has to be. Some form of elasticized bandage is therefore required. An ordinary cotton bandage gives too little support, but crepe, webbing, and elastic bandages are all suitable. A very important point is to put the bandage on tightly enough to be effective, but not so that it interferes with the circulation; the patient may then be in danger of getting gangrene. If the extremities (the toes in the case of a sprained ankle, and the fingers in a sprained wrist) go white or become numb or get pins and needles, then you have put the bandage on too tightly. If this happens you must take it off and start again, this time bandaging a little more loosely.

Q **I have heard a lot about cold compresses in the treatment of sprains. What exactly are they?**

A Very much what the name suggests. You take something like a piece of old linen, a dish towel, a handkerchief, or a roll of bandage and thoroughly soak it in cold, but not iced, water. You then wring it out so that it no longer drips, lay it on the sprained area, and bandage it in place. As soon as it begins to dry or get warm, take it off, soak it in cold water again, and repeat the process. To be at all effective in controlling the pain and swelling of a sprain, the cold compress must be applied within the first few minutes.

Q **Can massage help in the treatment of sprains?**

A Yes. Gentle massage can be started as soon as the immediate effects of the injury have worn off, usually on the second or third day. At this stage, the area will still be very tender, so only light pressure should be applied. The massage can become gradually more strenuous as the injury heals.

Most of us have sprained a wrist or ankle at some time. Fortunately the damage almost always heals by itself, with the help of simple home treatment.

A sprain is one of the most common of all injuries. It chiefly affects the tissues around a joint and generally rates as more serious than a strain, but considerably less serious than a dislocation or fracture.

Virtually any joint can be involved in a sprain, but some are far more likely to be affected than others because of their position and the strains they frequently have to bear. Thus the ankle is particularly vulnerable because it bears much of the body's weight and is often involved in potentially hazardous activities.

Causes
Sprains are usually the result of the sharp twisting or wrenching of a joint beyond its natural limits. If the force involved is very great there may, in addition, be dislocation or even a fracture. Most commonly, however, the ligaments are affected. These are very tough bands of fibroelastic tissue which hold the joint firmly in the correct position and protect it from dislocation (see Ligaments).

In trying to resist the force that is suddenly exerted on them, the ligaments may become stretched and some of the fibers may even be torn. It is rare, however, for the whole ligament to be pulled apart or ripped away from the bone. Any tendons (the thin, tough tails of muscle) may be similarly affected. Blood vessels in the tissues surrounding the joint are likely to be torn, causing bleeding and the bluish discoloration which is the feature of many sprains (see Bruises).

Any accident may bring about a sprain. People may sprain their ankles when tripping on the stairs or falling off a ladder.

Wrist sprains are also a common consequence of falls. The larger joints, such as the knee and hip, may be sprained in the course of a strenuous sport, and neck sprains may result from whiplash injuries when an automobile is brought to a sudden, violent halt (see Whiplash injury).

Accidents will happen when children become adventurous in their play; and a fall may result in a sprained wrist or ankle.

Sally and Richard Greenhill

Symptoms

There are several changes in the joint that indicate it has been sprained. The most obvious is sudden, severe pain in the affected area.

This comes from two sources: from the stretched or torn strands of ligament, and from distention of the surrounding tissue. This is brought about by bleeding and the secretion of fluid, which is part of the repair process.

The pain becomes dramatically worse if any attempt is made to move the joint or to make it bear any weight. As a result there is also disability in the sense that the joint is put temporarily out of use.

Any movement that is possible will be slight and of little practical value.

The swelling over the ligament usually develops quickly, and any bleeding into the underlying tissue will give it a blue or bruised appearance. As well as pain there will be tenderness. Even light pressure on the side of the joint will cause pain, but the actual site of the damage will be particularly sensitive. This is known as pinpoint tenderness, and it helps to indicate where the damage is in a swollen joint (see Swelling).

Treatment and outlook

Distinguishing between a sprain and more serious damage, such as a fracture, can be very difficult but it is essential. It should be remembered that the two types of damage are really different stages in the same process, and that both involve pain, tenderness, swelling, and loss of use of the joint.

Apparent sprains, unless they are obviously very minor, must therefore be treated with great caution until a doctor's opinion has been obtained. In this way

any aggravation of a possible fracture will be avoided. An X ray may even be needed to confirm the diagnosis (see X rays).

The treatment of sprains has undergone considerable changes over the last decade. Not all doctors, however, are in complete agreement with the newer approach, which recommends using the joint rather than resting it.

Immediate treatments, nevertheless, remain fairly standard. If a doctor is available when the sprain occurs (as may happen with a sports injury), he or she may inject the area with local anesthesia to minimize the reaction. A cold, but not ice, compress may be used for the same purpose, but not with such dramatic effect. The affected joint should then be firmly bandaged to limit the swelling and provide support.

Heat should never be applied to a new sprain, though it may well be helpful in restoring function from the second day onward. The patient may then start to use the joint gradually, perhaps with the help of a crutch. In most cases, however, healing will be rapid (see Healing).

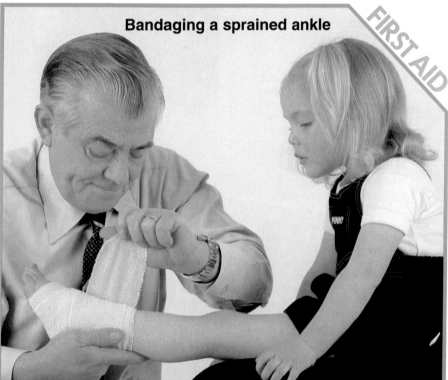

Bandaging a sprained ankle

FIRST AID

Ron Sutherland

- Stand in front of the patient and position the injured foot at right angles to the shin
- Use an elasticized bandage, unrolling it as you work and holding the remainder so that it faces upward
- Put the bandage on from below upward and from the inside outward

- Start off with a couple of firm turns to make sure it does not slip
- Apply the rest evenly and firmly. Each successive turn should cover two-thirds of the previous one
- Secure with a safety pin through the two outermost layers. If it works loose through wear, remove and reapply

Stammering and stuttering

Q My three-year-old daughter seems to be developing a stammer. Should I correct her speech or simply ignore it?

A Most children of this age go through a stage of normal nonfluency which can sound rather like a stammer. It happens because she doesn't have a big enough vocabulary yet to express herself properly. Don't correct her, this could make her self-conscious about her speech and she could develop a real stammer. Give her your full attention when she speaks to you and allow her enough time to say all she wants. Above all don't feel anxious, because this feeling will be communicated to her. She will then feel she is doing something wrong and become anxious about her speech as well. If it persists, you should seek advice from a speech therapist.

Q I have had a stammer for as long as I can remember. Since it is only a problem when I feel under stress, I haven't bothered to have any treatment for it. I have now been asked to give a speech at my son's school and don't want to let him down by refusing. At the same time I am afraid of stammering. How can I overcome this problem?

A You can buy a machine called a masker which emits white noise into your ears when you speak, thus preventing you from hearing your speech. Most people who stammer find that it keeps them fluent for such occasions as public speaking. But they are only usually prescribed as a last resort. Your local speech therapist may help you to get one and teach you how to use it, but a course of speech therapy would probably be of more long-term benefit.

Q Is it true that stammering is more common among boys than girls?

A Yes. The ratio is as high as four boys to every one girl who stammers. On the whole girls are more advanced in developing speech, which may be why they are less prone to stammering.

Stammering and stuttering are terms for the same speech difficulty—the hesitations that interrupt fluent speech. Speech therapy is now a great help with this problem.

Ray Duns

No one speaks with perfect fluency. It is common to hesitate and repeat phrases, but these interruptions are not usually noticed by either the speaker or the person listening. Normally the speaker is far more interested in what he or she is saying than how it is said.

People who stammer are, on the other hand, very conscious of how they speak and worry about getting the words out, although they can speak normally under certain conditions. They cannot, however, keep their speech fluent at all times. Stammering is more common among boys than girls, and often starts between ages three and eight.

Normal nonfluency
Most children go through a stage when they hesitate and repeat sounds. This usually happens at about three years old, when children are eager to explain their

Listen patiently when children try to express themselves with words. Hesitations will thus disappear and fluency develop naturally.

new experiences, but don't yet have the vocabulary to express themselves. While searching for words, he or she fills the pause by repeating the previous phrase, words, or the initial sounds of words. Repetition of sounds in normal nonfluency is relaxed, and the child does not notice it unless it is drawn to his or her attention. It is important to listen when a child is going through this phase without seeming to be worried about their speech. If a child catches any anxiety he or she will start to feel they are doing something wrong and become tense about speaking. This could lead to a real stammer developing. Most children learn enough words to express their ideas, and this phase of nonfluency disappears.

Primary stammering

The first stage of stammering commonly appears as repetitions of the initial sounds of words. The onset is often gradual and may progress from normal nonfluency, or it may appear after an illness or trauma. Hesitations and repetitions often increase as the child becomes more anxious about certain situations. This could be exacerbated by the parents' attitude to the child's speech problem. No one knows why some children become worried by a speech difficulty, but it is this anxiety about speaking which can result in a stammer. Often, in the early stages, the child's difficulty occurs only occasionally—such as when he or she is in a hurry, excited, or anxious to tell a story (see Anxiety).

Secondary stammering

The secondary stage of stammering involves further tension and embarrassment. Instead of repeating sounds the stammerer cannot get sounds out at all, or once started, cannot end them. These interruptions, known as blocks and prolongations respectively, are often accompanied by eye blinks, facial tics, and limb movements (see Twitches and tics). These often become part of the stammer, as a chance movement sometimes seems to help the stammerer to force out a word. In reality, however, it has nothing to do with producing the sound, since a stammer occurs essentially because the muscles of speech are not controlled or coordinated. There is too much tension in the muscles used for breathing and sound formation.

Points of difficulty

No particular sounds create specific problems for all stammerers, but individuals find certain sounds more difficult than others and will try to avoid them. For example, a person who thinks they will get stuck on *m*, will say "hill" instead of "mountain," or even use a whole phrase instead of the feared word. The stammerer may become so skilled at avoiding words that it passes unnoticed, but ultimately it only serves to reinforce their lack of confidence.

If a word cannot be avoided, it is a common trick to add a set phrase such as "that is to say," which the stammerer hopes will carry them over the difficult word. On the whole, consonants like *p*, *b*, *t*, *d*, *k*, and *g* create blocks, whereas sounds such as *f* and *s* result in prolongations.

The degree to which a stammer affects someone's sociability depends on their personality. Usually particular situations cause anxiety and tend to be avoided. Children and adolescents fear reading in class, and adults try not to use the telephone. Often the stammerer's fear of speaking does not relate to how much they are actually stammering: when they are feeling confident they notice the stammer less; when feeling less confident he or she will report the stammer as bad, even when speaking quite fluently.

Causes of stammering

No one knows what causes a stammer to develop, although many theories have been put forward. It was once thought that a left-handed person who was forced to use their right hand became a stammerer, because the normal situation, where one-half of the brain is dominant, was thereby upset, with conflicting messages being sent to the speech organs by both halves of the brain (see Speech).

Tests have shown that stammerers are as able to perform rapid and rhythmic movements as fluent speakers, that they have no particular hormonal imbalance, and are no more prone to psychological problems than other people. It is thought that most of a stammerer's personality problems are due to frustration and anxiety resulting from the stammer.

A stammer often occurs in a young child, when the control of the speech mechanism is unstable. As failure to speak fluently becomes habitual, and linked with anxiety, a child learns that self-consciousness in speech is normal. Any attempt to correct the child increases their anxiety, so that the symptoms of stammering become part of speech, and he or she learns to speak as a stammerer.

Assessing a stammer

Assessing the severity of a stammer in a variety of situations is crucial when devising any treatment program. Fluency must be measured by counting repetitions, prolongations, blocks, interjections, and revisions (starting a word and changing it) during reading, monologue, and con-

This woman is undergoing biofeedback training, with visual and auditory stimuli. When combined with relaxation techniques, stammerers can use it to control anxiety.

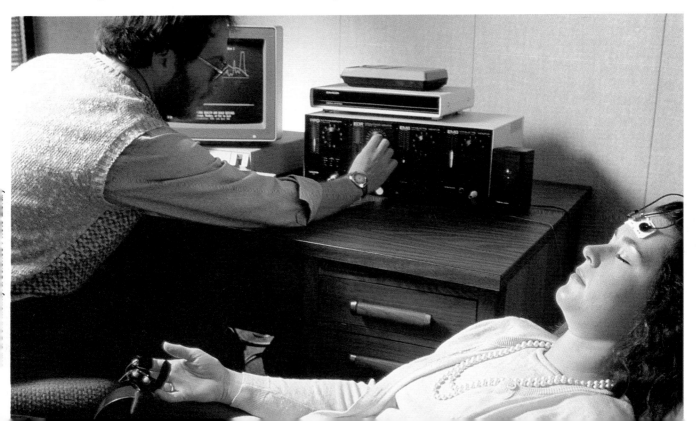

Central Press

A stammer is especially disabling for public figures. The British king, George VI, overcame this handicap with the help of speech therapy and sheer perseverance. The machine (right) slows down the speed at which a stammerer hears his or her own speech. This boy is rewarded with a token as he reads a paragraph without hesitation.

versation. The incidence of these impediments is noted (see Speech therapy).

The attitudes of adult stammerers to speaking are deduced through standard questionnaires and tests. With young children, the parents are asked to report on their speech at home and in school. The kinds of pressure felt by a child have to be clearly understood so that they can be reduced or alleviated in ways devised by parents and speech therapist together.

Treatment

Any adequate treatment of stammering must treat the person as a whole. Several types of treatment work for a short time by lessening the stammerer's anxiety about speaking, since fear and the expectation of stammering are major factors in maintaining the stammering habit. However, proper speech therapy aims to teach the stammerer how to control their speech, as well as helping to alter their self-image. Any therapy will only be truly effective in conjunction with the stammerer's own hard work.

Ray Duns

Q Is it possible to inherit a stammer?

A Studies have shown that the predisposition to stammering is inherited. However, a parent may stammer and all the children have normal speech, or one child may stammer without influencing the speech of other children. Unconscious imitation of the speech of a parent or another child may also occur, which could give the appearance of a true stammer.

Q My four-year-old son cannot say *s* properly. I have been correcting him and now he seems to be developing a stammer. What should I do?

A It is quite normal for four-year-olds to lisp slightly. It is very likely that he hasn't developed full control of his speech muscles yet, and if he becomes excessively aware of a speech difficulty he could well develop a stammer. Advice should be sought from a speech therapist who will be able to organize a course of treatment to prevent a stammer developing.

Q Is it true that forcing a left-handed child to use his right hand could cause him to stammer?

A This was thought to be true. However, many left-handed people learned to use their right hand successfully without any interference to their speech. Fear of punishment for failure to use the more awkward hand is more likely to cause a stammer in most cases. Nowadays children are rarely forced to use their right hand when they are naturally left-handed, so it isn't usually a problem anymore.

Q Is learning to relax useful in helping a stammerer?

A Yes, it usually does have a place in treatment. Most stammerers are fluent when they are relaxed. The problem, which a worthwhile treatment will seek to solve, is how to carry any feeling of confidence and relaxation that the stammerer has into situations which make them feel particularly anxious about speaking.

Jedcom (UK) Ltd.

This woman is using a masker: a portable white noise machine. The patient learns to speak above the noise, heard through earphones, which masks the sound of his or her own voice, thus aiding more fluent speech.

The most common methods currently in use for learning fluency are slowing down the speed of speech, or prolonging the sounds of words. All stammerers can speak fluently if they allow themselves enough time to control their speech. This also enables them to speak as normal speakers do, in phrases rather than single words. As their speech control improves under the guidance of a speech therapist, they speed up their speech. Fluency programs are often used with young children, where they learn to speak single words fluently, then progress to two words, three words, and so on, to continuous speech.

At the same time, the stammerer has to become accustomed to the role of a fluent speaker. Stammerers view themselves essentially as stammerers, and find it threatening to change. It is rather like a fluent speaker being told that all the world stammers and they must do so too. As part of the treatment, therefore, he or she has to try out their newfound fluency in the real world. This is done in stages, starting with the least threatening of a series of feared speaking situations. The stammerer's therapist comes along at first, but eventually is confident enough to go on these assignments alone. After several successes the patient's confidence as a fluent speaker improves.

Courses for stammerers are frequently run in groups so that they can give each other support and learn from each other's mistakes. Social skills training needs to be included in the treatment since stammerers often find it difficult to approach people and talk to them in a relaxed way. The courses are usually intensive; every day for two to three weeks. Most stammerers need to attend more than one course, following up with a weekly class between courses. They can continue with classes until they feel confident enough to maintain fluency without further help.

Outlook

As there is no cure for stammering, a stammerer may experience setbacks even after learning fluency. It is important to remember that these do not signify a permanent regression. If he or she takes care to control their speech, fluency will return and be sufficiently maintained for the listener not to be aware of the problem. The stammerer's own persistence is thus crucial in sustaining, as well as achieving fluency.

Starch

Q Is starch more fattening than other foods?

A There is nothing about starch that makes it particularly fattening, but we eat more starch and sugar than any other class of food. We tend to think of starch as being fattening because reducing our intake of starch happens when we reduce our total food intake. Fatty foods are the ones to avoid.

Q Is it possible to live without eating any starch at all in an everyday diet?

A Yes, but it would not be good for you since starch is a valuable and easily obtainable source of energy. The other thing about starch is that starchy foods are our normal source of fiber, and fiber is very important in keeping the body working well. For instance, whole wheat bread contains starch and also has a lot of fiber.

Q If you eat lots of starch, why is it that you become overweight when the body does not store it?

A The body does in fact store some starch in the form of glycogen, in the liver and muscles, for use when blood sugar concentrations are low, but this is not very much. It is the excess glucose in the blood (the end product of the digestion of starch and sugars) that may be converted to fat and deposited as fatty tissue. It is best to regard starchy foods as hidden reserves of sugar.

Q When I was young, people used to use bread and starch as poultices on their skin. What were these for and why were they commonly used?

A Poultices, or fomentations, are warm masses of pulpy material that are applied to the body in order to relieve pain and inflammation. Various kinds were used, and bread and starch poultices were cheap and easy to make. Starch poultices were used for the removal of scales on the skin, as well as to relieve pain.

Traditionally, starch has been thought of as a very fattening part of our diet. But, in fact, it is no more so than many other readily available types of food.

Sugar and starch between them are major sources of energy for the body and provide the energy that we require for movement, breathing, and all internal metabolic functions. However, anyone who consumes more of these carbohydrates than are burned naturally as fuel may find that the excess is converted to fat deposited around the body.

Starch in the diet

We tend to eat a large amount of starch in our diets because foods rich in starch are usually cheaper and more readily available than proteins. In itself starch has no special properties that make us fat; it simply provides a ready supply of glucose that the body requires for its metabolism to work (see Metabolism).

Many weight-loss diets claim that you should cut down on starchy foods. This is based on old-fashioned nutritional ideas. Current medical evidence shows that starch is the best thing you can eat. If you need to lose weight you should cut down on fat (see Slimming).

Sources of starch

Plants manufacture carbohydrates by the process of photosynthesis, whereby they convert carbon dioxide gas from the atmosphere and water from the soil into a simple sugar, utilizing the energy from sunlight in the presence of the green pigment chlorophyll. The sugar is soluble in water and is transported to the parts of the plant that need energy for growth or repair. The excess sugar is converted into insoluble starch and stored, ready to be converted back into sugar when the plant needs it. Plants such as potatoes that have a large storage capacity therefore contain a large quantity of starch.

The digestion of starch

The process of digesting starchy foods begins in the mouth. Food is first broken into manageable pieces by the teeth and mixed with the saliva produced by the salivary glands in the mouth. The saliva contains a starch-digesting enzyme called ptyalin, or amylase, which is capable of breaking down the starch into simpler sugars (see Saliva).

There is, however, little time for the starch-digesting enzyme to act before the food is swallowed and passed into the stomach. In the stomach there is no digestion of carbohydrates.

The starch in our diet comes in many forms, from what are known as "junk" foods, such as French fries, to the healthy apple. Only excess starch is fattening.

Phil Babb

Starch metabolism

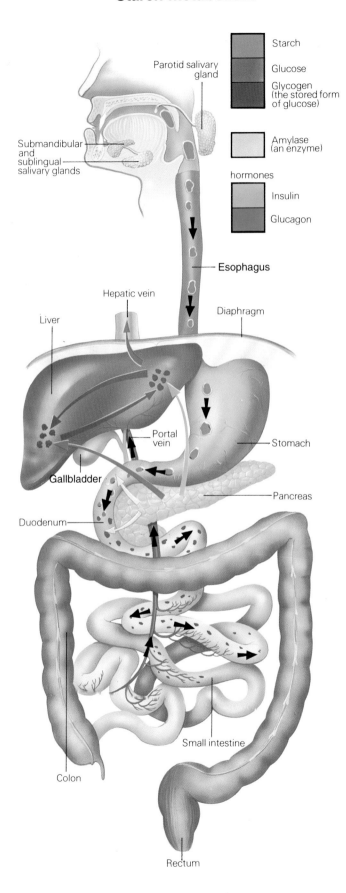

Parotid salivary gland

Submandibular and sublingual salivary glands

Esophagus

Hepatic vein

Liver

Diaphragm

Portal vein

Gallbladder

Stomach

Duodenum

Pancreas

Small intestine

Colon

Rectum

Starch

Glucose

Glycogen (the stored form of glucose)

Amylase (an enzyme)

hormones

Insulin

Glucagon

When the stomach contents are passed into the duodenum, or small intestine, enzymes from the pancreas continue to break down all carbohydrates into the simple sugars like glucose that make them up. This end product of digestion is absorbed into the body, enters the hepatic portal vein, and is transported to the liver before entering the bloodstream (see Digestive system).

The liver and glycogen

In the same way as plants store starch for use when sugar supplies are low, so the body also stores a form of starch called glycogen, or animal starch.

Glucose absorbed in the small intestine can be converted to glycogen in the liver which usually holds about 3.5 oz (100 g). The muscles also contain substantial quantities. As glucose is used up in the body to provide energy, so the equivalent amount of stored glycogen is broken down by enzymes to glucose. In this way the concentrations of glucose in the blood and body fluids can be kept within limits (see Glucose).

The deposition of glycogen and its reconversion to sugar is controlled by hormones, most importantly insulin from the pancreas. When we eat meals that contain a lot of starch and sugar, then the amount of sugar in our blood can double within a matter of minutes. This rapid increase causes the pancreas to pour out insulin, which acts on the muscles and the liver and instructs them to withdraw sugar from the blood before it is lost in the urine, and to store it as the starch glycogen (see Insulin). However, the muscles and liver can only store a limited amount of starch; the excess is either converted to fat and laid down in fatty tissue or burned off.

Several other hormones are also related to glycogen breakdown and storage. Epinephrine and thyroid hormones accelerate the conversion of glycogen to glucose and tend to act when the body is active. Corticosteroids increase its manufacture from proteins, while a hormone called glucagon (from the pancreas, like insulin) inhibits the storage of glycogen and helps break it down to glucose.

During digestion, starch is broken down into glucose by the enzyme amylase. Glucose is carried by the blood to the liver. If the level of glucose is high, insulin, a hormone from the pancreas, causes the free glucose to be converted into glycogen, which is stored in the liver. When blood glucose levels become low, the pancreas releases another hormone, glucagon, which causes the stored glycogen to be released as glucose, which the body uses as a fuel to provide the energy it needs for movement.

Sterilization

Sterilization is an effective, once-and-for-all method of contraception, and for some women it may be a suitable step to take. However, the woman must be prepared to rule out any possibility of ever having another child.

Q How easy is it to reverse a sterilization operation?

A This depends on the method used. It is possible to attempt to reverse sterilization operations where only the fallopian tubes have been obstructed. Because this is a major operation that is expensive to perform, you will have to check your health insurance policy to see if you are covered in this instance. Moreover, the operation has only a 50 percent chance of success, and for this reason it is important to realize that, if you are sterilized, it is very likely that you will never have another pregnancy even if you are prepared to undergo major surgery. You must be absolutely certain, therefore, that you wish never to become pregnant again before being sterilized. This may save much heartache later.

Q What are the dangers of having a sterilization procedure reversed?

A Every operation involves a small risk, but probably the greatest risk of this kind of procedure is the possibility that, if you later conceive, the embryo will grow in one of the fallopian tubes until it bursts through, causing severe internal hemorrhage. This is called an ectopic pregnancy.

Q When I recently had an abortion I asked to be sterilized at the same time since I do not want any more children. The doctor advised me against this. Can you explain why?

A There are two main reasons. Probably the most important is that you are marginally more likely to develop blood clots if you are sterilized during an abortion. These clots can travel to your heart or lungs which is obviously dangerous. The other reason for your doctor's advice is that he or she may be worried that you could be too distressed at that time to make the correct decision on such a radical matter. For much the same reason, doctors prefer not to sterilize a woman immediately after childbirth.

Anthea Sieveking/Vision International

The term *sterilization* is now used more loosely than it was when the procedure was first put into practice. This is because occasionally an operation is performed to attempt to reverse a sterilization operation.

Nevertheless, any woman choosing this method of contraception must be confident that she will want no more children even if her personal circumstances were to change, since it is potentially irreversible.

Methods of sterilization

For a woman to be fertile, she must be able to release eggs from her ovaries; she must have intact fallopian tubes along which the eggs can pass to the womb; and she must have a normal womb in which the fertilized egg can embed itself

and develop into a fetus and eventually a baby (see Conception). All methods of sterilization work by permanently blocking one or more of these stages.

Most sterilization procedures consist of blocking the fallopian tubes in one of a number of ways. This method is particularly popular since it involves relatively minor surgery, though it is still a slightly more risky procedure than sterilizing a man by vasectomy (see Vasectomy). Women sterilized in this way do not have sudden menopausal symptoms (as happens when the ovaries are involved), and their periods continue, though these may be slightly heavier.

The function of the fallopian tubes may be permanently interrupted in a variety of ways. First, they may be completely removed, a method of steril-

When a woman makes the decision to be sterilized, the first step is for her to visit her gynecologist to discuss the issues involved. Before proceeding with surgery, most gynecologists prefer to include the husband or partner in the consultation to insure that both partners are fully aware of the implications of the operation.

ization that is unlikely to fail. Alternatively, a portion (about .33 in or 1 cm) may be cut away from the middle of each, or they may be cut through or burned—a method called diathermy. The burn is made in only two places, but the effect will travel along the tubes, thus damaging them (see Tubal ligation).

In some cases, clips are placed on both tubes, or a loop of each is pulled into a tight plastic ring. All these procedures, except for total removal of the fallopian tubes, are potentially reversible, but any woman undergoing one of these operations should assume that it will make her permanently sterile. They are probably the methods most often used, and seldom have any complications.

Unfortunately, between one and four women in every thousand who have this type of surgery subsequently become

Before performing a sterilization, a doctor will have to be convinced that a woman will want no more children. In the right circumstances, sterilization can be an ideal form of contraception, and one which has no side effects, such as the Pill does. Sex, too, may become more enjoyable since the woman no longer has the inhibiting fear of an unwanted pregnancy.

pregnant. This is probably because the tubes get unblocked. Another rare problem is that a fertilized egg can be trapped in one of the fallopian tubes, where it grows until it ruptures the tube and passes into the abdominal cavity. This potentially extremely dangerous condition is called an ectopic pregnancy, and is treated by surgically removing the affected tube (see Ectopic pregnancy). These problems are nevertheless uncommon, and many women are very happy with this type of sterilization.

There are other methods which are not often used as they are less satisfactory. It is possible, for example, to sterilize a woman by removing or damaging her ovaries, but she will then rapidly develop menopausal symptoms such as hot flashes. This method is usually contemplated only if the ovaries are already damaged or diseased.

Women and doctors seldom consider hysterectomy (the removal of the uterus) as a form of contraception because it involves major surgery (see Hysterectomy). It may be a sensible choice if the woman has gynecologic problems such as large fibroids (see Fibroids) or heavy periods, both of which may be effectively cured by hysterectomy.

Q If my sterilization procedure failed how would I know if I were pregnant?

A You would have the same signs of pregnancy as you would have had before you were sterilized. For example, you would miss a period, your breasts might feel tender, and you may also feel nauseous. If you feel pregnant and have a sharp pain on one or other side of your lower abdomen, you should see a doctor immediately since there is a chance that the pregnancy is in one of the fallopian tubes (an ectopic pregnancy). This condition needs urgent treatment.

Q Will I still have a menopause now that I have been sterilized?

A The menopause occurs when your ovaries can no longer release eggs. Most sterilization operations are performed on the fallopian tubes, which means that the ovaries are unaffected and continue to function normally. The eggs will simply pass into the abdominal cavity, instead of into the womb. The ovaries will stop releasing eggs and ovarian hormones at menopause, so that you will have the normal menopausal symptoms.

Q Is sterilization ever performed on women who have not had any children?

A This depends on whether or not the doctor consulted believes that the woman's request is reasonable. He would probably consider it more reasonable if she suffered from some major physical illness that would make a pregnancy unwise, or if she carried some hereditary defect or disease.

Q Will I be less feminine or put on weight if I am sterilized?

A Provided you are not sterilized by having your ovaries removed (which is very unlikely), you will have all the normal female hormones in your blood. This means that you should feel just as you did before and that you are unlikely to gain any weight.

Sterilization by cutting the fallopian tubes

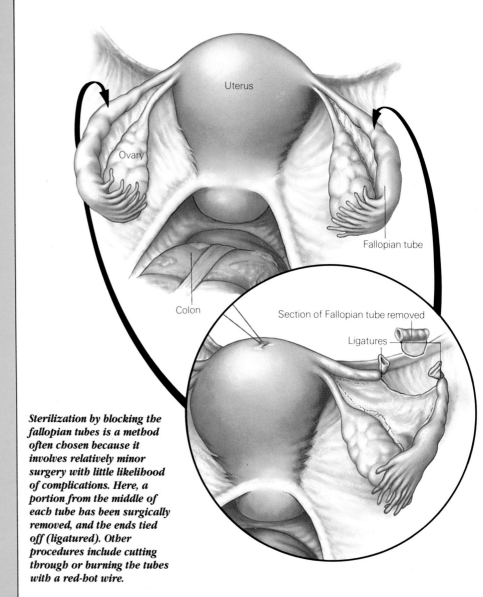

Sterilization by blocking the fallopian tubes is a method often chosen because it involves relatively minor surgery with little likelihood of complications. Here, a portion from the middle of each tube has been surgically removed, and the ends tied off (ligatured). Other procedures include cutting through or burning the tubes with a red-hot wire.

Advantages and disadvantages

When a woman decides to be sterilized she is making a major irreversible decision about her life that can yield many benefits. She will not have to make regular visits to the family planning clinic, and she will not have to worry about the side effects that she might otherwise have suffered with another form of contraception. She may even find that she enjoys her sex life more because she is free from the fear of an unwanted pregnancy.

On the other hand, some women find that they enjoy sex more when they are running the risk of becoming pregnant. Moreover, there is always the possibility that a woman may at a later date want more children, for example if she were to form a new relationship, or if any of her children should die.

Doctors are also very worried about sterilizing women who are unmarried, have no children, or are very young, especially since there are successful reversible forms of contraception on the market that may suit them better. Of course, in every case the decision to sterilize a woman will depend ultimately on the individual herself and her doctor.

For this reason it is extremely important for any woman contemplating sterilization to weigh the advantages and disadvantages as rationally and as carefully as possible. If she has any worries or questions, her physician may be able to set her mind at rest. Moreover, although the decision rests ultimately with her, she should also discuss her thoughts and feelings with her husband or partner.

Sterilization procedures

Site of sterilization	Procedure	Surgical method used	General remarks
Ovaries	Removal of both ovaries	Transverse incision in the abdominal wall just above the pubic hair line	Usually used only if the ovaries are diseased since this method precipitates menopause
	Radiation of both ovaries	No surgery required	Only used if a woman is very obese and requires sterilization—she will readily become menopausal
Fallopian tubes	Removal of both fallopian tubes Removal of midportion of both tubes Cutting or burning of both tubes Placing clips on both tubes Pulling a loop of each tube through a tight plastic ring	Incision through vaginal or lower abdominal wall Incision through vaginal or lower abdominal wall or use of the laparoscope	Very unlikely to fail as a form of sterilization Probably the most common methods used since they are relatively minor operations with a low incidence of complications
Uterus	Removal of uterus (hysterectomy)	Incision in the lower abdomen	A method used if a woman has completed her family and has other gynecologic problems such as heavy periods or large fibroids
		Removal through the vagina	This method used if the woman has completed her family and has a vaginal prolapse

Why choose sterilization?

There seem to be three important times in a woman's life when she may consider sterilization as a form of contraception. The first may be when she is having an abortion. Although her decision is often completely rational, many doctors prefer not to sterilize a woman at the same time as performing an abortion. There are two main reasons for this. First, she runs a greater risk of developing blood clots in her leg and pelvic veins during the operation. This is because she still has in her blood the altered levels of clotting factors that are associated with pregnancy. Second, many women may make the wrong decision at a time when they are undergoing severe emotional turmoil (see Abortion).

Similar arguments apply against sterilizing a woman immediately after having a baby, as well as the further argument that it is sensible to be certain that the new baby will thrive. Often, however, women and doctors feel that the convenience of the mother being sterilized while still in the hospital with the baby outweighs the disadvantages. Women also choose sterilization as they approach middle age rather than continuing to take the Pill.

Arranging to be sterilized

Women can arrange to be sterilized by asking their gynecologist. Many gynecologists prefer to interview the woman together with her partner to be certain that they both understand exactly what

the surgery entails, and the disadvantages as well as the advantages of this form of contraception. If the gynecologist is convinced that sterilization is appropriate, given all the circumstances of a case, he or she will arrange a convenient date for the surgery to be performed.

It is important that the couple continue to take contraceptive precautions until the surgery has taken place since it is possible for a pregnancy to continue normally if conception took place just before the surgery (see Pregnancy).

Surgery

An instrument called a laparoscope is often used in sterilization (see Laparoscopy). The laparoscope is a fine rod that allows a clear view of the fallopian tubes, and along which the necessary instruments can be passed to perform the operation. Laparoscopic sterilization is occasionally done while the woman is conscious, but of course the area where the laparoscope is to be inserted is first made completely numb so that the operation is relatively painless.

The majority of sterilizations are, however, performed under general anesthesia, and the woman is allowed home the next day. The scar will be tender for several days, and most women prefer to rest as much as possible during this time, though this, of course, is difficult if a woman has a large family.

Unlike male sterilization, female sterilization is effective immediately so that a

couple need not use any other form of contraception after the procedure.

Most women wait a week or so after being sterilized before having sexual intercourse so that their scars will have time to heal. If the woman has been sterilized by hysterectomy her scars will take even longer to heal, and she should wait a month or even six weeks before attempting intercourse (see Healing).

Outlook

Stories abound about the disastrous consequences for a woman who has her fallopian tubes blocked off. Most of these are completely untrue. The woman will not look different, become less feminine, or lose interest in sex. She will probably enjoy it more since she no longer has to worry about the possibility of pregnancy. The surgery will not make her put on weight, she will still have periods and go through menopause in exactly the same way as if she had not been sterilized (see Menopause, and Menstruation).

Most surgeons performing a sterilization are well aware that a woman does not want an unsightly scar—and in most cases it will eventually be hidden at the umbilicus or by her pubic hair as it regrows (see Scars).

It is important for every woman to continue having routine Pap smears after sterilization, as she will still need to be screened against the possibility of developing cancer of the cervix (see Cervix and cervical smears, and Pap smears).

Steroids

Q My doctor keeps wanting to reduce the dosage of my steroids, despite the fact that they make my asthma better. Why is he doing this now that I am feeling so much better?

A There is no doubt that steroids can help in asthma, particularly in severe attacks. However, there is also no doubt that they can have serious side effects, and that these effects are inevitable if the dose is high enough for long enough. This is the reason your doctor is trying to keep the dosage as low as possible. It is important that he finds the right balance.

Q I have been found to have Addison's disease, and have been put on steroids for it. Does this mean that I am going to get all sorts of side effects?

A No, this is one situation where giving the drugs is free of side effects. Addison's disease is the disease resulting from failure of the body's adrenal glands to produce an adequate amount of steroids. The missing steroids can be replaced by steroid tablets. Since this is simply replacement treatment which does not raise the level of steroids in the body above normal, there is no risk of side effects.

Q If you need steroids, do you have to have them in tablet form or are there other ways that they can be given?

A Steroids can be given in many different forms, but the method used depends on what condition the steroids are treating. Where the aim is to control the effects of some aspect of the immune system, then the steroids are usually given by mouth. But more localized inflammation can be treated differently. Skin creams, ointments, enemas, and inhalers are all examples of how steroid treatment is applied to a specific area for a specific purpose. There are also injectable steroids, and these can be given in very big doses to prevent the complications of conditions such as shock. Steroid treatment is often used in this way in emergencies.

Treatment with steroid drugs is one of modern medicine's most powerful weapons. But, although they can be life-saving, they can also have serious side effects.

Transworld

In accepting a new kidney from his twin brother, Darryl (right) was given high doses of steroid drugs. This treatment suppressed the body's rejection of the new organ.

Steroids are produced naturally in the body by the adrenal glands, and these hormones are a normal and essential part of the body's endocrine system (see Adrenal glands, Endocrine system, and Hormones).The drugs that are referred to as steroids are either exactly the same as the body's naturally occurring steroids— that is, either cortisone or hydrocortisone—or else they are very closely related both in their chemical structure, and in their function.

Steroid drug treatment is now widely used to fight both inflammation and disease, and to reduce the activity of the body's own defense system. But the treatment can have serious side effects. Consequently, steroid treatment must be a skillful balancing act.

The use of steroid drugs

One of the natural effects of steroid activity is to control excessive inflammation. When the body's defense system responds to infection, some of the cells that take part in attacking the infection have their activity suppressed by steroid treatment, so that their response is not so vigorous as to damage the body itself. This action is of interest with regard to allergy diseases, and steroids are now widely used in controlling the symptoms of these allergies (see Allergies). For example, in the case of asthma, part of the allergic reaction to the pollen may include severe obstruction to breathing. It is a sign of the body's defense system overreacting. This response can be considerably reduced by steroid treatment. It is also possible to reduce the strength of any side effects by giving the steroids in a locally active form, such as in an inhaler.

Steroid drugs are also widely used against a group of diseases in which the body's immune system turns against itself. These include the generalized inflammatory disease known as systemic lupus erythematosus, and a similar disease, rheumatoid arthritis. There is no doubt that in the short term steroids can do much to alleviate the symptoms of these diseases. However, in the case of rheumatoid arthritis, if the treatment is used over a long period of time then the side effects will outweigh the benefits. Consequently in treating rheumatoid arthritis, it is more usually used as a short-term treatment (see Rheumatoid arthritis, and Systemic lupus erythematosus).

There are many other unusual and ill-explained inflammatory diseases that respond rapidly to steroids. A good example is the condition called temporal arteritis, where the lining of the arteries becomes inflamed for no obvious reason. This condition affects elderly people and is common in the arteries in the head, causing headaches and even blindness. Once the diagnosis is made, it improves within 24 hours of being treated with steroids (see Arteries and artery disease).

Steroids are also the basis of the treatment of organ rejection after transplantation. The patient may be given high doses for some time to suppress substantially the body's natural response of rejecting foreign tissue (see Transplants).

Various tumors also respond well to steroids, as do joint inflammations like water on the knee and tennis elbow.

Side effects

The unwanted side effects of steroids occur because they are given in much higher amounts than would normally be found in the body. These side effects are very similar to the symptoms of Cushing's syndrome, a disease where the adrenal glands become overactive and so produce excessive amounts of steroid hormones in the body.

These symptoms include excessive weight gain, with the tendency for the fat to be found on the face and trunk, and

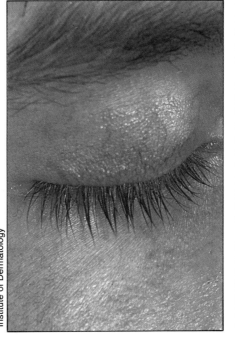

Institute of Dermatology

One of the side effects of steroid drug treatment is the appearance of prominent blood vessels on the eyelids. This soon disappears when treatment stops.

the loss of protein leading to weakness of muscles, bones, skin, and gut linings (leading to ulcers). Diabetes frequently occurs and the blood pressure is raised; there may even be severe mental disturbance.

However, steroid treatment also tends to suppress the body's own adrenal activity. As the dose is reduced it is possible for the body to become short of steroids. The main danger of this is that there is a reduced capacity to respond to stress, so that there might be a sudden collapse with loss of blood pressure during a minor illness, for example. To avoid this possibility the dose is very carefully reduced, giving the adrenal glands time to recover their own activity.

Steroids are very much a mixed blessing. There is no doubt that they save many lives, and prevent even more unpleasant symptoms. However, anything but the smallest of doses results in some side effects. Doctors try to keep doses as low as possible, and only use the drugs when there is no suitable alternative.

Steroid structure

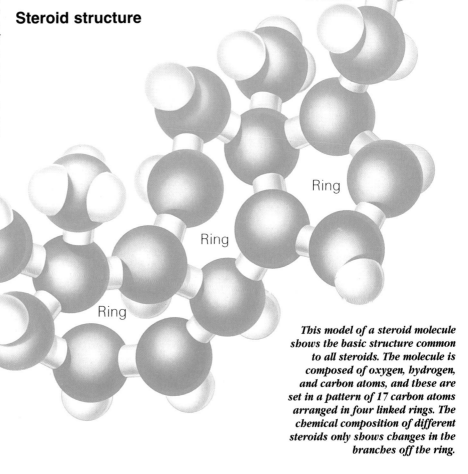

This model of a steroid molecule shows the basic structure common to all steroids. The molecule is composed of oxygen, hydrogen, and carbon atoms, and these are set in a pattern of 17 carbon atoms arranged in four linked rings. The chemical composition of different steroids only shows changes in the branches off the ring.

Stethoscope

Q Why does a stethoscope have two pieces at the end?

A One of the pieces is called the bell, and it is indeed shaped like a small shallow bell. It is applied gently to the skin and it picks up any low frequency sounds from the heart (or any other organ). This means that it is most useful for hearing low-pitched rumbling sorts of sounds that happen as a result of heart failure or obstruction of the mitral valve. The other part is called the diaphragm and is made of plastic stretched out tightly over the mouth of a very wide and flat bell-like end piece. This is used to hear the very high-pitched blowing murmurs that can be heard when the aortic valve is diseased, for example. Almost all the other sounds that a doctor may listen for in the various organs are found in the middle of the frequency range and it doesn't matter if the bell or the diaphragm is used.

Q Why don't doctors use electronic stethoscopes; wouldn't they be able to hear better if they did?

A Electronic stethoscopes are available, but they don't help much in the routine practice of medicine. The sort of sounds that doctors are listening to are quite easy to hear; the difficulty lies in their interpretation. However, one area in which electronic help is often needed is in picking up the heartbeat of a baby in the womb.

Q My doctor thought he heard a murmur in my heart and sent me to a cardiologist. When the cardiologist listened through the stethoscope he asked me to touch my toes 10 times. Why?

A There are some sorts of heart murmur that get a good deal louder on exercise, and one of these is the murmur from an obstructed mitral valve in the heart. The specialist was trying to make any murmur that you have as loud as possible. However, if there was any doubt whether you have such a murmur then an ultrasound test to examine the mitral valve would have sorted the matter out.

Perhaps more than any other piece of equipment, the stethoscope is the doctor's badge of office. Used most often for examinations of the heart and lungs, it is also essential for measuring the blood pressure.

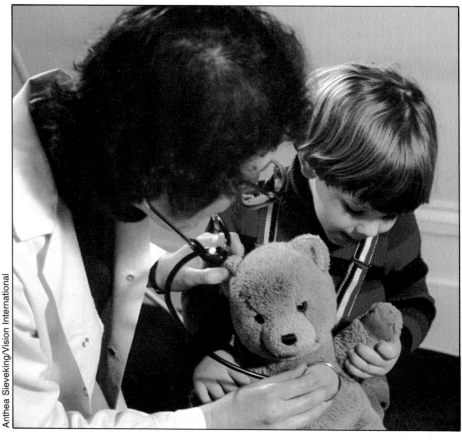

Anthea Sieveking/Vision International

For centuries doctors were unaware of the value of the various noises produced by such organs as the lungs and the heart in making a diagnosis. It was not until French physician Laennec realized the potential value of these noises that the stethoscope came into being.

Development

Laennec practiced in Paris at the end of the 18th century. At that time the new technique of percussion had recently arrived from Vienna. This is the method whereby doctors tap the chest to see whether the lungs sound hollow as they should, or dull as they do if fluid is present over the lung or if the lung is becoming solid as a result of infection.

The next step after percussion was the realization that the normal sounds of breathing and of the heartbeat carried much valuable information. Initially physicians such as Laennec applied an ear directly to the patient's chest, but it is not possible to hear very well in this way.

The stethoscope is the piece of medical equipment we are probably most familiar with. It can help in all manner of diagnoses, or, indeed, reassure us that all is well.

One day Laennec saw two children playing with a long piece of wood; one was tapping one end while the other picked up the message as he listened to the other end. This gave Laennec the idea that forms the basis of the modern stethoscope. Back at the hospital where he worked, he listened to the chest of a patient through a rolled up tube of paper. He was amazed at how much he could hear, and went on to develop a stethoscope. This was trumpet-shaped, and the doctor listened by putting his ear to the smaller end. The obstetric stethoscope that is used today for listening to the heart of the baby in the womb still retains much the same design.

The stethoscope then evolved to its current design, with a chest piece connected to the doctor's ears by tubing.

By the beginning of this century virtually all doctors were using such an instrument. The chest piece has varied considerably over the years, but now most stethoscopes are of the same pattern, with a bell and a diaphragm. The bell picks up a wide range of sounds, and it is essential for listening to the low-pitched rumbling noises produced by some diseases of the heart. The diaphragm picks up and sharpens high-pitched noises; there are various sorts of whistling and blowing murmurs from the heart that can be missed unless the diaphragm is used (see Heart disease).

The use of the stethoscope

Doctors find their stethoscopes of most value in diagnosing heart and lung troubles. In the heart most of the abnormal sounds are murmurs (see Murmurs of the heart). A murmur is invariably caused by blood rushing through a constricted channel of some sort which makes its flow confused and turbulent instead of smooth. This turbulent flow gives rise to the murmur. The doctor also listens for variations in the normal sounds of the valves as they open and close, and the possibility of extra sounds which happen in normal young people and children, but indicate that the heart is working under extra pressure in older people.

Turbulent blood flow can also be heard in blood vessels, and this indicates that the vessel is slightly blocked, or that the arteries are hardening.

In the lungs there is a normal rustling noise as air moves in and out of them. If there are wheezes this suggests that the bronchial tubes are constricted, as may occur in asthma, while crackling noises indicate that there is fluid in the tiny air

Organ or system	Use
Heart	Audible murmurs, caused by disturbance of blood flow in the heart, signify valve disease. Additional sounds may indicate the presence of other heart diseases
Lungs	Over a normal lung there is a soft rustling sound as breaths are taken. When this sound becomes harsh the underlying lung has become solid, usually as a result of infection. Additional noises, such as the wheezes that typify asthma, and fine crackling noises when fluid has collected in the alveoli, are the result either of infection or heart failure. Absence of the breath sounds suggests that there is a collection of fluid around the lung (pleural effusion)
Abdomen	Through a stethoscope soft sounds can be heard all the time. Their absence indicates that the intestines are not working, as after an operation, for example. In contrast, very overactive sounds may indicate that the intestines are struggling hard to overcome a blockage
Uterus	Special obstetric stethoscopes are used to detect the beating of the baby's heart during late pregnancy
Blood vessels	The stethoscope is used over the brachial artery in the arm to establish the blood pressure. Other arteries may also be examined: a whooshing sound of blood rushing turbulently through them indicates hardening of the arteries
Thyroid gland	Occasionally enlargement of the thyroid gland in the neck will result in an audible rush of blood

Uses of the stethoscope

sacs (the alveoli). Absence of the normal breath sounds may indicate a collection of fluid in the pleural space around the lungs, while alteration in the quality of the breath sounds themselves, or in the sound when a patient speaks the time-honored test phrase *ninety-nine*, suggest that the lung is becoming solid.

The stethoscope is an invaluable instrument and, when the doctor has been informed by the patient of other symptoms, will enable him to make or confirm most of the important diagnoses affecting both the heart and the lungs.

In addition, the stethoscope is used as a matter of routine over the brachial artery in the arm to pick up changes in sound as a blood pressure cuff is blown up. In pregnancy, the fetal heart is checked at every prenatal appointment after about 20 weeks, and while it is monitored carefully throughout labor, the stethoscope may now be replaced by sophisticated electronic equipment.

Design of the modern stethoscope

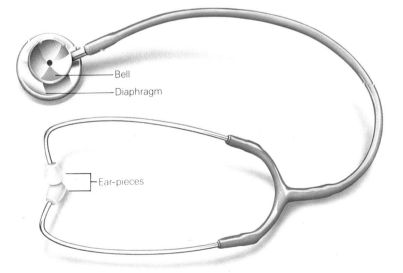

Bell
Diaphragm
Ear-pieces

The modern stethoscope consists of a chest piece with a bell and diaphragm connected to the earpieces by tubing.

Early stethoscopes were trumpet-shaped, with the doctor listening at the smaller end. Modern obstetric stethoscopes retain this design.

Mary Evans Picture Library

Stiffness

Q Is it better to rest or exercise a stiff limb?

A Initially a stiff limb should be rested in order to give the natural repair processes time to do their job. However, the part concerned should regularly be put through its full range of movements, supported in some way if necessary, so that adhesions and even greater stiffness do not develop. As the condition improves, rest should increasingly give way to exercise on a little-and-often basis until normal activity is regained. What is required at this stage is doing neither too much nor too little. Exercise to a point at which stiffness begins to be felt, but take care not to go beyond it. Five minutes' exercise every hour or so is ideal, rather than having long and possibly exhausting sessions only once or twice a day.

Q My mother has been told that she has a frozen shoulder. What does this mean?

A Frozen shoulder takes its name from the fact that the shoulder is literally immobilized. There are many conditions in which the shoulder may be stiff and movement of it painful. With a frozen shoulder it is not only difficult or painful to reach up and stretch the arm above the head, but it is also virtually impossible. Frozen shoulder is the most serious type of stiff shoulder, and can be difficult to eliminate. Various types of physical therapy are used to treat it, and sometimes injections of local anesthesia or steroids into the joint may help to restore movement.

Q I have been told that heat would improve my stiff back, but I don't have a heat lamp. Is there any other treatment that would be suitable?

A Yes, there is. If sensibly used, a portable heater can do almost as much good as a heat lamp. Put the portable heater on a table so that the heat is directly on your back. You should be close enough to it to feel the warmth, but not so close that you burn your skin. Do this for about 15 minutes at a time, three or four times a day.

However slight, any type of stiffness is inconvenient because it restricts movement and is often painful. Although, of course, prevention is best, knowing what to do when stiffness actually occurs will minimize the effects.

Stiffness is one of the most annoying and potentially disabling things that we can suffer from; only paralysis and severe pain interfere as much with full and free mobility—an essential part of normal life.

Common causes of stiffness

The most common and, fortunately, the least serious type of stiffness is one that we all suffer from at some time or another: muscles that we have not used strenuously for some time, or which are suddenly put to excessive or unaccustomed use, protest by becoming both stiff and sore—for example, as a result of a sudden burst of gardening.

There are two distinct types of muscle stiffness. One comes on in the course of exercise, the other does not develop until afterward. The first type of stiffness is due to the accumulation of waste products in the muscle tissue. In the performance of its work a muscle can be compared to an automobile engine (see Muscles). It requires fuel which is supplied by the bloodstream in the form of nutrients derived from the food we eat. This is mixed with oxygen and is then burned up to produce the energy required to make the muscle fibers contract, and produce movement. In the process, toxic waste products are produced and, unless they are removed, will give rise to pain and stiffness in the muscles concerned.

Usually, these waste products are removed without any problem and muscle activity is smooth and painless. But two particular circumstances may cause them to accumulate in the muscle to the point at which stiffness occurs: first, if the muscle is being used so intensely or strenuously that waste products are being produced faster than the blood can get rid of them. Second, in the case of a muscle that is not usually put to such energetic use, the network of blood vessels is inadequate to permit the extra blood required for both the provision of nutrients and the disposal of waste products to be supplied.

Stiffness that comes on after exercise is the most common form of stiffness. It is thought to be caused by some of the fibers of the muscle and the tissues that are intermingled with it and surrounding it being stretched, or even torn, by the unaccustomed use.

Effects of injury

Injury to muscles or joints occurs either from their being stretched or wrenched, or as a result of direct blows causing bruising and other tissue damage. The accompanying stiffness usually disappears within a few days, when the damaged tissue has had time for repair. In some cases, however, the stiffness does not go away, and this may be due either to the part not being allowed adequate rest or to the development of adhesions between two tissues that normally move freely across each other.

As with any type of inflammation, injury to tissues stimulates an outflow of fluid to protect and soothe the inflamed structures. This fluid is then usually reabsorbed into the blood circulation as the inflammation subsides (see Inflammation). However, in some cases the fluid thickens to form a gluey substance instead, and this

David Burnett/Colorific!

can have the effect of making neighboring tissues stick to each other. When an attempt is made to move the affected part, the adhesions make it stiff and resistant to movement.

Therefore, injured muscles and joints, even though being rested from their usual exertions, should regularly be put gently through their full range of movements so that adhesions do not have a chance of forming. When prolonged immobility of some part of the body is necessary—as in a fracture—this cannot be done and there is usually considerable stiffness when attempts are first made to start moving it again. This is usually overcome by physical therapy. Persistent adhesions, in which the stiffness does not respond to physical therapy, may require manipulation, if necessary under general anesthesia, to break them down and restore full mobility to the joint.

Stiffness disorders

Another common cause of stiffness is inflammation of joints and, as such, is a feature of all types of arthritis. It is particularly predominant in rheumatoid arthritis, the type of arthritis that primarily affects the smaller joints (see Rheumatoid arthritis). Indeed it is often the stiffness of the finger joints, rather

Spectrum

A sudden burst of strenuous work, such as digging the garden, is almost sure to result in a certain amount of stiffness if you are not used to it (above).
Sportsmen such as these footballers (left), need to limber up before a game; this helps to prevent muscle cramps occurring while they are playing.

than pain in them, that draws attention to the condition, and stiffness may be the only symptom for several years. With osteoarthritis, however, which mainly affects the larger joints, such as the hips and shoulders, pain usually develops first, with stiffness and disability following later (see Osteoarthritis).

Stiffness can be a problem for elderly people, both limiting their mobility and increasing their frustration. Often it is associated with particular types of arthritis and rheumatism, but more commonly there is a generally increased stiffness of all joints and muscles as part of the slowing down of physical activity with aging (see Arthritis, and Rheumatism).

How the body is affected

Stiffness affects different parts of the body in particular ways. Stiffness in the neck is most commonly caused by wrenching the neck, exposure to drafts, inflamed glands, or disorders of the joints between the vertebrae of the neck (cervical spondylosis).

1847

Q How does massage affect stiffness of the muscles? And how should it be given?

A Massage seems to work in two ways. First it has the effect of breaking down the small adhesions that are likely to have developed between some of the groups of tissues. Secondly, the physical friction of the massage stimulates the flow of blood through the part and therefore probably enhances the repair process. A massage is best given by a trained masseur or physical therapist.

When giving massage, remember that it is the friction that counts and not what you rub on, so you may just as well use something inexpensive like soap liniment.

Also remember that gentle rubbing will not achieve much. What is required is a steady kneading movement, getting the balls of the thumbs well into the part concerned. It should be administered with sufficient vigor for the massager to want to quit after 10 to 15 minutes!

Q My sister developed stiffness and pain in the ankle and was given an injection right into the joint. How does this work?

A The injection used was probably one of two kinds. The first would be an injection of one of the synthetic cocainelike local anesthetics such as novocaine or lignocaine. When you have a joint that is giving pain, the muscles and tendons around it tend to go into spasm to prevent it from moving and thus protect it from further damage. This may become counterproductive since it also gives rise to considerable stiffness. Injecting local anesthesia into the tissues around the joint overcomes the pain, the spasm is consequently relieved, and the stiffness goes. The second type of injection that might have been used is hydrocortisone, and that would have been injected directly into the joint cavity itself, the needle passing between the ends of the two bones. Hydrocortisone is a powerful anti-inflammatory drug, and by injecting it in this way it is able to act directly on the inflamed joint lining and thus bring about a speedy and often dramatic return to normal.

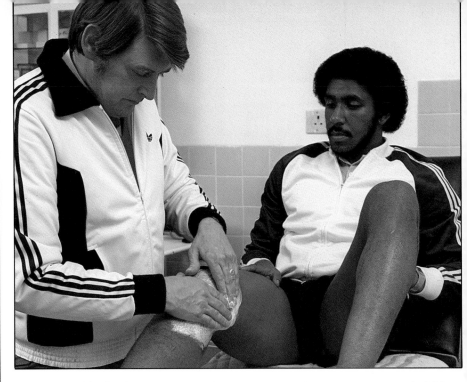

Stiffness of the back occurs in a variety of conditions and is often accompanied by backache (see Back and backache). Disorders of posture, such as round shoulders (kyphosis), a sideways curve (scoliosis), or a pot-belly posture (lordosis), may lead to stiffness of the back. Arthritis of any of the joints between the vertebrae will also restrict movement and give rise to stiffness. Any condition, such as lumbago or sciatica, involving considerable pain on movement of the back joints is usually accompanied by spasm or tightening of the ligaments and supporting muscles in an attempt to restrict movement, and thereby avoid pain. This spasm inevitably results in stiffness.

The shoulder, arm, and hand are parts of the body particularly prone to stiffness. Overuse, injuries such as sprains, arthritis, and other types of inflammation, reading in bed or driving in an awkward position, exposure to drafts or damp—all can lead to stiffness in some part of the upper limbs. In older people even minor falls or twists can cause the muscles, tendons, and ligaments that surround the shoulder joint to be damaged, resulting in extreme stiffness. With a frozen shoulder there is gradually increasing stiffness and pain on movement. Nevertheless, it is important to keep the joint moving, otherwise even more severe and long-standing stiffness will result. An injection of hydrocortisone into the joint may help to reduce the inflammation and loosen the joint, but manipulation is sometimes necessary.

Stiffness in the elbow or in the wrists is most frequently the result of arthritis, but may also be due to loose chips of bone. Stiffness of the fingers can result from a number of causes, including arthritis and accidental damage. Occasionally, there

Sports injuries are very common. And this is why it is so important to have someone around who knows how to administer some effective on-the-spot physical therapy.

may also be inflammation of the sheath of one or more of the tendons that operate the fingers, which makes movement stiff and painful.

Stiffness of the legs is mostly due to osteoarthritis, which frequently affects the hips and knees. Stiffness in the knee may be caused by a torn cartilage—though this more commonly results in episodes in which the knee becomes locked—or to the presence of loose bodies such as fragments of broken bone or torn-off cartilage. Stiffness in the ankles or the feet may be due to a previ-

Massage given by a trained masseur or a physical therapist can be an excellent form of treatment for muscle stiffness.

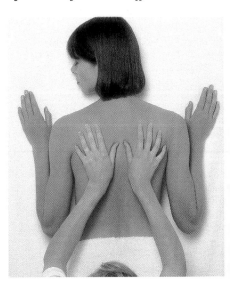

ous injury, inadequately treated sprains, badly designed shoes, foot strain, or inflammation of the tendons controlling the toes. The big toe is sometimes affected by attacks of sudden stiffness and pain which make walking difficult. This is called *hallux rigidus* and, even though its cause is not completely understood, should be treated promptly if permanent stiffness is to be avoided.

Treatment and prevention

A variety of treatments are available for stiffness, whatever its cause and no matter which part of the body is affected. Frequently a few days' rest from energetic use—and, in particular, from weight-bearing—is all that is needed to achieve full recovery. However it is important that passive or assisted movements of the part continue on a regular basis to prevent the development of adhesions. The common forms of stiffness are likely to be helped by simple home physical therapy. Both heat and massage are useful,

and progressive exercises will also assist in getting the affected part back to normal (see Massage).

Obstinate cases will require additional treatment. Physical therapy in the form of shortwave diathermy, hot packs, wax baths, hydrotherapy, and massage are some of the techniques that are presently available (see Physical therapy).

Persistently stiff or painful joints and tendons sometimes benefit from an injection of local anesthesia or of hydrocortisone, either to reduce the spasm of the surrounding tissues or reduce inflammation. If these measures fail, or adhesions are present, it may be necessary to manipulate the joint (see Manipulation) to achieve a return to a full range of movement. If the joint is permanently damaged it may be possible nowadays to replace it with an artificial joint.

Stiff joints and muscles can also be treated with drugs. Aspirin, by virtue of its anti-inflammatory properties, will often reduce stiffness as well as pain, and is

Soaking in a hot bath, the easy way to relax tired muscles and soothe away stiffness.

always worth trying. It should be given in soluble form or be enteric coated, so that irritation of the stomach is avoided. There are now a large number of specifically antiinflammatory drugs that do not contain steroids and that can achieve truly remarkable results. If steroids themselves are used, they are given as local injections wherever possible to avoid their serious side effects.

As always, however, prevention is preferable to cure. Regular suppleness exercises throughout the middle years of life will pay substantial dividends in avoiding premature or crippling stiffness in later years (see Physical fitness). And a gradual breaking-in period of progressive training will considerably diminish the likelihood of developing disabling and time-wasting stiffness in connection with sporting activities.

Stillbirth

Q My friend told me that she had held her stillborn baby. Isn't this rather morbid?

A Not at all: many parents find it easier to grieve for the dead baby if they have seen or held him or her and it makes the baby more a person to remember.

Q Do you still make milk after having a stillborn baby?

A Yes, lactation does occur, but without the stimulus of a baby sucking, milk dries up fairly quickly. Medication can help the process.

Q Who can I talk to about why my baby died?

A Your obstetrician will gladly see you at the time of the death, and again about six weeks later when you have got over the initial shock. He or she will answer any of your questions and tell you the result of the autopsy, if there was one, on your baby.

Q Why do doctors ask to do an autopsy on stillbirths? It seems very heartless.

A Sometimes, especially if the doctors are not sure why a baby died, it is important to find out so that they can tell the parents why their baby died, and to try to prevent it happening again. Often an autopsy is the only way of finding out the cause of death.

Q Is a woman more likely to have a stillborn baby as she gets older?

A Women over 40 do have an increased risk of stillbirth, although there are many tests which can be performed to minimize this slight risk.

Q Can alcohol or smoking cause stillbirth?

A There does seem to be a higher stillbirth rate in those women who smoke and drink heavily during pregnancy, although the occasional alcoholic drink will do no harm. Smoking should be avoided completely.

To lose a baby is shattering—the grief, sense of loss, and even guilt take a long time to fade. A period of mourning is necessary before the bereaved parents can come to terms with their loss and look to the future.

Steve Bielschowsky

At present, the term *stillbirth* is used when the death of a baby occurs before it is born, but after 28 weeks of pregnancy. Most deaths occur while the baby is still in the uterus, before labor begins, but about 10 percent occur during labor. If a fetus dies before 28 weeks of pregnancy, it is known as an abortion or miscarriage.

Causes of stillbirth
The cause of many stillbirths is still unknown, but there is a body of medical evidence that gives an explanation for some of them. It has been suggested that some stillbirths occur when there is an inadequate supply of oxygen in the blood to the baby from the mother via the umbilical cord and the placenta.

Placenta previa
When the condition called placenta previa occurs, the placenta lies too low in the uterus. When labor begins, the placenta can separate from the uterine wall, or be damaged by the baby trying to get out, and this can cause severe bleeding. This may end in a stillbirth, although an emergency cesarean section can be performed which can save the baby's life (see Cesarean birth).

Blood vessels in the placenta may clot (infarction); sometimes the placenta just

After the death of a baby there is usually a phase of shock during which the parents will need to express their grief, to cry, and to talk about their feelings. Sharing their sense of loss with each other will bring some comfort, but the time individuals take to come to terms with the experience, and to look to the future, will vary.

does not seem to work very efficiently; or it separates, either partly or wholly, from the wall of the uterus before birth (an abruptio placentae); all these conditions can predispose to a stillbirth.

Many mothers who catch rubella (see Rubella) in early pregnancy, or who have chronic kidney or thyroid disease, or a severe infection during pregnancy, may have a stillborn child. Some women suffer from toxemia of pregnancy, where the blood pressure is high and they lose protein in the urine and retain fluid. This condition makes them much more likely to have a stillborn child, and they need careful attention during pregnancy.

Problems during pregnancy
About 20 percent of stillbirths are caused because the baby has an abnormality—it may have a chromosome disorder such as Down's syndrome, or a congenital abnormality like spina bifida, or anencephaly. There may be heart or kidney abnormalities. These can be diagnosed by amniocentesis (see Amniocentesis) or with an ultrasound scan. Unfortunately despite a successful diagnosis, the stillbirth cannot always be prevented.

Rhesus factor
Rhesus incompatibility (see Rhesus factor) used to be a major cause of stillbirth, but this condition can now be prevented by giving every rhesus negative mother an injection of anti-D gamma globulin after delivery of a rhesus positive baby, or following an abortion or stillbirth. This destroys all the antibodies that she has formed during the pregnancy.

Problems during labor
A stillbirth can occur during labor. If the baby is very large compared to the size of the mother's pelvis, or is lying abnormally in the womb, or if there is more than one baby, it may be a difficult delivery and the blood and hence oxygen supply to the baby can become obstructed. The umbilical cord can come out before the baby, or be torn, twisted in a knot, or around the baby's neck—again all can interfere with the baby's supply of oxygen from the mother.

Premature babies are much more susceptible to trauma and lack of oxygen during delivery than term babies, and hence they are at a much greater risk of being stillborn.

Symptoms
Many women notice that their baby moves much less in the last few days before a stillbirth happens. Others will feel very jerky movements—as though the baby is trying to escape from the womb. Many women do not notice that anything has changed. Once the baby has died, no movements whatsoever will be detected by the mother.

Death is confirmed by the doctor or nurse being unable to hear any fetal heartbeat, and by there having been no movements for more than 12 hours. This can be checked with an ultrasound scan or, if the baby has been dead for several days, with an X ray.

If death does occur during a baby's delivery there will be no sign of life whatsoever (heartbeats, attempts to breathe, or movement) at birth.

After the death
Once the doctor is certain that the baby is dead he or she will tell the parents, preferably when they are together.

If the fetus is still in the uterus, labor will be induced as soon as possible. If left alone, it might take four weeks for labor to occur spontaneously; this would be extremely difficult for a woman to bear

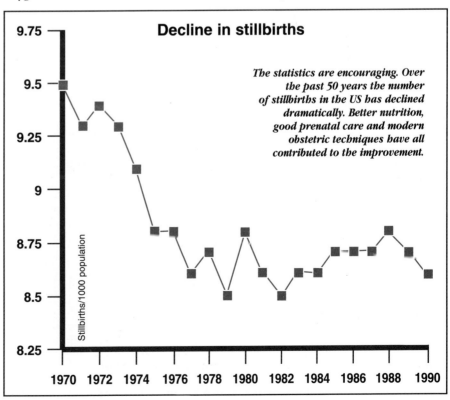

Decline in stillbirths

The statistics are encouraging. Over the past 50 years the number of stillbirths in the US has declined dramatically. Better nutrition, good prenatal care and modern obstetric techniques have all contributed to the improvement.

Q If the fetus dies in the womb, is it removed by a cesarean section?

A No, it is extremely rare for this to happen. Labor is usually induced by placing a prostaglandin pessary into the vagina, near the cervix. Sometimes an oxytocin drip is also needed and the fetus is then delivered vaginally.

Q When I went to visit my sister and her baby in the maternity suite, there was a woman in the next bed who had had a stillborn baby. This seemed cruel. Why wasn't she put on another floor?

A Sometimes women feel they must face other children immediately after losing a baby; sometimes there just isn't a single room or cubicle available for the mother. It is important, too, that she should not feel totally isolated from everyone else; she can derive support and comfort from the other mothers at this very difficult time.

Q My sister had a stillborn baby and was told to wait until she had recovered from the death before she became pregnant again. Wouldn't it be better to have another baby as soon as possible?

A No, it seems better for parents to learn to accept their baby's death, and this will take time. Another baby will not replace the child they have lost; it has a permanent place in the family and must be mourned properly.

Q I have diabetes. Does this make me more likely to have a stillborn baby?

A If you have diabetes there is a slightly higher risk of stillbirth. But if your diabetes is controlled properly at the time of conception, and during the pregnancy, there is a much higher chance of having a normal healthy baby. See your gynecologist as soon as you start thinking about having a baby. He or she will advise you on personal care before and during your pregnancy and will undertake the necessary prenatal checkups.

emotionally. The dead fetus can also cause the mother to bleed if it is not removed early enough.

Once delivered of the fetus, the mother needs the same care as if her baby had lived, but arrangements for her to go home as soon as possible will be made with her doctor, and an appointment booked for her postnatal check.

Registering a stillbirth

It is a legal requirement that the baby must be registered as being stillborn with the local authorities, and the hospital or your doctor will issue a certificate stating that your baby was born dead. The results of the autopsy will also be recorded on the certificate. This will be done as soon as possible so that burial arrangements can be made.

The administration department at the hospital will be able to advise on carrying out these procedures.

Grieving

Initially after the death of a baby there is a phase of shock. This can last about two months and many parents during this time will need to express their grief, to cry, and to talk about any guilt feelings they may have. Other children in the family will also need to be comforted.

By monitoring the heartbeat of the baby in the uterus, obstetric staff can determine whether he or she is showing any signs of distress. If the baby is being deprived of oxygen, a factor that may cause a stillbirth, a cesarean can be performed.

It is very common for the next phase to be one of depression, when some couples will search for someone, or something, to blame for the death: it may be a particular doctor, nurse, or hospital; it may be themselves.

The time it takes for different individuals to adjust will obviously vary, but eventually acceptance will be reached, and with it, a willingness for normal family life to continue.

Prevention

In nearly 40 percent of cases there are factors which, had they been detected and dealt with, the stillbirth might have been prevented. Good prenatal care and good obstetric care during labor are essential. The baby's growth, movement, and heart rate, as well as the mother's health, must be regularly checked throughout this time.

Unfortunately many women still do not have adequate prenatal checks or they start prenatal care late in their pregnancy. Sometimes it is because they dislike the formality, the size of, or the wait at the clinics; or there is no one to look after their other children. But it is these women who have the highest number of stillbirths (see Prenatal care).

Community hospitals may offer good prenatal care for women who do not have adequate health insurance.

Finally, any woman who suspects that her baby is moving less than it should, or who has any fears, should call her obstetrician as soon as possible to preempt a stillbirth if possible.

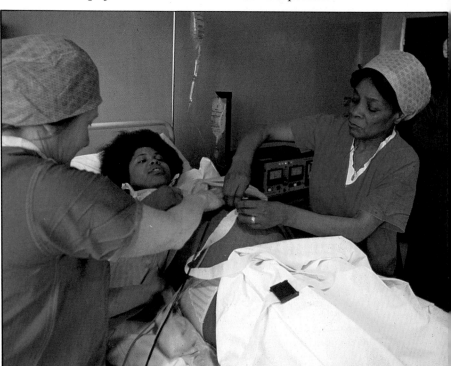

Stimulants

Q I feel tired and run down a lot of the time, and I'm sure some sort of stimulant would help. Which is the best?

A As you can imagine, the drug company that discovers a drug that lifts people up when they are run down is bound to make a fortune! The fact of the matter is that feeling run down on occasion—and even frequently—is quite normal. In some cases, however, the persistent feeling of being off-color and run down can be a symptom of depression, and here drugs may be very valuable. But there is no effective pick-me-up for those of us who are just feeling a bit down from time to time.

Q What is the difference between a stimulant and a tonic?

A There are various drugs that act on the nervous system, and indeed other parts of the body, to increase the level of activity; these are the true stimulants. Tonics, which were popular in the past, are harmless compounds that were given to patients in the hope of toning them up. If they were effective, it was because the patient and even the doctor believed in their effectiveness, not because they had any direct effect on the body's tissues. This effect is known as a placebo action.

Q If someone is suffering from heart failure, can you just give them a stimulant to make the heart work harder?

A Yes, this is an acceptable treatment. Indeed, for 200 years the treatment of heart failure depended on the stimulant activity of the drug digoxin. However, the reason why heart failure occurs is because the actual heart muscle is running short of the oxygen that it needs to do its pumping. By stimulating it you are not only getting more work out of it, but you are also increasing the demand for oxygen, so that overall you may have less effect with stimulant drugs than you had hoped. For this reason they are no longer the main way of treating heart failure.

Most of us use stimulant drugs more than once a day, like caffeine, the active ingredient in coffee and tea. But there are other stimulants besides: some of these are harmful, while others have specific medical uses.

For centuries, people have been looking for some substance that would stimulate the brain, and help them over the vague feelings of ill health and tiredness that are part of the human condition. The quest seems to be hopeless, and it is better to accept that we cannot feel 100 percent all of the time.

Amphetamines

One group of drugs that have come nearest to fulfilling this idea of an all-around tonic is amphetamines (see Amphetamines). These drugs have an effect at most levels in the nervous system: they are able to stimulate both thought and action, while putting off the need for either sleep or food. A price has to be paid, however: if fatigue is postponed for too long, it will eventually break through, and will be more severe than before. Prolonged use can lead to a nervous, agitated state that may progress to severe psychiatric disturbance.

Amphetamines are also addictive in the sense that people become unable to do without them, even though there are no serious physical withdrawal symptoms as there are with heroin. Amphetamines combined with barbiturates, which generally depress the nervous system, were

Since it was discovered that caffeine can mobilize fat stores early on, and delay the use of glycogen, some marathon runners have a cup or two of coffee before a race.

Courtesy of Nescafé

STIMULANTS

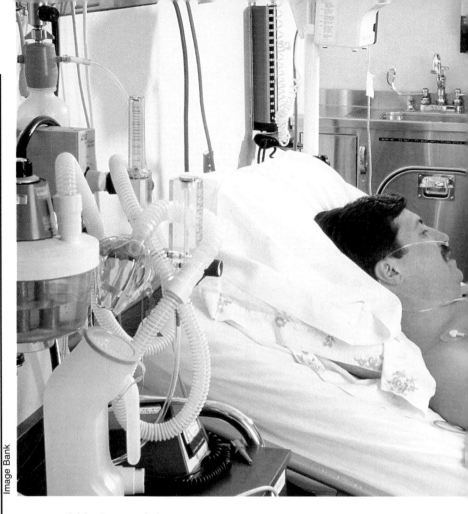

Image Bank

A patient who is having breathing difficulties may be put on a respirator, but occasionally the drug doxapram may be used to stimulate the lungs.

once available. Some of the most common types were known as purple hearts, and these led to serious addiction problems in the 1960s. Such combinations are no longer prescribed (see Barbiturates).

Nowadays, amphetamines have only the most limited of medical uses. They are used to overcome failures of the hypothalamus, and related parts of the brain which control such functions as eating and sleeping. Narcolepsy is a condition where there is a frequent and irresistible desire to sleep, even in the daytime. It often results from tumors in the region of the hypothalamus, and its effects can be combated with the use of amphetamines. Oddly enough these drugs have also been found to be useful in the treatment of overactive children (see Hyperactivity).

While doctors have become aware of the dangers of amphetamines as addictive drugs, there is no doubt that habituation to them is growing.

Caffeine

Caffeine has been with us a good deal longer than amphetamines. Coffee came into widespread use in the 17th century, and caffeine has become the most socially acceptable of drugs. It poses none of the problems that are associated with excessive consumption of alcohol, and none of the health risks of nicotine. Alcohol and nicotine are the only other drugs to rival caffeine with regard to the amounts in which they are consumed.

Coffee is not the only substance to contain caffeine. It is also found in tea, cocoa, and cola drinks that are made from the kola nut. All these substances also contain related compounds, for instance theobromine, and all belong to the group of xanthine derivatives.

Caffeine stimulates the central nervous system at all levels, although the extent of this stimulation is less than is found with the amphetamines. Caffeine has been shown to increase ability at a variety of tasks. However, overall caffeine is probably incapable of improving the level of intellectual performance, although it may be able to help in maintaining a high level of functioning thought processes in circumstances where they would otherwise be declining, either as a result of tiredness, or boredom.

There are other effects on organs outside the nervous system. Coffee or tea drunk in large amounts has a mild diuretic effect on the kidneys. Caffeine also affects the heart: the pulse rate tends to run a little higher after coffee and some people may even suffer from palpi-

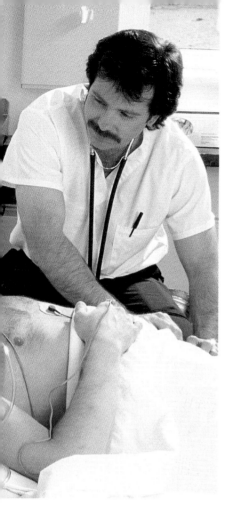

cells; this is a substance called cyclic AMP (adenosine monophosphate). This intracellular substance is responsible for turning on the various different activities of many of the body's cells. Aminophylline acts more on the lungs and the heart rather than on the brain, like caffeine. It is very useful in dilating the bronchial tubes that become constricted and lead to an attack of asthma, while it stimulates the heart to contract with more power. Because xanthine drugs and caffeine also magnify each other's effects, they should be used together with caution.

Other stimulants

Epinephrine, the body's hormone of fight or flight, is really the most powerful of the all-around stimulants. It increases the force of contraction of the heart, widens the air passages, and leads to an increase of blood flow to crucial areas like the muscles, while diverting blood from such areas as the skin and the stomach.

Many of the drugs that doctors use are based on molecules like the epinephrine molecule. There is a whole range of stimulating drugs designed to have effects like widening the bronchial tubes in asthma, or stimulating the power of the heart's contraction if cardiac failure occurs after a coronary or heart surgery. Another group of drugs is designed to block the effects on the heart, since over-stimulation can lead to angina (pain resulting from a loss of blood supply to the heart).

Occasionally doctors try to stimulate the breathing rather than put patients on a respirator. Of the small group of drugs that do this, the most commonly used is doxapram. This drug is related in its effects to the poison strychnine, and is one of the only drugs among a group known as the analeptics that is utilized in everyday medicine. These drugs cause significant stimulation of the entire nervous system, and the smallest doses are likely to cause fits or convulsions. Doxapram will do this in a large dose, but in smaller doses it has a useful stimulating effect on the respiratory system center (the part of the brain found in the medulla that controls breathing).

tations—or even panic attacks—as a result (see Anxiety). Additionally, many depressed patients abuse caffeinated drinks in order to mask their symptoms (see Depression).

Caffeine is not totally without adverse effects. Drunk in large amounts, caffeine can lead to a nervous and slightly trembling state. Some degree of addiction almost certainly happens. Much more important is the fact that coffee probably contributes to many attacks of migraine (see Migraine). Studies have failed to show evidence that coffee is involved in causing heart attacks. However, there is a relationship between drinking more than an average amount of coffee and smoking cigarettes, and cigarettes have been proved to be a cause of heart attacks (see Heart attack).

Although studies have never proved caffeine's deleterious effects for pregnant or nursing women, most obstetricians still recommend a decreased intake of caffeine (see Pregnancy). Caffeine can, however, cause the esophageal muscle to open, allowing digestive acids to flow back into the throat (see Heartburn).

Caffeine is closely related to another of the xanthine derivatives, a drug called aminophylline, which is one of the most useful stimulant drugs. Like caffeine, this drug works by increasing one of the messenger substances that is found inside the

Effects of stimulants

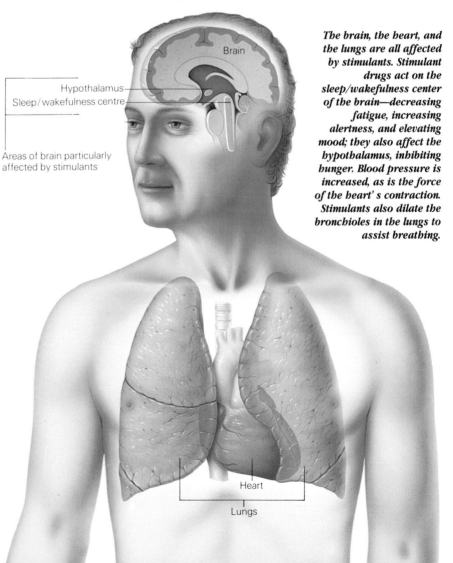

Brain

Hypothalamus
Sleep/wakefulness centre

Areas of brain particularly affected by stimulants

Heart

Lungs

Mike Courteney

The brain, the heart, and the lungs are all affected by stimulants. Stimulant drugs act on the sleep/wakefulness center of the brain—decreasing fatigue, increasing alertness, and elevating mood; they also affect the hypothalamus, inhibiting hunger. Blood pressure is increased, as is the force of the heart's contraction. Stimulants also dilate the bronchioles in the lungs to assist breathing.

Stitch

Q Why do I always get a stitch if I exercise directly, or even soon, after a meal?

A There are two possible reasons for this. First, after eating a meal the blood in the circulation tends to be diverted away from the muscles between the ribs to the digestive system, and this may cause a stitch, which is a kind of cramp. The second reason is that the full stomach may press on the diaphragm as you run, and this can cause a stitch.

Q Do athletes' warm-ups really prevent them from getting a stitch when they compete?

A The purpose of an athlete's warm-up is to ease muscles into well-oiled working order without overstraining them. Since a stitch is a muscular problem originating in the diaphragm, or the muscles between the ribs, then warming up should help prevent it. But a stitch can also come on when the body is fatigued and suffering from lack of salt, and warming up is not likely to make any significant difference to this.

Q I have a pain like a stitch that seems to come and go all day long. Is this just indigestion or some kind of persistent stitch?

A If you have a persistent stitchlike pain that doesn't seem to have any connection with exercise, then it would be advisable to see your doctor as soon as possible. It may simply be indigestion, but if this is causing you continual discomfort, you should have the problem diagnosed by your doctor and have it treated if necessary.

Q I read somewhere that bad diarrhea can give you a stitch. Is this really true?

A Because a stitch is a kind of cramp, it can sometimes be caused by severe diarrhea, which depletes the body muscles of water. This dehydration makes the muscles go into the painful spasm characteristic of a stitch.

The sharp, stabbing pain of a stitch is a sensation we tend to take for granted. It is usually caused by a cramp in the breathing muscles, and can be temporarily debilitating.

A stitch is a form of cramp that produces a stabbing pain in the front of the body around the area of the rib cage, or in the side just below the ribs. Like other kinds of cramp, it is most common during vigorous exercise, but can come on for no apparent reason. Although painful and temporarily debilitating, a stitch is usually more of a nuisance than a serious complaint. There are, however, some diseases whose symptoms can be confused with a stitch. For this reason, any persistent pain that resembles a stitch should be reported to your doctor (see Cramp).

How a stitch develops

A stitch has very localized effects, being confined solely to the muscles involved in breathing. These are the intercostal muscles between the ribs, which help the rib cage expand and contract, and the diaphragm, a sheet of muscle covering

A stitch is a common feature in the typical rough and tumble of childhood playtime. Impetuously returning to the fray too soon after eating is the most usual cause, but any burst of sudden exercise may be enough to bring on the stabbing pain of a stitch.

Corbis

the whole of the base of the rib cage (see Diaphragm, and Ribs). When you breathe in, the muscles of the diaphragm contract, pushing the muscle sheet flat; on breathing out, the muscles relax and the diaphragm assumes a domelike shape.

When a stitch comes on, a cramp occurs in the intercostal muscles, or the diaphragm, or both. If the intercostals are involved, the pain is usually toward the front of the chest. The effect of this kind of stitch is to make breathing painful. You feel a stabbing pain every time you breathe in because the muscles cannot contract properly; it may also be difficult to catch your breath (see Breathing).

When the diaphragm is involved in a stitch, the pain is usually felt at the side of the body. The cramp causes the diaphragm to develop a kind of tuck in it. Again, breathing is painful, with the pain bridging the gap between breaths so that

Dealing with a stitch

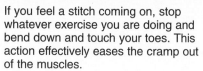

If you feel a stitch coming on, stop whatever exercise you are doing and bend down and touch your toes. This action effectively eases the cramp out of the muscles.

If this fails to work, sit down and bend over so that your head is between your knees. Relax and breathe slowly and deeply. The stitch should then quickly disappear.

Roger Payling

to the sufferer it feels continuous. The pain is felt in your side, rather than at the actual site of the trouble, because of the way in which the body's nerves are distributed (see Nervous system).

Causes of stitch

Like other forms of cramp, a stitch usually comes on during strenuous exercise. This is caused by an inadequate blood supply to the breathing muscles, due to diversion of blood to other parts of the body; constriction of the blood vessels supplying that part of the body; or failure of the blood vessels to stretch and so supply sufficient blood during exercise. In addition, a buildup of waste products—such as lactic acid—in the muscles can also cause a stitch (see Blood).

A stitch is most likely to develop if you do any exercise straight after a meal, or if you overstretch your body's resources. However, with regular exercise, the stitches become fewer as the blood vessels widen and become more elastic to take a greater blood flow.

But no matter how fit you are, exercising after meals may cause a stitch to develop because there is no way of preventing blood being diverted to the digestive system. So, always leave a gap of about an hour after a meal before taking any strenuous exercise.

A weakness in the diaphragm may also lead to a stitch coming on after even the slightest exercise, or just after a heavy

meal and without doing any exercise at all. What happens in this case is that the full stomach presses on the diaphragm and causes it to bulge upward. In very severe cases, the diaphragm may actually rupture under such pressure.

Treatment of a stitch

The best way to deal with an ordinary stitch is first to stop exercising, and then to bend down and touch your toes. This action stretches the diaphragm and intercostal muscles and so stops the muscular spasm that is causing the stitch. If this does not work, just sit down, relax, and try to breathe in and out as deeply as possible, keeping your head down between your knees. Again, this will help stretch the muscles and hopefully get them out of this unpleasant spasm.

Causes for confusion

A pain like a stitch, but which is not related to exercise and is generally more persistent than normal, can be a sign of serious illness and should not be ignored. Illnesses that result in stitchlike pains include pleurisy, inflammation of the diaphragm caused by infection through bacteria or viruses, or problems of the spleen or colon.

Accordingly, a pain that initially feels similar to a stitch, but which is particularly associated with severe pains in the chest or abdomen, should be brought to the attention of a doctor without delay.

Stomach

Q How do people manage when they have had their stomachs removed? Can they eat normally, and what happens to their digestion?

A Most people who have an operation to remove the stomach only have part of it removed. This can still affect them in many ways, however, and they usually find that they feel full after a small meal and have to eat little and often. They must see a doctor regularly as, in the long term, they may become anemic and develop other nutritional deficiencies. If the whole stomach is removed, and this is not always necessary, then they have more severe symptoms and also require regular injections of vitamin B_{12}, since the stomach is necessary for the natural absorption of this vitamin.

Q How big is the stomach and does its size vary?

A The stomach can, in fact, vary considerably in size. It may be the size of a large pear or so large that it almost reaches the pelvis. Eating a lot of food may cause it to enlarge and any blockage to the outlet of the stomach could have the same effect. However, when someone is said to have a large stomach, this usually means that the abdomen is fat.

Q Is the stomach ever empty, or does it always contain some food or digestive juices?

A Food entering the stomach usually takes an hour or so, depending on the nature of the food, to pass into the intestines. After this, apart from a small amount of digestive juice which remains, the stomach is empty.

Q Is drinking alcohol on an empty stomach harmful?

A Apart from the fact that the alcohol would be more quickly absorbed into the bloodstream, it is probably inadvisable to drink alcohol without food since it can actually damage the lining of the stomach, causing inflammation and bleeding.

Mick Saunders

The stomach is the body's natural reservoir. It holds the food we eat and breaks it down in preparation for its journey through the intestines.

The stomach: site and structure

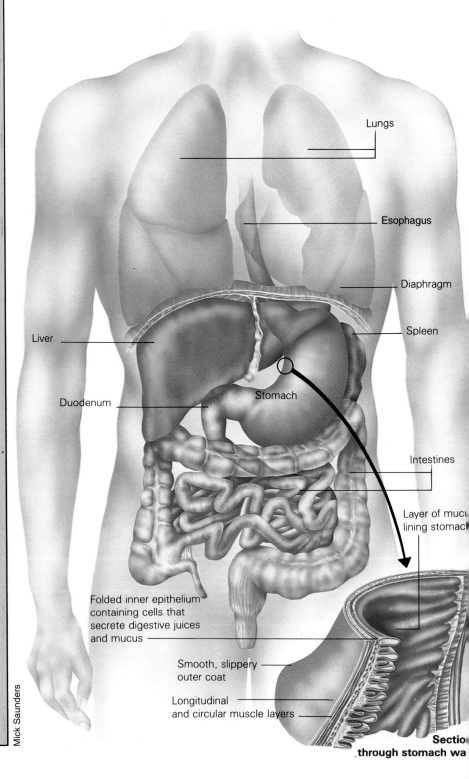

Lungs

Esophagus

Diaphragm

Spleen

Liver

Duodenum

Stomach

Intestines

Layer of mucu lining stomac

Folded inner epithelium containing cells that secrete digestive juices and mucus

Smooth, slippery outer coat

Longitudinal and circular muscle layers

Sectio through stomach wa

The stomach is a muscular bag situated in the upper part of the abdomen. It is connected at its upper end to the esophagus (the gullet), and at its lower end to the duodenum (the first part of the small intestine). The wall of the stomach consists of a thick layer of muscle lined with a special membrane called epithelium.

Function

First, the stomach acts as a reservoir for food. The lining membrane then produces a juice that contains acid and enzymes to break down the food and thereby aid digestion.

In the stomach the food is mixed together with the digestive juices until it has formed a pulp, which is then forced out into the duodenum. At the junction between the stomach and the duodenum there is a ring of muscle, the pyloric sphincter, which relaxes from time to time to allow the food to pass into the duodenum. The food is then pushed along the intestines to be further digested and absorbed (see Digestive system).

Common problems

At some time or other most of us have experienced that queasy feeling when the stomach contracts forcibly. When this happens the contents of the stomach may be ejected up into the esophagus, an action known as vomiting. Vomiting can have several causes: any disturbance of the central nervous system, which controls the contraction of the stomach; any irritation of the lining of the stomach; or an obstruction of the outflow from the lower end of the stomach (see Vomiting).

Frequently, vomiting may be associated with a common condition known as gastroentiritis. This is when the lining of the stomach becomes inflamed as a result of a viral infection, eating spicy foods, drinking alcohol, taking certain drugs, stress, or for no particular reason at all. A mild attack of gastritis produces symptoms of nausea, vomiting, and occasionally some pain in the upper abdomen. Severe attacks can result in bleeding from the stomach lining (see Gastroenteritis).

The treatment of gastritis is to remove the cause wherever possible, and to drink lots of bland fluids. Sometimes drugs which prevent vomiting may be prescribed by a doctor. Fortunately gastritis is usually a self-limiting condition once the primary cause has been removed.

The stomach is situated higher up in the body than most people think—in fact, it is found just under the diaphragm. It is a muscular bag with a smooth, slippery outer coat and a corrugated inner lining that is protected from its own acidic digestive juices by a layer of mucus.

Roger Payling

Stomach problems such as gastritis or ulcers can flare up for a variety of reasons, but perhaps most frequently as a result of eating spicy food, drinking alcohol, and taking certain drugs.

Gastric ulcers

Ulcers occurring in the stomach are thought to be related to the breakdown of the mucous layer that protects the lining and prevents it from being affected by the strong acid and enzymes naturally present in the gastric juices (see Ulcers).

The acid can erode the mucosal layer, then penetrate the muscle layer. This can then lead to perforation of the stomach wall, causing an ulcer. Many gastric ulcers appear to be present for many years before medical advice is sought, because there is often a great deal of scarring and fibrous tissue around the ulcer.

People who develop gastric ulcers do not have a high level of acid in the stomach, unlike those people who develop duodenal ulcers. In fact, some patients with gastric ulcers have a low level of acid secretion.

Symptoms and dangers

Gastric ulcers are most commonly found on the upper aspect of the stomach (the lesser curve). They tend to appear, grow bigger, and then disappear. Although no one really knows the exact cause of gastric ulcers, spicy foods, alcohol, smoking, and stress seem to be contributory factors. The symptoms are characterized by burning pain, which comes shortly after eating, nausea, and sometimes weight loss. There may be episodes of these symptoms followed by long periods without any symptoms at all.

If a gastric ulcer is left untreated for a long period of time, several things can happen. First, if the ulcer is situated over a main blood vessel supplying the wall of the stomach, it may eventually erode through the blood vessel, leading to a massive hemorrhage (see Hemorrhage). Second, the ulcer can perforate through the wall of the stomach so that a hole appears suddenly in the stomach wall. The stomach contents can then leak out into the peritoneal cavity, causing peritonitis. Third, repeated attempts at heal-

Jerry Harpur

Q My husband is 60 years old and he has just recently started getting persistent indigestion pains. Antacids, such as milk of magnesia, do not really seem to be helping much. What should he do next?

A It is important for someone of his age who has developed persistent indigestion to have proper investigations to make sure that he has not developed a stomach tumor. Your doctor should arrange for him to have a number of tests. These tests will probably include a barium meal X ray, followed by a gastroscopy. The latter enables the doctor to see into the stomach by means of a flexible telescopic instrument (a gastroscope) passed through the mouth and esophagus.

Q Is it normal to lose weight with an ulcer?

A It depends on what sort of ulcer it is. If the ulcer is in the duodenum, eating relieves the pain and so the patient may put on weight. However, if the ulcer is in the stomach, eating brings the pain on and so the patient tends to lose weight because he or she is afraid to eat.

Q I recently had an attack of vomiting and loss of appetite. My doctor said that I had gastric flu. Is this possible?

A Yes. You probably developed a viral infection of the stomach, causing its lining to become inflamed. However, there is no way of proving that this is what it was. The symptoms of viral gastritis, as it should be called, are usually short-lived, and respond to simple measures such as drinking bland liquids, and possibly taking antivomiting tablets.

Q Does a stomach tumor always cause pain?

A No. Sometimes there is no pain at all. The patient simply notices a loss of appetite, or loss of weight. Pain can often confuse the issue, sometimes leading to a misdiagnosis if the patient is simply thought to have indigestion.

ing the ulcer may lead to scarring and contraction of the tissues around the ulcer. This may eventually produce a narrowing in the middle of the stomach so that it assumes an hour-glass appearance.

Treatment

Diagnosis of a gastric ulcer is usually made by means of a barium meal X ray, followed by a gastroscopy to make sure that the ulcer is benign. Treatment is in the form of tablets for a period of about three months. If the ulcer does not heal, or if the patient develops any complications, then surgery is usually required, and the affected part of the stomach has to be removed.

Cancer of the stomach

Gastric cancer is one of the most common malignant tumors, and it affects men more than women. It can start as a small ulcer or as a small polyp and eventually grows bigger to obstruct the passage of food through the stomach (see Cancer).

Because the tumor involves the lining of the stomach, patients may lose blood into the stomach, and it may be anemia that brings the illness to light. Others feel constantly nauseated and lose their appetites, and consequently lose weight. Other patients may develop pain in the upper part of the abdomen. Because the pain can be very similar to that caused by a benign gastric or duodenal ulcer, these patients can often find that they are treated for a long time with antacids with no relief of symptoms. It is for this reason that any patient over the age of about 50 years coming to the doctor complaining

The stomach processes the food we eat, but sometimes the going gets a little rough. Unripe fruit, picked directly from trees, can often play havoc with the digestion.

of indigestion should be treated with caution. If he or she does not respond quickly to conventional treatment for indigestion, further investigation of the case will be essential (see Indigestion).

Like a benign ulcer, gastric cancer is usually diagnosed by means of a barium meal X ray and a gastroscopy. The sooner this is done the better, since there is evidence that an early diagnosis improves the overall outlook of the treatment. Wherever possible the treatment of gastric cancer involves the surgical removal of the tumor, which often means removing the whole stomach. Patients who have had their stomach, or a major portion of it, removed are usually unable to eat large meals, but in other respects should be able to carry on as normal. They do, however, have to be seen at yearly intervals since they are more likely to develop anemia and nutritional disturbances, which can usually be corrected.

Pyloric stenosis

Sometimes the outlet of the stomach, the pyloric canal, becomes blocked, leading to a buildup of stomach contents and eventual profuse vomiting. In infants this can occur as a result of overgrowth of the muscle in this region, the cause of which is unknown. In adults, it is caused either by a cancerous growth or by a longstanding duodenal ulcer, which has caused fibrous scarring.

Stomach pump

A device for washing out harmful substances from the stomach before they have been absorbed, the stomach pump is used most often in cases of drug overdose.

Q Is having your stomach pumped at all dangerous?

A The procedure is not usually dangerous, although a lot depends on the skill of the people using it. The chief problem that may arise is that fluid may accidentally be aspirated into the lungs, causing pneumonia.

Q What is the outlook in people who have had their stomach pumped after taking an overdose?

A Provided they get to the hospital alive after taking the overdose, most people survive as long as they are handled properly and their vital functions are given adequate supportive treatment. Survival also depends on the nature of the drugs that they have used.

Q Can an unconscious person have his or her stomach washed out safely?

A Yes. Initially, however, a special protective airway is put into the windpipe to prevent any of the stomach's contents from passing into the lungs. A serious type of pneumonia would result if this happened.

Q Is the stomach pump really a pump as the name suggests?

A No. The procedure involves washing out, rather than pumping out, a harmful substance which has been swallowed. The pump itself is a tube which is passed through the mouth down through the esophagus and into the stomach, enabling water to be flushed down and sucked back up again (this is called a gastric lavage). The process is repeated until the entire contents of the stomach are gradually removed including the substance in question. A sample is usually kept for analysis. A similar, although finer, kind of tube is used in feeding people who cannot swallow, while tubes, called endoscopes, can be inserted into the body to investigate a patient's symptoms.

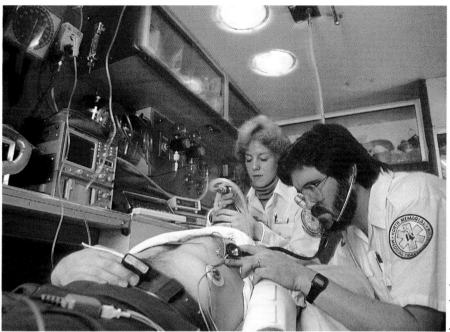

Image bank

When a stomach pump is used, a tube is passed from the mouth to the stomach and water passed down it. The water is siphoned out or aspirated, bringing with it the unwanted substance, usually tablets taken in overdose. The procedure has to be done before they can be absorbed and do any harm to the patient. The procedure is known medically as gastric lavage.

When it is needed

Drug overdose, either accidental or deliberate, is a common cause of hospital admission. Accidental overdoses often occur when children swallow their parents' pills or household remedies, such as aspirin, by mistake (see Overdoses).

In adults, it is most likely that the overdose has been taken as a deliberate suicide attempt, although not all people who take overdoses actually have their minds set on dying (see Suicide).

Whatever the reason, acts of self-poisoning are common. The drugs used are not only those obtained on prescription, but ones which can be bought over the counter, such as aspirin and acetaminophen. Apart from these, the drugs most commonly used are tranquilizers and antidepressants (see Tranquilizers). The drugs are often taken in combination and, in a high proportion of cases, alcohol is also consumed.

When dealing with an emergency case of drug overdose, the first priority is to insure the patient's vital life functions. Drugs may be given to help stabilize the blood pressure, and blankets used to prevent hypothermia.

Intensive care

Emergency room treatment aims to keep alive the patient who has taken an overdose. This means that it is more important for the trauma team to check and maintain the vital life functions, rather than immediately try to wash out the drug from the stomach (see Emergencies). They must clear and maintain an airway, perhaps by inserting a tube to assist breathing, or even by putting the patient on a machine called a respirator which will help him or her to breathe.

It is also important for the medics to check the blood pressure, and give drugs if this has fallen dangerously low. These in turn can cause irregularity in the heart's action, and this must also be checked and corrected. Occasionally the patient becomes very cold (a condition which is known as hypothermia; see Hypothermia), and this has to be treated as soon as possible.

The drug that has been taken must be identified. For this reason, it is extremely important that anyone who accompanies the patient to the hospital takes

Q Who actually performs the procedure?

A The stomach pump is used at the direction of a doctor and usually inserted by a nurse who is experienced in the technique.

Q When is the stomach pump commonly used?

A It is most often used in the treatment of people who have taken overdoses of such drugs as tranquilizers or antidepressants. It is particularly useful as a treatment up to four hours after the drug has been taken, but it is often used up to 10 or even 12 hours afterward.

Q Is there any danger of internal damage when a stomach pump is used?

A This is most unlikely. A similar principle is involved when a patient has abdominal surgery. The same kind of tube of a smaller size is inserted into the stomach so that secretions can be sucked out while the intestines are not functioning. Likewise, a patient who is unconscious will have to be fed by a tube inserted through the nose and passed down into the stomach. This causes no harm to the patient but enables him or her to receive, in liquid form, all the elements of a normal diet.

Q Is the normal digestive process likely to be upset after the stomach has been subjected to a pump?

A Usually a patient who has taken an overdose is in no mood for eating. He or she may indeed not be able to if they are still unconscious. By the time the patient has regained consciousness the digestive processes should be restored, having received no damage of any kind from this procedure.

Q Why is lukewarm water always used?

A Quite simply, the water needs to be the same temperature as the body. If too hot, it could burn the internal organs; if too cold it may cause shock.

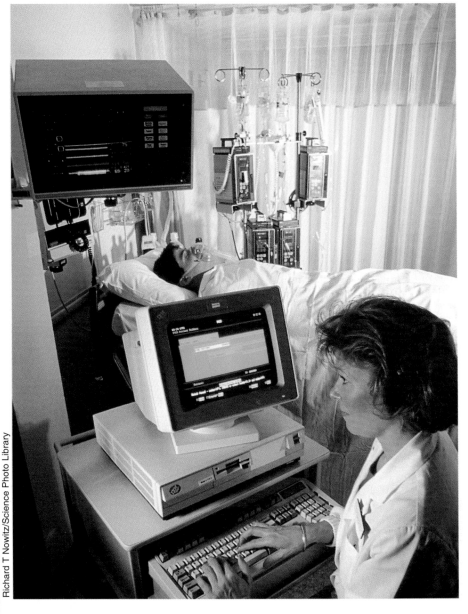

Richard T Nowitz/Science Photo Library

along the empty pill container. In cases of doubt, physicians should take samples of blood and urine for drug analysis (see Specimens). When these procedures have been carried out, the medics will decide whether or not the use of a stomach pump is appropriate.

Use of the stomach pump

A stomach pump should be used fairly soon after the overdose has been taken; that is, before the drug has disappeared from the stomach and been absorbed via the intestines. This usually means that it is most likely to be effective within four hours of taking the drug.

The decision whether or not to use the stomach pump is based on evidence of the type and number of pills that have been taken. Obviously if someone has swallowed only two or three pills as a

Washing out a drug from the stomach may not be the complete solution. Where the poison has had sufficient time to pass into the bloodstream, prolonged treatment in an intensive care unit may still be required.

symbolic gesture there is little point in subjecting him or her to a stomach pump. It may be worth attempting to remove certain drugs, such as acetaminophen, up to 12 hours after they have been taken.

Dangers and precautions

The chief danger of the stomach pump procedure is that fluid may accidentally be aspirated into the lungs and may cause pneumonia (see Pneumonia). It should never be used on any patient who has taken paraffin, or strong acid, or alkali solutions (these can do more damage

The stomach pump procedure

● The patient is positioned with his or her head down and a rubber tube, about ⅜ in (1 cm) in diameter and 18 in (45 cm) long, is passed into the stomach via the mouth.
● A funnel is attached to the end of the tube, its position checked and ½ pt (250 ml) of lukewarm water introduced.
● This is left for two or three minutes, then allowed to flow out by a siphon action.
● The process is repeated until up to 3½ pt (2 liters) of water have been used. The pumping of fluid is done with the aid of gravity.

as they are brought up. It is also dangerous to perform the procedure on an unconscious person without establishing an airway into his or her windpipe. Afterward, some people may suffer from chest complications (see Chest).

It may be possible to induce a conscious patient to vomit by means of a special drug called an emetic, thus avoiding the need for a stomach pump (see Emetics, and Vomiting). Emetics can be very useful in treating children who have taken overdoses, but should never be used in any patient who is drowsy, drugged, or unconscious.

If doctors do decide to use a stomach pump on an unconscious patient, it is essential that the windpipe or trachea is blocked off so that no stomach contents can enter the lungs. This is done by means of an endotracheal tube (a tube placed in the trachea and then sealed off with an airfilled balloon).

Effectiveness

The reliability of the stomach pump technique has been debated by doctors for many years, but essentially it depends on the experience of the people who decide on and perform the procedure.

In addition, it should be pointed out that, since the use of the barbiturate family of sedatives has declined, the number of patients who actually die from overdose has fallen considerably. In one survey of 236 patients admitted to a major hospital, not one died after admission. This group of people had often taken tranquilizers, anti-depressants, acetaminophen, and aspirin, sometimes in combinations of two or more. Less than 3 percent had taken barbiturates. In the majority of cases a stomach pump was used, and it was, as a conclusion, recommended for the treatment of patients who have taken more than 10 tablets, particularly those of the aspirin family.

One of the great advantages of putting a tube into the stomach is that not only can the stomach then be washed out but substances can also be introduced that are able to slow down the absorption of poisonous drugs. For example, a special form of activated charcoal will inhibit the absorption of acetaminophen, and a special chemical binding agent called desferrioxamine is used in the case of iron tablets, which are sometimes taken accidentally by young children.

The decision to use the stomach pump should really be based on the doctor's interpretation as to whether or not the patient has taken potentially lethal quantities of a drug. A frequent problem is that the patient, if conscious, may not give a clear account of the type and quantity of drug he or she has taken. For example, the patient may say that he or she has only taken a mild tranquilizer, in which case it would be safe not to use the stomach pump. The doctor may, however, have reason to doubt the patient's accuracy, and, in such cases, it is clearly in the patient's interest for the procedure to be carried out, unpleasant though it may be. The stomach pump thus plays a necessary part in the medical management of the patient who has taken an overdose, although the most important factor in saving his or her life is immediate intensive life-support treatment.

How the stomach pump is used

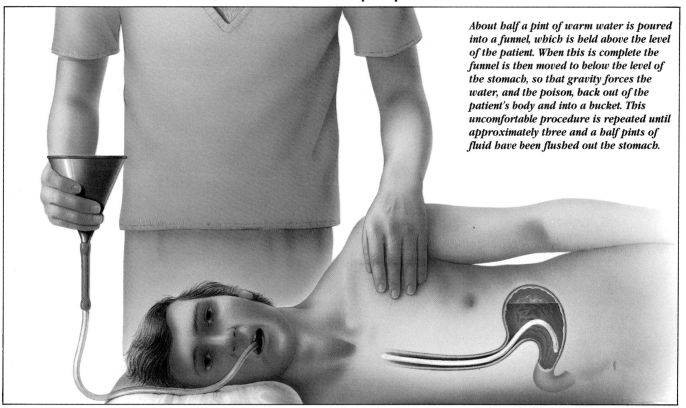

About half a pint of warm water is poured into a funnel, which is held above the level of the patient. When this is complete the funnel is then moved to below the level of the stomach, so that gravity forces the water, and the poison, back out of the patient's body and into a bucket. This uncomfortable procedure is repeated until approximately three and a half pints of fluid have been flushed out the stomach.

Strangulation

Q The doctor has told my father that he has a strangulated hernia and that he must have surgery right away. Is this true?

A Yes. A strangulated hernia is a dangerous condition and must be dealt with immediately. What happens is that a loop of bowel (intestine) passes through a narrow opening in the abdominal wall and its blood supply is cut off. This means that the piece of bowel dies and the bowel contents cannot move through normally. To rectify this, the loop has to be removed, the cut ends joined together and replaced into the abdomen, and the opening stitched up.

Q What happens when a strangulated hernia becomes gangrenous?

A When any part of the body is deprived of blood it soon dies and becomes gangrenous. The only possible treatment is to cut away all of the dead gangrenous tissue and join together the healthy cut ends of the intestine.

Q My baby was born with a bowel obstruction and had to have surgery. How did this happen?

A Doctors call this unusual condition volvulus neonatorum. While the baby is developing in the mother's womb, part of its intestine twists around itself because it is not held together tightly enough, causing an intestinal obstruction. Immediate surgical correction is needed to prevent the affected portion of the intestine from dying and becoming gangrenous.

Q Can a baby be strangled by its own umbilical cord during birth?

A This can happen but obstetricians are normally well aware of the danger. The baby's heartbeat is usually monitored during birth and would show some abnormality if strangulation were to occur. This would normally be dealt with by delivering the baby by emergency cesarean birth.

Internal strangulation occurs when the constriction of a tubular structure of the body, such as the windpipe, intestine, or a blood vessel, prevents normal functioning and circulation. In some of its forms it is potentially fatal.

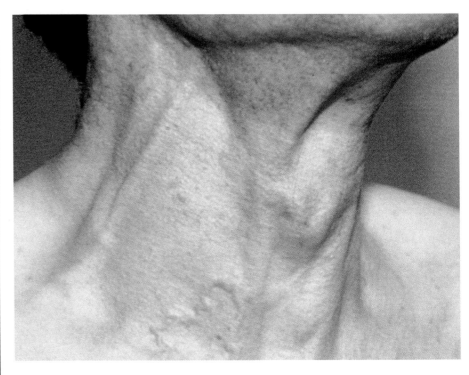

The word *strangulation* immediately conjures up an image of someone struggling desperately for breath while another person grips them tightly about the throat. There is, however, another meaning since strangulation or compression of other parts of the body can also take place. Areas of the intestine or sections of blood vessels in the limbs, for example, can be strangulated so that circulation is interrupted and function impaired. This strangulation can lead to an inadequate amount of blood reaching the area (a condition called ischemia), and possibly death and decay of the affected tissue (see Gangrene). The outcome is extremely serious, and surgery must usually be performed.

Intestinal strangulation

Intestinal strangulation occurs when the blood flow to the intestine is interrupted, leading to swelling (edema), discoloration (cyanosis), and gangrene. This condition is usually caused by a hernia (see Hernia), the prolapse of one segment of intestine into the cavity or lumen of another segment (called intussusception), or a twisting of the intestine onto itself to cause an intestinal obstruction (called volvulus).

External strangulation occurs when violent pressure is exerted on the neck's carotid artery, starving the brain of oxygen. Similarly, internal strangulations occur where the body's organs become deprived of blood, usually as a result of hernias.

Intussusception occurs mainly in babies and small children, and is characterized by abdominal pain, vomiting, and bloody mucus in the stool. A barium enema (see Enema) can be used to confirm the diagnosis and the obstruction is corrected surgically.

If a case of volvulus is left untreated, the section of obstructed intestine involved will die, peritonitis (inflammation of the peritoneum, or covering of the abdominal wall; see Peritoneum) will occur, the intestine will rupture, and the patient may die. Early signs of intestinal strangulation resemble those of intestinal obstruction, namely severe pain, vomiting of fecal matter, dehydration, failure of the contents of the intestine to pass through the bowel, and abdominal distension. Peritonitis, shock, and the presence of a tender mass in the abdomen are also found with intestinal strangulation. The level of intestinal obstruction and its cause can be revealed by X-ray examination. Treatment includes the removal of intestinal contents using a special tube and sometimes surgical repair. In the case of intestinal strangulation, surgery is always required.

Hernias

A hernia, or rupture, occurs when an organ or part of an organ becomes displaced through the lining of the cavity in which it is normally situated (see Hernia). One of the most common types of hernia occurs when a section of intestine protrudes through the front wall of the abdominal cavity, often as a result of muscular strain or injury.

The most feared complication of hernia is strangulation. Like all other organs of the body, the intestine has a blood supply consisting of arteries carrying blood to it and veins carrying blood away. Arteries are high-pressure vessels whereas veins are low-pressure ones. Because of this, the walls of the veins are much thinner and softer than those of the arteries. When a loop of intestine passes through a constricted opening, as in a hernia, the blood continues to pass into the loop via the arteries. However, constriction on the easily compressed veins soon means that the amount of blood in the loop increases. This causes the hernia to swell, which in turn causes further constriction and increased compression of the veins.

Eventually the return of blood via the veins stops altogether. There is massive swelling and soon the arterial blood supply is also cut off. The result is a strangulated hernia, which is a highly dangerous condition. Any part of the body deprived of blood soon dies and becomes gangrenous. In the case of a strangulated hernia, the passage of the normal intestinal contents is also totally obstructed.

Surgical treatment

Surgery is the only treatment possible in the case of a strangulated hernia (see Surgery). The situation cannot be remedied simply by replacing the loop into the abdomen, which could be fatal. The gangrenous piece of intestine must be removed surgically, and the two healthy cut ends joined together. Sometimes the two cut ends cannot be joined up immediately and the upper cut end must be brought out to the exterior through an artificial opening in the abdominal wall. This is called a colostomy (see Colostomy), or a jejunostomy, depending on which part of the intestine is involved.

Hemorrhoids

Strangulation can also affect parts of the body other than the intestines. Veins that become swollen and twisted in the region of the anus and lower rectum are called hemorrhoids (piles), and are often painful and bleeding (see Anus, Hemorrhoids, and Rectum). When hemorrhoids pass outside the anal opening they are called prolapsed. They can become trapped by the anal sphincter, the tight muscular band that closes the anal opening, and their blood supply can be cut off.

Strangulation is sometimes used deliberately to treat anal piles; tight rubber bands are used to encircle the hemorrhoids and cut off their blood supply so that they fall away in time.

Intussusception

Intussusception is a condition in which a segment of the intestine slides inside the adjoining segment in the manner of a naval telescope being closed. This process is called invagination, and it usually occurs at the point in the intestine where the lower part of the small intestine (the ileum) joins the wider large intestine (the colon). Understandably, invagination can occur more easily at this junction than at any other point in the entire intestine. Intussusception is the most common cause of strangulation and blockage of the intestine in the first two years of life. Surprisingly, it is three times as common in male babies as in females.

In most cases the condition occurs without any cause being discovered. Sometimes the process starts as a result of constipation, with hard fecal material in the intestine (see Constipation). Occasionally swelling of the lymphoid patches in the lining of the small intestine result in their being pushed by moving bowel contents into the colon. Small benign fatty tumors of the intestine called lipomas can act in the same way. Intussusception is a fairly common feature of cystic fibrosis (see Cystic fibrosis).

To understand how intussusception causes strangulation of the intestine, it is necessary to appreciate that the coils of the intestine are suspended from the inner back wall of the abdomen by a thin membrane called the mesentery. The mesentery contains the arteries and veins that carry blood to and from the intestine. When the intestine telescopes, part of the mesentery, with its blood vessels, is dragged into the wider part of the large intestine

The first result is that the veins, in which the pressure of blood is lower than in the arteries, become compressed. This means that blood being pumped into the walls of the intestine through the arteries is unable to get out so the affected part of the intestine quickly swells up with the increased volume of fluid. The resulting increase in compression closes off the arteries also.

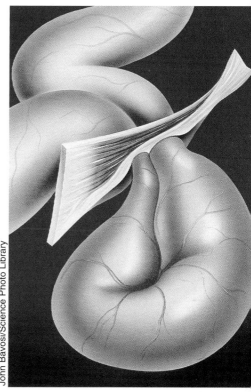

In this illustration of an intestinal hernia, the intestine (orange) has burst through the abdominal wall. The protruding region (pink) has impaired blood supply and requires urgent surgical treatment if gangrene (tissue death) is to be averted.

John Bavosi/Science Photo Library

Any part of the body wholly deprived of its blood supply must necessarily die. This is a critical state of affairs because dead bowel will soon perforate, releasing the highly contaminated contents into the sterile area in the peritoneal sac that surrounds the intestine. The result is infection of the peritoneal membrane, a condition known as peritonitis. Unless urgently treated by surgery, peritonitis is usually fatal.

Intussusception is thus a surgical emergency that will tolerate no delay. Obviously it is extremely important to avoid intestinal perforation and peritonitis if at all possible, so the earlier the diagnosis is made the better. The symptoms are characteristic. The baby suddenly develops attacks of screaming and drawing up of the knees. Soon after this vomiting nearly always begins. Within 12 hours or so the baby passes blood and mucus in its stools. The child's abdomen is distended and is exquisitely tender to touch. Careful feeling will reveal a sausage-shaped mass: the thickened and swollen length of double bowel.

Attempts are usually made to relieve intussusception by nonsurgical means. This is done by giving a barium enema drip, through the rectum, without applying more pressure than is provided by keeping the barium container at a height of approximately 3 ft (1 m). Applied in time, the gentle, internal hydrostatic pressure of the barium solution will reverse the intussusception in 75 percent of cases. Barium is opaque to X ray, so success can be proved by observing on X ray the free flow of barium back into the small intestine (see X rays).

If this method fails, there is no choice but open surgery to pull out the segment of telescoped intestine, and, if necessary, to remove a length of necrotic (dead) bowel and join the free ends together. Unrelieved intussusception is almost always fatal.

Other types of strangulation

An unusual cause of strangulation is the growth of tumors inside the neck (see Neck). Cancers of the thyroid gland (see Thyroid), for example, can grow extremely rapidly and can spread locally to compress adjacent structures. This can lead to strangulation by compression of the great blood vessels of the neck, or even by compression of the windpipe or voice box. Pressure on the two main arteries of the neck, the carotids, deprives the brain of blood and leads to loss of consciousness. Pressure on the great veins prevents the return of blood from the brain and has the same effect. The term *carotid* and the word *garrotte* come from the Greek word meaning "to stupefy," and it is clear that the Greeks were aware that strangulation had its effect at least partly by compression of these arteries.

When neck tumors press on and obstruct the airway, an emergency tracheostomy (an operation that makes a new opening into the windpipe in order to allow breathing) may be necessary (see Tracheostomy). Urgent surgery to remove the tumor will also be necessary.

Strangulation of the heart (see Heart disease) is a very rare condition that can occur when an opening in the fibrous bag that surrounds the heart (the pericardial sac) allows part of the heart to herniate through.

Severe abdominal injuries as a result of automobile accidents, for example, can result in various abdominal organs herniating through the diaphragm and into the chest, where they may strangulate.

Similarly, with severe head injuries (see Head and head injuries) that involve bleeding within the skull, the increased pressure can force the brain to herniate

downward through the large opening at the base of the skull (the foramen magnum), compressing part of the brain called the brain stem, and causing fatal strangulation. This complication is one of the most serious intermediate and late effects of head injury and may occur with or without fracture of the skull.

Typically an injured person is briefly unconscious and then recovers, but later within hours or days develops a severe headache with vomiting, drowsiness, and confusion, and then lapses again into unconsciousness (see Unconsciousness). This dangerous situation, which is inevitably fatal unless treated, is the result of the formation of a blood clot (hematoma) on the outer surface of the

brain that increases in size. Because the skull is unyielding, the brain is gradually forced downward. The vital centers for respiration and heartbeat are in the brain stem, and compression of these, or of their supplying blood vessels, against the edge of the foramen magnum is a common cause of death.

This form of strangulation of nerve tissue and small blood vessels is remediable only by neurosurgery. The procedure involves folding back a flap of scalp, temporarily removing a rectangular area of the vault of the skull to expose the hematoma, sucking it out, securing and closing any bleeding points, and replacing the bone and scalp. Performed in time, such surgery is lifesaving.

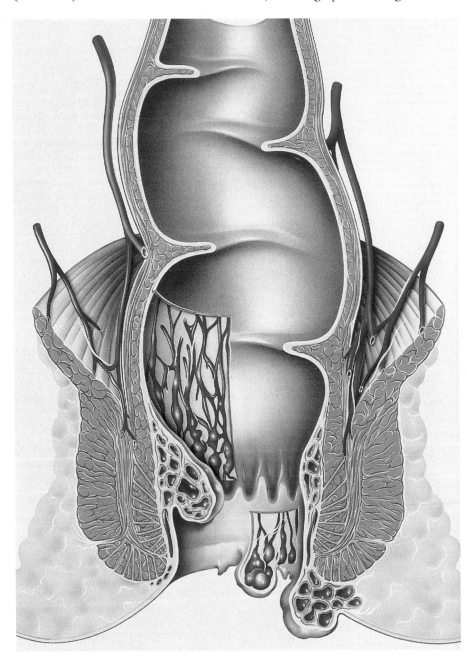

Illustration of a section through a human anus showing internal and external hemorrhoids (lower center, blue)—swollen and strangulated veins.

Stress

Q Does everyone suffer from feelings of stress?

A Yes. Stress is an integral part of life. It is unlikely that we could survive without it. But you have to be clear about what you mean by stress. It is not, for example, necessarily unpleasant. Participating in, or even watching, competitive games, involves considerable stress.

Q So there is good stress and bad stress?

A Yes, in a way, but what you call bad stress might be very important to you. It might, for example, result in a lifesaving level of arousal and physical capability. In acute emergencies, people can perform amazing feats of strength or agility. These would be impossible without stress.

Q Surely stress can't ever be pleasurable, can it?

A Tell that to a young stockbroker, champion skiier or tennis player. Many occupations and activities involve pleasurable stress. Sometimes stress is necessary to achieve a certain minimum standard of performance.

Q But if stress is damaging, how come all these people don't die from heart attacks?

A Stress is not necessarily damaging. Some stress can be damaging to some people, but others can withstand enormous strain without suffering any harm. The idea that a lot of stress will inevitably cause heart attacks, ulcers, skin disease, or even cancer isn't borne out by the facts.

Q You mean that there's no scientific evidence that stress is harmful?

A No, that's not what I'm saying. Severe, acute stress, such as life-threatening situations, can be harmful. Posttraumatic stress disorder is a real medical entity. But the occasional stresses of minor emergencies are things we can't do without. We need them.

The popular view is that many diseases are caused by stress and, while this view is not universally accepted by doctors, the medical profession is now beginning to acknowledge that some stress can result in sickness.

Corbis

The popular medical media have had a wonderful time with stress. For years, writers of books and articles for lay consumption, have been stating or implying that almost any organic disorder can be attributed to stress. Such claims have met with a ready public response. Nearly all of us are familiar with the unpleasant feeling of being stressed, and we would not be human if we did not fear that it was doing us harm.

One of the reasons for the appeal of the early writing on the subject in the 1960s and 1970s was that it seemed to be new. The term *stress* was unfamiliar. In those days, we were accustomed to talking about strain and, suddenly, everyone was talking about stress. These terms come from engineering, and are not widely understood. They are often confused. Stress is the force exerted on a body that tends to cause it to deform. Strain is a measure of the extent to which a body

The hectic yet often monotonous life many of us are forced to lead makes a certain amount of stress unavoidable. What we can do, however, is take positive steps, whenever possible, to insure that the pressures of life are kept to a minimum.

actually is deformed when it is subjected to stress. The terms can, of course, be applied to human bodies in exactly this mechanical way, but when we talk about biologic stress we are usually speaking metaphorically, if not always logically.

The theory of biological stress

The man who brought stress into the limelight was the Austrian-born Canadian physician Hans Selye (1907–1982), whose initial papers on what he called the stress-adaptation syndrome were produced in the early 1950s. Selye was a well-qualified man who studied medicine in Prague, Paris, and Rome before working at McGill

University, Montreal, Canada. In 1945 he became director of the Institute for Experimental Medicine and Surgery at the University of Montreal, which he had founded. From then on Selye produced book after book: *The Story of the Adaptation Syndrome* (1952); *The Stress of Life* (1956); *From Dream to Discovery* (1965); *The Case for Supramolecular Biology* (1967); *Stress without Distress* (1974). These books were directed at the general public, and they made Selye and his ideas famous.

Selye was a physiologist who knew all about the hormonal changes that occur in the body under conditions of anxiety. The production of epinephrine and the steroid hormone cortisol was known to be necessary for survival in fight or flight situations. Without these aids to alertness and sudden physical exertion, few primitive humans would have survived to take part in the evolutionary process. So, by natural selection, they became part of our physical and physiologic makeup. None of this was controversial (see Anxiety, and Hormones).

Selye first thought of the idea of biologic stress when he was a medical student. It occurred to him that all sick patients, however diverse their conditions and symptoms, had this in common: they looked and felt sick. His professor dismissed this idea as childish nonsense. Ten years later, while working at McGill, Selye discovered that rats who were given various damaging injections, or who were kept cold or persistently overworked, developed enlargement of their adrenal glands, the glands that produce epinephrine and cortisol (see Adrenal glands). They also often developed stomach ulcers. These rats were showing a general, and identical, reaction to a variety of stress-producing events (stressors). Was this, he wondered, the thing that all sick people had in common?

His further research and thought led him to propose what he called the general adaptation syndrome. Stressors, whatever their nature—physical threat, actual injury, bacterial infection, social or marital problems, perceived danger of any kind—all caused, Selye claimed, much the same effects. The adaptation syndrome was divided into three parts: the alarm stage (previously described as the fight or flight reaction); the resistance, or adaptation, stage; and the exhaustion stage.

The alarm stage features:
- secretion of epinephrine
- a rise in the pulse rate and in blood pressure
- rapid breathing
- tense muscles
- trembling

- feeling of butterflies in the stomach
- slowed digestive processes
- reduced blood supply to the skin
- release of sugar fuel into the blood
- an increase in the clotting power of the blood

Some of these symptoms will be all too familiar to us all.

Stressors, Selye suggested, may force the alarm stage to persist for long periods, even for months. If the stressor persists, the level of arousal drops a little but remains high, and in the resistance stage the body tries to repair damage caused in the alarm stage. Eventually, if the stressor persists, we enter the stage of exhaustion in which we become highly vulnerable to bodily damage.

Selye was convinced that this mechanism was an important element in the production of such disorders as hardening of the arteries, heart disease, high blood pressure, strokes, stomach and duodenal ulcers, colitis, arthritis, pre-

Different people have different ways of alleviating stress, but unfortunately some methods, such as excessive smoking (above) or alcohol consumption, can be extremely destructive to your health.

menstrual syndrome, and diabetes. Selye called these disorders diseases of adaptation. (see Arteries and artery disease, Blood pressure, Premenstrual syndrome, and Ulcers.)

Stressors

Many of these stressors are obvious, and many people feel that they can rate them by the strength of the physiologic effects they produce, often by the amount of muscle tension felt in the upper part of the abdomen. These stressors include anxiety, frustration, discomfort, conflict, alarm, excessive ambition—all the things we have come to think of as the stresses of modern life. They also include physical insult to the body, whether from infec-

Physical exercise and pampering of the body, such as indulging in beauty treatments (left) or massage, can help to alleviate the stresses of everyday life.

tion, mechanical trauma, burns, radiation, intake of toxic substances, drug side effects, exposure to allergens (substances provoking allergic reactions), overcrowding, atmospheric pollution, and so on. There is a real distinction between acute (short and sharp) stress, such as a severe physical assault or a major psychological trauma, and chronic (long-term and less intense) stress, such as being disabled.

One of the most potently perceived stressors is frustration. Our motivation, or goal seeking, is central to our success and satisfaction, and when this is thwarted we are apt to suffer a strong emotional reaction that is felt as frustration. Motivation encompasses the whole spectrum of our desires, and none of us is free from frustration. Thwarting of major motivation may be an almost lifelong process, but we are also beset with numerous small frustrations related to different minor matters. Many people set their goal higher than is appropriate to their innate abilities. In such cases frustration is likely to be prolonged and may be very severe, causing stress.

In 1967, inspired partly by Selye's work, the psychologists Thomas Holmes and Richard Rahe, working at the University of Washington, came up with a new set of stressors relating to life changes. Selye had already decided that stress was caused by both bad events (distress) and by good events (eustress) and that both kinds could cause disease. He postulated that bad stress was usually the more serious because it was nearly always more severe and more persistent

At times even the most patient of mothers will find it hard to cope with the task of looking after demanding young children.

than eustress. Holmes and Rahe now came up with a table of events graded in terms of their severity in causing harm. They arbitrarily allotted the figure of 100 to what they considered the most stressful life event—the death of a spouse—and smaller numbers for less severe stressors, such as moving house, going on vacation, or financial troubles.

It is easy to criticize this scheme on the grounds that, for different people, different events can have widely varied significance and, consequently, different stress values. Moreover, most of these events can be quantified over quite a wide range. Trouble with the boss, for example, might range from a minor disagreement to a major, livelihood-threatening row. Some of the categories actually involve clusters of other changes. Even so, tables of this kind have won a fair measure of acceptance as a guide to the totality of stress suffered by a person.

Conclusions

What is significant about all this research is that Holmes and Rahe claimed to have found that about 80 percent of people whose total stress events added up to more than 300 points in one year developed serious illness. This compared with about 30 percent of those whose totals were less then 150 in a year.

It has to be said, however, that the ability to withstand stress varies enormously with the person. Some people thrive on it; other people break down under a minor level. The reasons for this variation remain obscure, but may have something to do with personality types.

Scale of life event units	
Death of a spouse	100
Divorce	73
Marital separation	65
Jail term	63
Marriage	50
Being fired	47
Retirement	45
Pregnancy	40
New baby	39
Death of a close friend	37
Large mortgage	31
Son or daughter leaving home	29
In-law trouble	29
Trouble with employer	23
Change of residence	20
Change of school	20
Vacation	13
Minor law violation	11

A type and B type personalities

In 1974, the heart specialists Meyer Friedman and Ray H. Rosenman, while researching the causes of heart disease, suggested that many people create their own stress. These are the A type people: impatient, competitive, driven, and constantly under pressure. A type people do everything in a hurry. They are always early for appointments, go crazy in traffic jams, and demand perfection of themselves in everything they undertake. The two cardiologists concluded that A type behavior was a more accurate predictor of heart attacks than almost any other combination of factors (see Heart attack, and Heart disease).

B type people are laid-back, relaxed, patient, easygoing, and much less prone to heart attacks. This concept aroused much interest and, for a time, it featured

Anthea Sieveking/Vision International

strongly in the medical literature. There were, however, some strong medical criticisms of it, and the initial enthusiasm for the idea was not sustained. Most doctors, however, would admit that there are certainly A type people around, and that they are more susceptible to certain diseases, especially heart attacks.

Public and scientific response

Selye's ideas, and those of his followers, have aroused enormous public interest. The response of the medical profession, however, has been muted. Some doctors have accepted the ideas without question. Many who are cautious about adopting new ideas without strong scientific evidence have been more critical. Some voiced strong skepticism; many ignored it in their books and papers or explicitly stated that it was all nonsense.

Selye's assertions have never gained the unequivocal support of the scientific establishment. Even today, when stress has become a household word, his name is conspicuously absent from biographical dictionaries of scientists. There are some reasons for this that are not necessarily related to the intrinsic merit of his ideas. His habit of passing his ideas direct to the public by way of books that ordinary people could understand, for example, did not always endear him to the medical profession, and this may have been the origin of some of the prejudice against him. Doctors like to announce medical advances by way of the medical press, where they are subjected to the criticism of their colleagues. This is called peer review. They are not happy when this process is bypassed by those who appeal directly to the public. Selye died without ever having gained full medical acceptance of his ideas.

What is stress?

The real basis for medical doubts, however, arose from the nature of the subject. For a start, there is the question of definition. What, in short, is stress? It is, of course, entirely subjective. Stress is what people feel, and one person's stress is another person's challenge. What is painfully stressful to one person may be excitingly gratifying to another. Stressors are not, in themselves, stressful. It is the interaction of the stressor and the individual that creates the stress, and we are all different in our responses. These points have not always been adequately appreciated, and there has been considerable confusion between cause and effect. Selye, himself, admitted that his English was not quite good enough for him to appreciate the difference between stress and strain and that he got his terms the wrong way around.

Critics of Holmes's and Rahe's life event stress factors have pointed out that the results of the research might equally be explained on the hypothesis that people predisposed to physical or psychological disease (see Psychology, and Psychosomatic problems) may be just the kind of people whose lives involve a greater number of stressful changes. Spouses and long-term partners share influences that commonly lead to the development of similar disorders. People with a predisposition to certain types of illness have a higher than average history of being fired from work. And so on.

As to the question of the A type and B type personality, critics remind us that most people do not fall into these clearcut categories. Certainly there are people at both extremes of the spectrum.

There are some people who are obvious A types, and others who are obvious B types, just as there are obvious introverts and extroverts. But the number who are in either of the extreme groups is a small proportion of the whole. This makes the entire concept open to debate. Nearly all the evidence for linking A type personalities with heart disease is in the popular literature.

Current medical views

Although doctors are still arguing about stress, the term, perhaps significantly, is cropping up far more frequently in textbooks and medical papers than ever before. A search on the word *stress* in any medical database will turn up thousands of examples. This is partly because the word has become so fashionable that it is

Relax and get away from it all; perhaps take yourself on a trip to the amusement park—this activity certainly looks hair-raising, but it will take your mind off your problems, and this level of fear is considered to be a healthy, invigorating form of stress!

used in all kinds of contexts and with a range of meanings.

Many diseases are now believed to have at least some basis in stress. Typical is the state of opinion on stress and peptic ulceration of the lining of the stomach and the first part of the small intestine (see Duodenum). Most of the research into this question has been in the form of retrospective studies looking back to see whether people with peptic ulceration were people who had been stressed. This is not considered the ideal method, and too much is left to the opinion of either the patient or the doctor.

Prospective studies to see whether stressed people later develop ulcers are better. One 13-year prospective study of over 4,000 people with no history of ulcers showed that those who were aware of stress in their lives were more likely to develop peptic ulcers than those who were not (see Ulcers). Again, however, the assessment of stress has to be subjective, and this makes convincing research difficult to organize. Only objective evidence is fully acceptable to science. One study, however, found many more personality disturbances in people with peptic ulcers than in those with kidney stones or gallstones. Currently it is agreed that more prospective studies are needed to determine the role of emotional stress in peptic ulceration.

These doubts have not prevented many scientific doctors from trying to produce theories to explain the relationship between stress and the processes that lead to disease. New models of how stress might operate appear regularly in the medical and psychological journals. A review of the medical literature indicates some support for the opinion that stress operates on the immune system. There is an awareness of the link between the immune system and brain processes concerned with thought, environmental perception, behavior, appreciation of stress, and so on (see Immune system). The immune system does not work in isolation in its defense against infection, tumors, and foreign material. A new branch of medical science, called psychoneuroimmunology, is concerned with the study of interactions between the mind and the immune system (see Mind).

Psychoneuroimmunology

Doctors are now gaining a clearer understanding of the ways in which hormones can affect the immune system. They are also discovering that immune system regulation can be mediated by direct nerve connections to the lymphoid tissue of the system (see Lymphatic system). These advances begin to explain much that was previously obscure about the way in

If a mother has to look after the children all day, there are many ways in which the father can help to ease the stress. He could play with the children when he is not working or he could take over the nighttime feeding of a bottle-fed baby.

which the body can respond to stress. This research also promises to advance our understanding of how human behavior can control the function of the immune system and how psychosocial factors and emotional states can affect the development of diseases such as infections and cancers.

The science of psychoneuroimmunology is still in its infancy, but remarkable advances in our knowledge of both neurologic and immunologic control mechanisms are making it increasingly clear that there are previously unsuspected ways in which stress can cause various diseases (see Nervous system, and Neurology and neurosurgery).

Posttraumatic stress disorder

For those who respond badly to stress, there are certain warning signs suggesting danger. These include increasing irritability, loss of appetite, sleeping difficulties, loss of concentration, greater difficulty in making decisions, inability to relax, short fuse, and anger over trivial matters. All these are commonplace.

Less common is the acute stress reaction that relates obviously to a particular event, and which is followed within about an hour by obvious symptoms. These may include anger, aggression, withdrawal, despair, or excessive grief. The outlook in this condition is good, but time is required for recovery. No one would try to deny that there are levels of

stress so severe that many people exposed to them would suffer psychological damage. Again, the outcome in such cases varies with the personality. When people are involved in major disasters, such as train or plane crashes or earthquakes, many come through the experience apparently unharmed; others react very badly.

In World War I, soldiers were exposed to appalling stress from long periods of intense artillery or mortar bombardment and small arms fire. These unfortunates were frequently required to get up out of their trenches and run across open terrain in the face of machine gun fire and almost certain death. Those who broke down were said to suffer from lack of moral fiber. Those who ran away were tried for cowardice and shot. Thousands who survived these ordeals subsequently suffered from what was then called shellshock, and what we now call posttraumatic stress disorder.

This disorder features a repetitive reliving of the stressful event or events, with intrusive flashback memories and nightmares. Any event or circumstance that the sufferer associates with the event causes serious distress. The features of stress mentioned above are often present, and there is sometimes loss of memory (amnesia) for the stressor event. If not treated, the disorder may become permanent (see Posttraumatic stress disorder).

Stress management

Q My friends see my job as stressful because it is mentally demanding and I often stay late. But I get a lot of satisfaction from doing it well. Is stress always such a bad thing?

A Individuals vary in their ability to cope with stress and you evidently thrive on some pressure, seeing it as an opportunity to achieve. However, make sure that the demands of your job don't throw your life off balance: make sure you're eating well, relaxing, and having a social life. Make time for leisure pursuits and exercise to throw off the tensions of the day.

Q Over the last few years I've experienced various problems, ending in the breakup of a long-term relationship. My mother thinks I'll feel better if I tell her about it, but I find it very hard to talk about that sort of thing. Surely there's no harm in keeping my feelings to myself?

A Showing a brave face isn't a good way of dealing with stress. Most people find it helps to air their emotions so that they can grieve for a loss such as yours, or put their fears into perspective. That doesn't mean you have to discuss this with your mother if you don't want to. Consider talking to a friend or someone more detached, such as a counselor. Or, you could write your thoughts and feelings in a private journal or in a letter that you may or may not send.

Q I always seem to have more than my fair share of work; then, when I get home, my husband expects me to do all the chores. I'm stressed and tired. Are there any quick relaxation techniques that will help?

A You could take 10 or 20 minutes a day to focus on slowing your breathing and relaxing all your muscles. But you could also ease your stress by changing your lifestyle. Discuss your workload with your supervisor and with your husband! Assertiveness training might help you gain the confidence to refuse to take on more work than you can cope with.

Everyone is subject to stress at some time, but it can take a serious toll on general health if it is ignored or tackled in the wrong way. Recognizing the need to deal with stress is the first step to successful stress management.

Rex Features

The hectic yet often monotonous life many of us are forced to lead makes a certain amount of stress unavoidable. What we can do, however, is take positive steps to ease the tension, by getting pleasurable exercise such as swimming or other sports.

When someone is subject to pressures or tensions, his or her body reacts by triggering the production of various chemicals or hormones, such as epinephrine, that prepare for flight from danger or fighting back against attack. The heart rate speeds up, boosting the blood supply to the muscles; glucose and fats flood into the bloodstream to supply extra energy; blood pressure rises and blood flow is diverted away from the intestinal tract to more immediately useful areas. In complex modern societies, there is no place for this kind of reaction since it is often counterproductive. If the body regularly experiences this physiologic reaction to stress without any outlet, the result is likely to be some kind of stress-related illness, from tension headache or backache to serious or even fatal illness. Prolonged stress is known to play a role in heart disease and high blood pressure, which can lead to stroke. Psychological problems resulting from stress include irritation, anxiety, and exhaustion, while chronic stress can contribute to mental breakdown. Stress may also be a significant factor in encouraging smoking, heavy drinking, and drug abuse, all of which produce ill effects. Successful stress management aims to avoid these consequences by teaching people the best strategies for responding to pressures.

Recognizing and facing up to stress

Various lists have been compiled that rate different situations according to the degree of stress involved: life-changing events such as bereavement, job loss, and relationship breakup alongside less unpleasant sources of stress such as getting married or moving house. The type of event experienced, however, is less important than the individual's perception of it—for example, a change of job may be very disrupting for one person but is a pleasant change for another. Personality makes a difference, as well: some people naturally take setbacks in their stride or see a problem as a challenge, while others tend to become very anxious or depressed (see Depression).

The important thing is to remember that stress is not a force outside our control, although this may be the feeling of those suffering from it. Keeping a stress diary for a few weeks is one way to assess the amount of stress in your life and its source. This involves setting aside a few minutes at the end of each day to describe

Stress: how well do you cope?

Natural reactions to any stressful situation may be positive or potentially damaging. Adaptive or positive tactics are those that help you face the problem causing the stress, and so find a solution. These tactics include:

- Expressing emotions, whether sadness or anger
- Talking over the problem with friends
- Thinking through the problem to try to understand it
- Seeking support from others
- Setting priorities for tackling problems
- Acting to solve a problem

Negative tactics involve avoiding the issue and may enable someone to cope in the short term, but over time will aggravate the stress. These tactics include:

- Bottling up emotions
- Avoiding other people
- Worrying
- Losing sleep
- Eating more or not eating
- Fantasizing about outcomes without taking any action
- Keeping busy or finding distractions
- Drinking or smoking more, or resorting to drugs

gaining a better job or learning to say no to a friend's demands, will help you work out which tasks are important and which are unnecessary. Write down a list of things to do, ranked according to priority, then concentrate on the highest priority tasks. This time-management strategy will let you spend more time on enjoyable or important activities, and feel a sense of achievement and control.

Some form of assertiveness training may help counter stress caused by overwork, or caused by conflicting demands at work and home. Nonassertive people find it hard to refuse others' demands and to express their own needs, laying them open to stress at work or in personal relationships. It is possible to learn assertive behavior skills, and this is very different from behaving aggressively, from self-help books or organized programs.

Another approach to dealing with stress is to try to change the way stressful experiences are perceived, a process sometimes called cognitive reappraisal. Some people respond to distressing events with thoughts like: "I'll never be able to manage this," "What if I fail?," or "I really hate this person." The object is to rewrite this mental script, turning it into lines such as: "This is a challenge" or "It'll take a bit of effort to get along with her." If you learn to recognize such negative thoughts and worries, tactics can be developed to resist them, such as steering your thoughts to a more enjoyable area.

Relaxation and support

Relaxation techniques offer a way to counter the effects of stress. Various methods have been developed, involving exercises such as tensing then relaxing muscles in different parts of the body, visualizing a peaceful place, and concentrating on breathing slowly and deeply. Learning to pause and relax for a few seconds before tackling a stressful situation is a useful technique.

More formal methods of relaxation include autogenic training, or self-hypnosis, and meditation, both of which need training by an instructor or therapist. One type of meditation, TM (transcendental meditation), has been widely studied in the context of stress management and has been shown to reduce anxiety and improve performance, as well as having long-term benefits in the treatment of high blood pressure and other stress-related diseases (see Meditation).

Leisure activities that offer a respite from the day's strains are helpful, and physical exercise is a good counter to stress. Research shows that aerobic exercise such as swimming, running, cycling, or dancing can improve people's psychological ability to deal with stress, reduce depression, and aid sleeping, while competitive sports provide a harmless way to take out frustration. Poor nutrition, with a high intake of sugary, fatty, and processed foods, can reduce resistance to stress, while using caffeine and high-sugar snacks will sap energy levels. Eating a balanced diet will provide more energy to cope with stress (see Nutrition).

A way of countering stress for many people is sharing their feelings with friends, coworkers, or family; bottling up emotions is rarely helpful. However, being able to turn to others for social activities is valuable. Those without social support networks are more prone to stress-related disease and depression.

Meditation, particularly outdoors, is one way of helping to alleviate the stresses and tensions of everyday life.

when you were tense or upset, or events that made you feel anxious, noting your reaction and any other way you feel you should have dealt with the event. A pattern may well emerge, showing that most stress comes from work overload or from difficulties with personal relationships. This can be used to help develop an action plan that will help you regain control and draw on strategies to tackle stress produced by different problems.

Taking control

If stress seems overwhelming, it is helpful to take a little time to think about your life and what you want from personal relationships, work, and self-fulfillment. How much time and energy do you allocate to each area of your life? Is this unbalanced? For example, are you putting too much into work at the expense of a personal life? Setting goals, such as

Corbis

Stretch marks

Q I developed a lot of stretch marks when I was a teenager. My daughter is now 12 and beginning to put on weight. Are stretch marks hereditary or can anything be done to stop her from getting them?

A Just because you got stretch marks during puberty does not mean that your daughter necessarily will. The best thing you can do is to make sure that she eats sensibly. It may be that stretch marks are unavoidable if she develops fast, but excess weight is often the main cause of stretch marks during adolescence.

Q I am three months pregnant, and so far I don't have any stretch marks. A friend told me she used a special liniment when she was pregnant, and she got very few stretch marks. Is this worth trying?

A It is very unlikely indeed that any cream or liniment can actually prevent stretch marks, although there are a number of myths about such substances. Oil or cream rubbed into the skin of your breasts and abdomen can help with any dry or flaky skin, but it won't stop the stretch marks.

Q I am expecting a baby, and my doctor told me I should watch my weight. What should the normal weight gain be?

A It is normally suggested that the average weight gain during pregnancy should be about 22 lb (10 kg). Anything much over this will increase the risk of stretch marks. Ignore people who tell you to eat as much as you can and ask your doctor or the prenatal clinic about the correct diet.

Q My husband has recently put on weight and seems to have stretch marks around his hips. Is this normal?

A Men can get stretch marks if they put on weight rapidly, just as women can. This is not dangerous, but your husband should lose the excess weight since it is bad for his health.

Anyone can develop stretch marks, and many women frequently do because of a sudden increase in weight, as happens in pregnancy. But do preventive measures work?

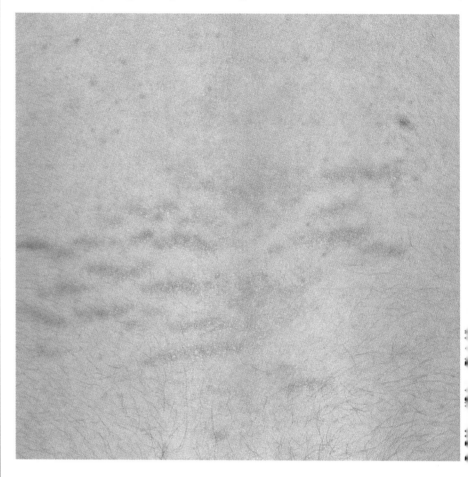

Stretch marks on the back of a teenage boy who had been overweight. Stretch marks (shiny streaks that appear on the skin) most commonly appear in adolescent girls and in women during pregnancy, but can occur as the result of any sudden weight gain.

Human skin is naturally elastic, and can normally stretch considerably to accommodate a sudden change in weight or in the shape of the mass that it covers. The tissue beneath the skin surface develops as we grow so that the skin area above it gradually increases. But if very rapid physical expansion takes place, the elastic tissue may be put under intolerable strain so that it tears and stretches the skin above it. This will show as a stretch mark—a red line on the skin surface.

The redness of the mark fades in a matter of months, but the skin surface can never go back to its previous condition. A papery kind of scar tissue will remain, and the stretch marks will look like pale or silvery threadlike lines (see Scars).

When stretch marks occur

Stretch marks can occur during puberty (see Adolescence, Puberty). As the hormonal balance changes, teenage girls may quickly put on weight in specific areas.

The sites most likely to be affected are the breasts, hips, thighs, and buttocks. Stretch marks are more likely to occur in girls who are already somewhat overweight, although they can affect girls who have developed large breasts at a particularly fast rate during puberty.

Stretch marks that appear during pregnancy can also be caused by hormonal changes that result in weight gain (see Pregnancy). Women with small breasts may be especially prone to stretch marks when they are pregnant, since the breasts will need to enlarge considerably in readiness for lactation (milk production). If the breasts are small, the skin may not be sufficiently elastic to be able to cope with this change. Stretching of the abdominal wall is, of course, bound to happen in pregnancy, and there may also be a significant increase in fat deposits around the hips and thighs.

These marks will stay a reddish color throughout the pregnancy, but will usually gradually lose their color in the months after the baby has been born. Some marks may hardly show after a few months, but others will be visible indefinitely. Affected

skin can also be shinier and thinner than the surrounding skin and may become less elastic. In some cases, stretch marks may be so severe that they resemble surgical scars, such as the abdominal scar left by an appendectomy.

Pregnant women often find that stretch marks appear on their breasts and abdomen. Generally they will find that the marks fade quite rapidly after the birth.

Prolonged treatment with steroid drugs can also cause stretch marks, since this can cause weight gain (see Steroids).

Can stretch marks be prevented?
The changes in shape that accompany both puberty and pregnancy are clearly unavoidable, but some women put on far more weight than others at these times. Adolescent girls who are putting on excess weight may have to change their eating patterns if stretch marks are to be avoided. Exercise is also very important since it helps to burn up the extra calories needed for the increase in muscular activity (see Exercise).

Women who are careful about what they eat and how much weight they put on during pregnancy are less likely to develop stretch marks than those who tend to eat to excess. Even though stretch marks on the breasts and abdomen may be inevitable, those on other areas of the body (the legs, arms, hips, and thighs) are almost always the result of being overweight. There is no evidence that one type of skin is more prone to stretch marks than another.

If you find you are developing stretch marks during pregnancy you should immediately review your diet. Hormonal changes mean that calories are burned less efficiently than before the pregnancy, so to compensate for this you may have to eat less fat and carbohydrates (see Diet). Your doctor or prenatal clinic will be able to advise you on what your weight should be during pregnancy, and help you plan your diet accordingly. Some marks are unavoidable, but early preventive action will minimize the possibility of getting more marks later in the pregnancy.

Some people maintain that oils or creams rubbed into the skin of the breasts and abdomen will prevent stretch marks, but most doctors will point out that no amount of lubrication of the skin surface affects the changes beneath it. However, many women find that the skin becomes dry and flaky during pregnancy and that an oil or cream helps considerably with this. There is certainly no harm in using these products, and if a pregnant woman takes care of herself in this way she will also quickly become aware of unnecessary weight gain and so be more careful about her diet.

Stretch marks are likely to be worse in women who are carrying twins because the abdomen will be stretched far more than in a single pregnancy.

Extreme fluid retention or an excess of amniotic fluid can also result in particularly severe stretch marks. In these cases plastic surgery may be advised after pregnancy, but this is unusual for the majority of women (see Plastic surgery).

Image Bank

1875

Stroke

Q My mother had a serious stroke when she was 53. Does this put me at risk of having one too?

A Not necessarily. Your chances of having a stroke depend to some extent on what caused your mother's disease. If high blood pressure was behind it, then it may be advisable to have your blood pressure checked so that, if high blood pressure is found, suitable treatment can be given. If there is a long history of strokes in your family, then it is important that you do not add to the risk by smoking.

Q Does taking the Pill increase the risk of having a stroke?

A In a tiny number of women, strokes have occurred while they were on the Pill. For this reason doctors try to discourage women who are over 40 from taking the Pill. There is far less risk in women who are under 40. However, doctors will try to dissuade women under 40 from continuing with the Pill if they have a history of migraine, as it does slightly increase the chances of having a stroke at a younger age.

Q Is there any surgery available to treat people who have had a stroke?

A In the past, surgery has been used in an attempt to unblock the artery whose obstruction has caused a stroke. These were not successful and often made things worse. Occasionally one of the larger arteries in the neck may be narrowed or roughened inside, and surgery to correct this may prevent further damaging strokes. For most people who have had a stroke, however, surgery has little to offer.

Q My father recently had a stroke, and he seems to have lost his ability to speak. Will it return?

A It is very likely that his speech will come back, at least to some extent. Sometimes people are not able to speak at all in the first few days after a stroke, but later recover almost completely.

With little or no warning a stroke can cause sudden weakness, paralysis, or even death. Nevertheless, however fearsome this common affliction may be, rehabilitation can help survivors overcome any resulting disability.

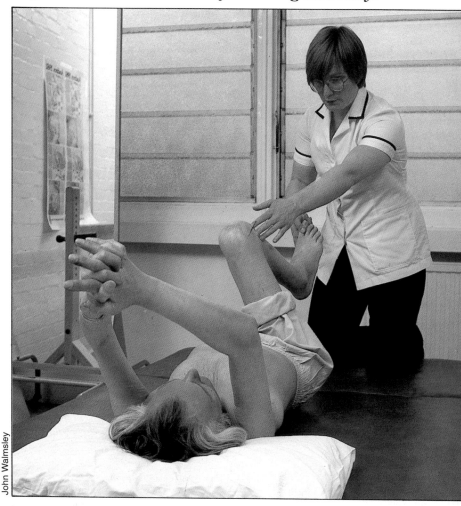

John Walmsley

A stroke need not signal the end to a person's active life. With physical therapy, it is often possible to restore the function of affected limbs to varying degrees.

Strokes often (though not exclusively) attack older people and are one of the most common causes of death throughout the Western world. However, present advances in medical research, particularly in connection with the role of high blood pressure, have helped our understanding of this illness. Many strokes are now preventable through early identification and treatment of those at risk.

What is a stroke?

Most people have some idea of what a stroke is, which is a testament to how often the disease occurs. The common factor in all strokes is that, due to a disease of the blood vessel that supplies a particular part of the brain, a section of the brain suddenly stops working. This means that the person involved often has little or no warning that something is wrong before he or she is struck down with weakness or paralysis down one side of the body. This condition may be accompanied by aphasia (loss of speech; see Aphasia) or by other problems in higher brain functions. A small number of strokes occur in parts of the brain that do not control the body's movement, so that paralysis does not occur.

What causes a stroke?

Like the rest of the body, the brain must have a constant supply of blood reaching it through its arteries (see Brain, and Brain damage and disease). If one of these arteries becomes blocked, the part of the brain that it feeds will die because of the lack of oxygen. Fortunately in the brain there are many cross-connections between neighboring blood vessels so that the area of damage is generally restricted. However, even that part of the brain that does not die may swell and damage the rest of the brain. The other way in which strokes may be caused is when blood vessels in the brain burst. When this happens the blood rushes into the brain under pressure, severely damaging nerve fibers.

These two basic mechanisms, cerebral infarction (when the artery is blocked) and cerebral hemorrhage (when there is bleeding into the brain), can be brought about by a number of different disorders.

Diseases that cause strokes

Obstruction of an artery in the brain can result from a disease that produces a blockage in the artery itself (a cerebral thrombosis; see Thrombosis), or when a blood clot passes up the blood supply to the brain artery and gets stuck there. This is called a cerebral embolism.

Thrombosis (or blood clotting) generally occurs when an artery of the brain becomes narrowed: fatty material accumulates in the walls of the artery. This is typical of a disease called atherosclerosis, which also causes the heart's blood vessels to clot, resulting in heart attacks (see Heart attack). Occasionally other problems in the arteries can cause thrombosis. These include inflammation of the artery, which can occur on its own or as a result of some serious infections.

Embolisms can be caused by heart diseases or by disorders in the main arteries in the neck from which the blood enters the brain. Heart disease and strokes are thus linked, not only because the same disease of the arteries can cause trouble in both the heart and the brain, but also because in many diseases of the heart, blood clots form on the valves or on the damaged inside walls of the heart and these then fly off as emboli.

Cerebral hemorrhages (when the blood vessels in the brain burst) also have a number of causes. The most common is when there are weak places (called aneurysms) in the walls of the brain's arteries which then burst, often under the influence of a higher than normal blood pressure. In the larger brain arteries at the base of the skull these aneurysms may be congenital, though they may not rupture until late in life, if at all.

Less common causes of cerebral hemorrhage can occur as a result of the presence of small, abnormally formed blood vessels in the brain, rather like the strawberry marks that are a similar abnormality of the blood vessels in the skin. This is called arteriovenous anomaly, and again this condition is congenital.

Who is at risk?

Certain people have a higher risk of having strokes than others. The main conditions that predispose a stroke are diabetes, high blood pressure, having a high

Strokes can be caused by hemorrhages or blockages (infarctions) in the brain. Many hemorrhages are caused by the rupturing of weakened arteries (aneurysms). Infarctions are caused either when a blood clot forms in a diseased cerebral artery (thrombus), or when a clot travels from another area of the body, such as the damaged walls of the heart, and lodges in the brain (embolus).

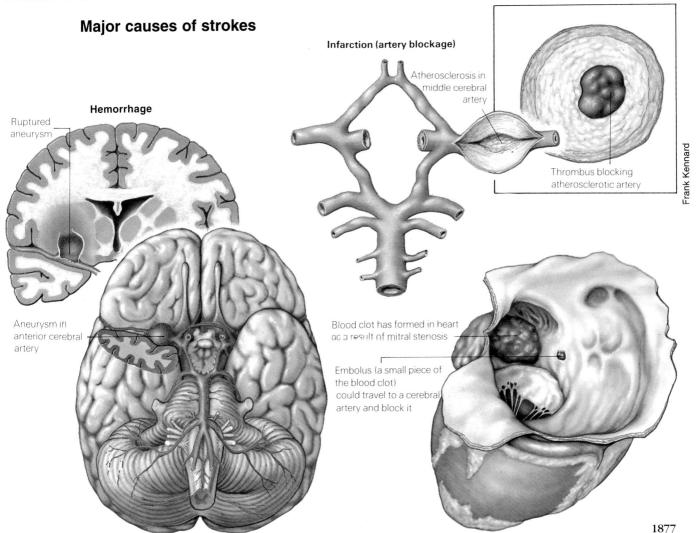

Major causes of strokes

Hemorrhage

Ruptured aneurysm

Aneurysm in anterior cerebral artery

Infarction (artery blockage)

Atherosclerosis in middle cerebral artery

Thrombus blocking atherosclerotic artery

Blood clot has formed in heart as a result of mitral stenosis

Embolus (a small piece of the blood clot) could travel to a cerebral artery and block it

Frank Kennard

Q Does everyone who has had a stroke have to be hospitalized?

A This would depend on the severity of the stroke, and whether or not the facilities available in the stroke patient's home enable him or her to be properly looked after. In some areas, special teams of physical therapists are available to treat people in their own homes. However, people with strokes often need to remain in the hospital while they are very disabled so that their stroke can be properly assessed, both in terms of treatment and of prevention of further strokes.

Q Is there any point in having someone's blood pressure treated after they have suffered a stroke, or is this like shutting the stable door after the horse has bolted?

A Immediately after a stroke, the blood pressure is usually left alone for a few days, since a sudden drop may impair the flow of blood to the damaged areas in the brain. However, careful studies have shown that it is important to treat the blood pressure vigorously to prevent further strokes, which might cause further disability.

Q My uncle had a bad heart attack and a few weeks later had a stroke that paralyzed his left side. Was this connected with his heart attack, and why did this happen?

A After a heart attack, blood clots form on the inside wall of the chamber of the heart. Occasionally part of this clot can become dislodged and fly upward to block off one of the brain's blood vessels, thus producing a stroke. This can be prevented to some degree by giving those patients who have had very serious heart attacks anticoagulant drugs.

Q Is it possible to prevent people having strokes?

A Yes. If patients with high blood pressure are identified and treated early, this can greatly reduce the risk of a stroke.

Mick Saunders

serum cholesterol, and smoking cigarettes. In addition, strokes seem to run in some families, though because the conditions is so common, this is difficult to prove. Finally, there are people with heart diseases that can cause a stroke by embolism. Thus people with a high risk can often be identified, and preventive measures taken to reduce the chances of a stroke occurring.

Symptoms

Some stroke patients have a warning attack in the weeks or months before a major stroke. These warning attacks can take the form of short-lived episodes of weakness down one side, or transient blacking out of vision in one eye—a sign of blockage in one of the blood vessels to the retina. Most stroke patients, however, do not get any warning. What really typifies a stroke is the suddenness with which it happens. In most cases, disabili-

A stroke can be caused by a blockage in any of the four pairs of cerebral arteries. Each type has different results, depending on the area of the brain that is affected. A blockage in an anterior artery is common, and one in the basilar is usually fatal.

Damage caused by a stroke

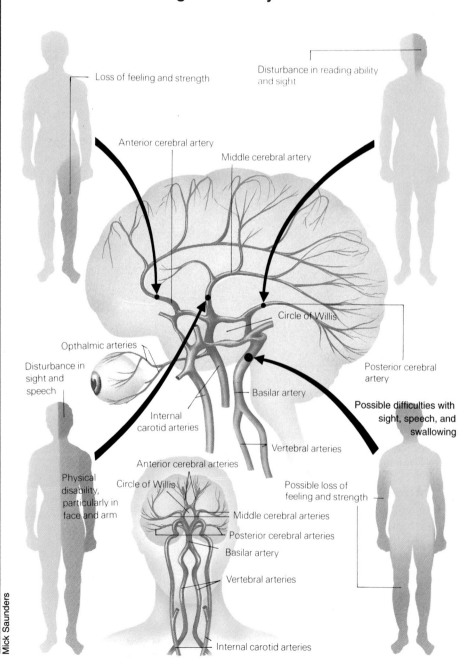

Loss of feeling and strength

Disturbance in reading ability and sight

Anterior cerebral artery

Middle cerebral artery

Circle of Willis

Opthalmic arteries

Disturbance in sight and speech

Posterior cerebral artery

Basilar artery

Possible difficulties with sight, speech, and swallowing

Internal carotid arteries

Vertebral arteries

Physical disability, particularly in face and arm

Anterior cerebral arteries

Circle of Willis

Possible loss of feeling and strength

Middle cerebral arteries

Posterior cerebral arteries

Basilar artery

Vertebral arteries

Internal carotid arteries

ties such as loss of function on one side of the body, or loss of speech, reach their maximum within minutes, though occasionally it may take hours. In the following days and weeks, there will be an improvement as some of the brain cells recover. After six months the disabilities will be considerably less than they were at the onset of the stroke.

Other symptoms may include loss of vision in the right or left-hand half of each eye (visual field defect), difficulty in dressing or finding the way around familiar surroundings, and a host of other subtle difficulties in brain function. If a large area of the brain was damaged at the start of the stroke, the patient may not have a clear awareness of what has happened, or may ignore everything that happens on one side of his or her body. As the damaged brain swells, he or she may become drowsy or lose consciousness. This may happen much more quickly in brain hemorrhages, since the surge of blood into the brain causes damage to the mechanisms that maintain alertness.

Treatment

Initial treatment consists of limiting the amount of damage that may be caused by swelling spreading to the unaffected parts of the brain. This is done by paying close attention to the blood pressure and administering certain drugs, particularly steroids (see Steroids). Very seldom can surgeons remove the blood clots that are causing pressure since they are often situated in inaccessible parts of the brain.

However, the main care of patients who have had strokes lies in the hands of

One of the most important stages in the recovery of a stroke patient takes place at home, where the support of family and friends becomes vital. However, it is very important for patients not to be pampered: stroke victims need to adapt and learn to do things for themselves again. The architect below, who had a stroke, is relearning to use the tools of his trade, this time with his nonaffected hand.

nursing staff, physical therapists, speech therapists, and occupational therapists. Careful nursing is very important to prevent the emergence of bedsores (see Bedsores) and chest troubles, which can seriously impair a patient's recovery from a stroke. During this vulnerable period when the stroke patient is often unable to undertake his or her own care, good nursing can literally save a life.

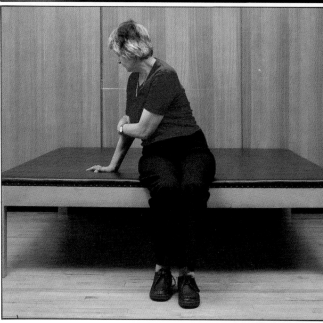

Stroke patients can exercise in their own homes. Exercises include using the strong arm to support the weak arm (above left) or paralyzed side (above) by pulling it up. Additional strengthening can be achieved by doing swiveling (far left) or pressing exercises (left), which require propping up the weak arm. Better balance can be gained by raising the body to a half-sitting position (below).

Physical therapists maximize the effect of movement as it returns to affected limbs. Later they become even more vital because the therapy they suggest may make the difference between a patient becoming seriously disabled or able to fend for himself or herself despite residual disabilities (see Physical therapy).

Treatment takes two forms. In the early stages, physical therapists insure that the unused limbs remain supple and that unnecessary stiffness does not set in. Later, when the patient is ambulant (and this happens early since prolonged periods in bed can be dangerous), the physical therapist concentrates on overcoming the abnormal reflex movements that interfere with the return of more useful muscle power (see Reflexes).

Speech therapy (see Speech therapy) plays an important role when the stroke has affected the power of speech. Speech therapists will be able to identify the dif-

ficulties the patient has and will work to encourage the return of speech, which often does happen to a greater or lesser extent. Further treatment by speech therapists consists of retraining patients with aphasia to make the best of the speech faculties that are left (see Speech).

Occupational therapists try to prepare the patient for a return to as normal a life as possible. The therapist assesses the patient, and works out ways of overcoming problems that resist physical therapy (see Occupational therapy).

The stroke patient at home
Many stroke patients are hospitalized while they are physically dependent (often in special stroke units), and then further recovery can be looked for when they go home. This means that the patient's family will need a lot of support and guidance to make sure that they are not so overprotective that they slow his or her recovery. Thus, the work of the physical and occupational therapists often extends to the home, where they can continue to supervise the patient's

recovery. Special aids are available for facilitating such everyday tasks as taking a shower, cooking, or eating, which often present difficulties.

Preventing a stroke
The recent advances in stroke research have been concerned with prevention. The fact that in recent years in the United States the number of strokes has declined is indicative of the effectiveness of the research. This is due to the successful identification and treatment of high blood pressure (see Blood pressure).

In fact it has been shown that careful treatment of high blood pressure can significantly reduce the risk of developing a stroke. Often the difficulty is that most people with high blood pressure feel perfectly well and may need some convincing to take their tablets religiously to keep it down. Generally your doctor will take your blood pressure as a matter of routine when you consult him or her, and he or she will be able to detect high blood pressure before it leads to trouble.

After minor strokes from which the patient may have recovered completely, it is an important part of treatment to try to prevent another more serious episode occurring in the future. Surgery can sometimes be performed on the large blood vessels in the neck. This may be done if the blood vessels have roughened parts in their lining from which clots fly off as emboli.

Small doses of aspirin are also being tried for stroke prevention. It has been found that small amounts of the drug can affect the clotting ability of the blood to a degree sufficient to prevent the brain's blood vessels from becoming obstructed (see Preventive medicine).

Anticoagulant drugs reduce the blood's liability to clot, and these are used to prevent a stroke when one of the predisposing heart conditions is identified. Many other drugs that can prevent a stroke in those at risk are now undergoing trials.

Outlook
Although a stroke can be fatal, the majority of victims recover to some degree. At least half of those who have had a stroke progress to a point where they can look after themselves, and most people paralyzed by strokes learn to walk again. Only about 5 percent of patients require long-term institutional care.

While the remainder of stroke sufferers may have to depend on relatives to look after them at home, they or their caregivers should make full use of the variety of home aids and of the hospital and therapeutic treatments available to them to help the patient overcome or live with their disabilities.

Speech therapy is essential for many stroke patients. Where speech has been lost, the patient practices lip movements in front of a mirror (left) or points to cards to test recognition of everyday objects (above). Where a patient's selected language response has become confused, he or she will try to fill in the missing letters in words that refer to the pictures on a set of cards.

Sty

Q Is it true that sties are caused by dandruff?

A Sties do seem to occur more commonly in people suffering from seborrheic dermatitis. This condition affects the scalp and produces dandruff, and causes a scaly inflammation of the eyebrows and eyelids. When the dandruff is treated the sties often clear up too.

Q I have heard that sties are very infectious. Is this true?

A The bacteria causing sties are infectious and certain virulent types seem to be responsible for recurrent infections. Anyone with a sty should therefore avoid rubbing the eyes since this can spread the infection into other sebaceous glands. A separate towel and washcloth should be used to stop the infection spreading to other members of the household. An antibiotic ointment may prevent the discharging pus from infecting other glands, although they cannot do much to a sty once it has formed.

Q Is it safe to pull out the eyelash over a sty?

A Yes, it will help the pus to drain out. Soften the eyelid with a hot compress first—this will also help to ease the pain. The eyelash can then be pulled out easily with a pair of tweezers and the sty should discharge spontaneously. If the relevant eyelash is not obvious, the eyelids should be left alone. Either the sty is not yet ripe or it may be an internal sty, in which case there is no related eyelash to be removed.

Q I have a small, painless nodule under my eyelid. Is this a sty?

A What you describe could be a meibomian cyst, which is the end result of an internal sty. The infection has been conquered by white cells but a pocket of sterile pus is left behind and is felt as a persistent hard lump that resembles a small hailstone. There is no need to do anything about it, but it can be removed surgically for cosmetic reasons.

Children and adolescents often suffer from sties—painful and unsightly swellings of the eyelid. While minor surgery may be required in some cases, antibiotic ointment and first aid are usually all that is needed.

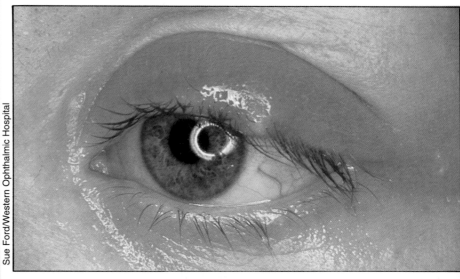

Sue Ford/Western Ophthalmic Hospital

Infection of one of the sebaceous glands in the eyelid can produce an external sty—an obvious red, angry pustule (above) that causes pain, and a feeling of grittiness.

There are two types of sty, depending on which of the eyelid glands is affected. On the outside are sebaceous glands associated with the eyelashes, which secrete greasy sebum to protect the surface of the eye (see Sebaceous glands). However, this sebum may block the gland and trap bacteria, and an external sty will then result. On the inside the eye has a further special line of glands called the meibomian glands. These are also sebaceous glands, but have no associated hair follicles. They open through the conjunctiva to the back of the eyelid and the secretion they produce may also block the gland: trapped infection then leads to an internal sty.

Causes

Sties are associated with a general tendency to dry skin and eczema, as in seborrheic dermatitis (see Dermatitis, and Eczema). Dandruff and flaking skin around the eyelashes and eyebrows are all related to this condition, and sties may be a complication of it. However, many children get sties with no underlying skin disease, and in these cases the cause is unknown. If sties recur, an underlying condition must be suspected. As in all infections, ill health and lack of physical fitness will make sties more common.

Symptoms

The eye may be troublesome for a day or so before the sty appears. During this time itchiness and a sensation of something in the eye may be felt. The actual sty comes up over the course of one to two days, starting as a local painful spot and then swelling to an obvious red, angry pustule. An external sty is easily recognized on the eyelid, but to see an internal sty the eyelid must be turned out to expose the back. Internal sties are usually more painful than external ones, since the distending meibomian gland will stretch the whole eyelid.

As the sty forms, the pain in the lid and the feeling of grittiness get worse. Bright light aggravates the pain (photophobia) and the eye seems to be continually weeping. A fretful child with photophobia, a runny nose from crying, and eye problems may be diagnosed as having a more serious illness such as measles; but detection of a sty and the absence of symptoms in the other eye should clarify the problem.

Treatment

If recognized early enough, antibiotic eye ointment or drops can prevent a sty forming. However, it is much more common to find that by the time the diagnosis has been made, the pustule is already formed, and antibiotics are then ineffective. The only treatment at this stage is to encourage the pus to discharge.

If sties keep recurring, a course of antibiotic eyedrops may help to prevent any discharging pus from infecting other sebaceous glands in the eyelid.

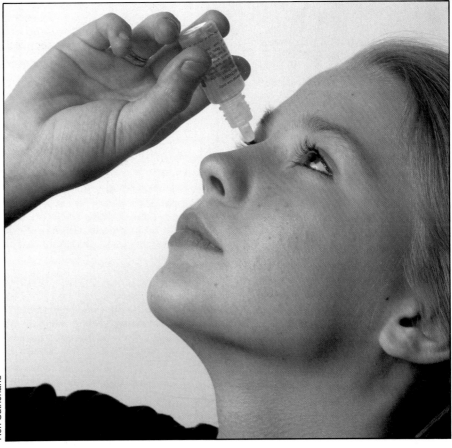

Local warmth from a hot compress will increase the blood flow and soften the eyelid, relieving pain, and encouraging the infection to clear. A simple hot compress can be made by using a clean washcloth wound on a wooden spoon and held under the hot faucet. It should be as warm as can be tolerated and held in contact with the closed eye for 10 minutes at a time. For an external sty the offending hair follicle can easily be identified. If the eyelash is pulled out with tweezers the sty will often discharge spontaneously, relieving the pain and the swelling.

Unfortunately internal sties are more difficult to deal with. The infected meibomian gland tries in vain to discharge to the surface, but the tough eyelid prevents this. The result is that the white cells eventually overcome the infection—so the symptoms go away—but they remain in situ as a cyst of sterile pus. This meibomian cyst can be felt as a little painless nodule under the eyelid and a small surgical operation is required to remove it. Under local anesthesia the eyelid is turned back and the cyst incised; the pus discharges and the conjunctival surface swiftly heals (see Pus).

With recurrent sties, antibiotic ointments may be helpful in preventing discharging pus from infecting other sebaceous glands on the eyelid (see Ointments). Rubbing the eye should be avoided as this can transfer the infection, and controlling dandruff is also impor-tant since this condition seems to cause sties. Where inflammation of the eyelids (blepharitis) is the cause, a prolonged course of antibiotics in conjunction with mild steroid drops may be helpful.

Some children suffer from recurrent sties in multiples. These do not harm the eye but they are painful and unpleasant. Unfortunately the cause is still unknown in most cases, but you should discuss the problem with your doctor since there may be an underlying associated problem, such as seborrheic dermatitis, which will respond to treatment.

Ron Sutherland

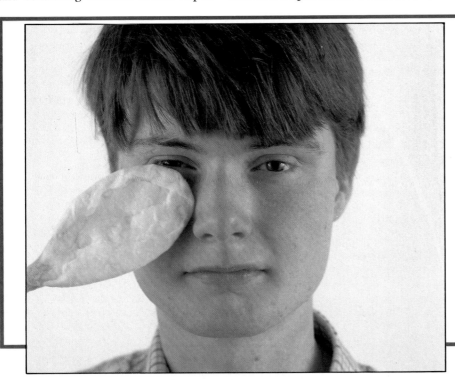

FIRST AID

If you have a sty

Do ...
- take steps to control dandruff. Wash hair regularly with an antidandruff shampoo to prevent recurrence
- apply a hot compress—a wooden spoon wrapped in a washcloth held under hot water will suffice. Hold to the eye for 10-minute periods to relieve pain and inflammation
- remove the offending eyelash if the sty is external; it will then discharge

Do not ...
- rub the eye, however tempting, as it risks spreading the infection to other sebaceous glands
- share a towel or washcloth

Subconscious

Q Do dreams come from the subconscious?

A Not necessarily. Some dreams reflect conscious joys or worries, others may derive from quite random electrical activity in the brain. Other dream images, however, may stem from subconscious thoughts, or desires, and so they are often used by some therapists as a good starting point for drawing out the dreamer's innermost feelings.

Q Do artistic people have particularly active subconscious minds?

A According to many artistic people, there is much truth in the old saying, "creativity is 1 percent inspiration, 99 percent perspiration." The subconscious thus plays only a small part in creation. Since it is also difficult to measure the activity of something that is by its very nature not available to conscious thought, the question is impossible to answer.

Q I am interested in having some psychotherapy, but I'm worried about what I might discover in my subconscious mind. Should I go ahead?

A This is a very normal fear, but, like most fears, is harder to cope with in imagination than it is in reality. With a psychotherapist whom you respect and trust, you will find that he or she will support you through the journey of self-discovery. You will probably find that the more you understand about yourself, the stronger and less fearful you will feel.

Q Whenever I do something my sister dislikes, she says it is because I subconsciously resent her. Is she right?

A Your sister may be right or wrong, but such an observation is not, by itself, helpful. It is used merely as a weapon in an argument. Explain to her that you can both only sort out your feelings if you trust one another at least enough to talk them through without such accusations.

There is a part of the mind where our deepest fears, childhood experiences, and primitive memories reside: this is the subconscious, and charting the terrain is both unnerving and rewarding—but never boring.

Human behavior is largely conditioned by past experience, beliefs, and feelings of which we are usually very much aware. Sometimes, however, our actions may seem out of character: they appeared to be all right at the time, but subsequently we would find it difficult to explain why we acted as we did. This is just one piece of evidence for the existence of the subconscious mind.

There are other pointers: for example, we will often hear our name mentioned in a conversation—even if we were not listening for it and could not hear anything else that was being said; or we will frequently notice a clock has stopped ticking—even though we were unaware of the clock's existence before it stopped! The occasional ability some people seem to possess that enables them to solve a problem in an apparent flash of insight, rather than by conscious thought, also betrays the existence of the subconscious activity of the mind (see Mind).

Development of a subconscious

From the moment of birth, feelings and images bombard the consciousness, and the mind begins the process of trying to understand them and record them. Some of the images and feelings are almost certainly wrongly recorded and fail to fit later

There are many more facets to memory and thought than we realize. A recollection of childhood, or even an entire way of feeling, can be triggered off by something as simple as the smell of a newly mown field.

sensations and impressions; additionally, there is far too much information soaking into the brain for items to be recorded individually. Instead, general impressions and rules of behavior begin to be learned. These rules, however, are the individual's rules rather than the rules someone teaches him or her.

Later, though, when the individual's experiences and rules come into conflict with what he or she decides are the wiser and stronger rules of others, his or her rules and particular experiences are filed away at the subconscious level. Yet forgetfulness does not prevent a later event from triggering off the original feeling or the original reaction: most people have by chance experienced a sound or a scent that vividly brings back a childhood feeling without being able to place the original event linked to the stimulus.

Some of the experiences buried in the subconscious may be common to many people. This led Swiss psychiatrist Carl Jung to postulate the existence of a racial subconscious that contained a set of memories common to those of a particular ethnic culture. Such a group memory would help to explain how myths, legends, and fairy tales that come from many countries often contain the same elements, even when the people of one country have no direct contact with the inhabitants of another (see Memory).

Dealing with the subconscious

Most subconscious memories and feelings are harmless enough. However, strong feelings of anger, fear, or desire, which have become buried in a person's subconscious mind because they are regarded as unacceptable, will almost certainly emerge unexpectedly from time to time as behavior that is destructive to the possessor, or to another person. In such circumstances it must be helpful to draw out from the subconscious the memories and feelings that cause the unfortunate behavior in order that the person may recognize them for what they are and come to terms with them (see Psychotherapy).

This process of examining the subconscious is the basis for many types of psychotherapy, and psychoanalytic therapy in particular. Because present thoughts can sometimes trigger subconscious memories under relaxed conditions, the examination of dreams (for which we seldom feel responsible) and the use of free association are practices that can be of value (see Dreaming). In free association the patient is asked to say whatever comes into his or her head, wandering from image to image with the expectation that any pressure coming from the subconscious will emerge into consciousness by suddenly remembered associations.

It must not be assumed, though, that the subconscious mind is the repository of the worst aspects of personality, or thoughts that ought to remain hidden. The subconscious mind is also likely to contain the unexpressed visions of the creative person, and joys and happinesses of which we remember little. Many people who have explored the subconscious through psychotherapy say that the journey can be life transforming.

Fairy tales and folk stories are a possible expression of the most mysterious part of our common experience. They can also act as a focus for nameless childhood fears, and by making them fanciful, diminish them.

Ron Sutherland

Suffocation

Q Is it true that you can suffocate if you swallow your tongue?

A Yes. If someone swallows his or her tongue and in so doing blocks the internal airways, suffocation will result unless first-aid measures are given immediately. You should not try to pull the tongue back into its correct position. Lie the person on his or her back with the head tilted backward. Pull the chin forward so that the tongue falls backward and creates a space through which air can flow. Having done this, give mouth-to-mouth resuscitation if necessary, and keep the chin forward at all costs until expert help arrives. Never leave the victim unattended.

Q My daughter always sleeps with her head buried under the blankets. Am I right to worry that she might suffocate?

A It is very unlikely that your daughter will be at any risk from suffocation by sleeping in this way. Not only are blankets porous, but if the waste carbon dioxide built up to a dangerous level in your daughter's blood, her body's natural defense mechanism would come into operation and force her to come up for air in good time.

Q I was in a very crowded train the other morning and was really worried that I might be suffocated by the crush of people. Would this have been possible, and what could I have done to prevent it happening?

A Being pressed in a crowd can certainly be a frightening experience and a dangerous one too. If you feel there is a real risk of suffocation, the most important thing is to position your hands near your face in such a way that you create an air space between you and the next person. Failing this, try to make movements with your head to create the same effect. Above all, don't panic, since this could endanger your own safety and that of other people in the crowd. Panic can rip through a crowd like wildfire.

Suffocation is a medical emergency in which the body's airways are prevented, either through accident or disease, from conducting oxygen to the lungs.

Suffocation can be caused in a variety of ways. To appreciate what happens when the body is deprived of oxygen like this it is necessary to understand the normal breathing process (see Oxygen).

The basis of breathing

As you take in a breath through your mouth or nose, air enters the body and travels down a series of tubes to expand your lungs. To help make this lung expansion possible, the ribs are pulled up and out and the muscular diaphragm below the lungs is pushed downward. In tiny sacs (alveoli) deep within the lungs, the oxygen in air breathed in is exchanged for waste carbon dioxide. Oxygen now enters the bloodstream and, assisted by the pumping of the heart, is carried to all parts of the body. The carbon dioxide rich gas is breathed out as the rib cage contracts and the diaphragm retracts upward (see Breathing, and Diaphragm).

About 20 times a minute, for an entire lifetime, this mechanism continues without the need for conscious control on our part. The body also has a built-in emergency mechanism designed to protect vital organs from lack of oxygen—particularly the brain, in which cells begin to die after only five minutes without oxygen. If for some reason the amount of oxygen in the blood falls too low and the carbon dioxide content rises too much, this is monitored by special cells in the brain. In response, breathing becomes deeper and more rapid, the blood vessels widen and those to all but essential areas are shut down. If necessary and feasible, the body is driven to move to a situation where more oxygen is available.

Suffocation from within

Despite the body's fail-safe mechanism, suffocation can occur from within the body if the airway is so obstructed that oxygen is prevented from reaching the alveoli or, having reached them, is prevented from getting into the blood. Choking on swallowed objects, swallowing the tongue in accidents, swelling of the tissues of the airways as a result of disease, or an intense allergic reaction can all cause suffocation (see Allergies). Even if oxygen enters the lungs, suffocation will result if, for example, the lung tissues are damaged and cannot exchange oxygen for carbon dioxide as they should.

All diseases of the lungs and airways can cause suffocation. These include asth-

Any crowded place carries the risk of suffocation, and bleachers in sports venues are no exception. Someone trips, the whole crowd shifts, and suddenly people are toppling like a pack of cards. Those trapped underneath can easily suffocate.

First-aid measures

If someone is in danger of suffocating because of a throat obstruction, you must act quickly. Grasp a small baby by the ankles and turn him or her upside down to try to dislodge the obstruction.

If a light adult loses consciousness, as a last resort hold head down over your knees and give a few sharp blows between the shoulder blades with your palm. Lie a heavier adult on his or her side and give similar blows.

Tony Randell

If the airway is blocked from the outside, or the chest is being crushed, do all you can to remove the obstruction or free the victim from a trapped position. If there is an obstruction inside the body, and the patient is still conscious, stand behind him or her and place both your arms just above the belt line. The victim's head, arms, and upper torso should hang forward. Grab your fist and press firmly inward and upward into the abdomen. Alternatively, ask him or her to cough as hard as possible to try to dislodge the obstruction, and to breathe as slowly and deeply as possible. If this fails, try to scoop out the obstruction using two of your fingers.

If the patient is weak or unconscious, the best way to remove an obstruction depends on his or her size and weight. For an adult, lie him or her on his or her side and give a few sharp slaps with the palm of your hand between the shoulder blades. For a child or light-weight adult, hold him or her head down over your knee and give similar blows. For a child light enough to lift, grasp him or her by the ankles and turn him or her upside down.

If these measures do not work, lose no time in starting artificial respiration by the mouth-to-mouth method. Speed is essential—not only is a life at stake but there is also a risk of brain damage if oxygen lack in the bloodstream goes over the all-important five minutes.

As well as giving first aid, you must obviously call for help, but never stop artificial respiration for this purpose or leave the patient unattended. If you are alone, shout out as loudly as you can between each breath into the patient's lungs; or try to pull the victim toward a door, a window, or to the telephone so that you can summon expert medical help without placing the victim at any further risk.

ma and bronchitis, which narrow the airways, emphysema, which overdistends and may partially destroy the alveoli; and cancer, which eats its way into normal lung tissue. In patients suffering from pneumonia, oxygen is sometimes prevented from entering the bloodstream.

External suffocation

Suffocation from forces operating outside the body is usually the result of some kind of accident. The nose and mouth, the exit and entry points of the airway, may be blocked if someone is crushed in a crowd accident, for example. A strangling constriction of some kind around the neck can also cause suffocation.

Symptoms

The exact symptoms of suffocation depend on its cause, but there are standard signs to look for. If there is some kind of obstruction, the neck muscles may make enormous, powerful contractions in an attempt to get rid of the blockage. At the same time, breathing will be labored and noisy and a bubbly fluid, possibly pink or red in color, may emerge from between the patient's lips. Other signs are a gradual increase in blueness of the skin, progressively deeper and more rapid breathing, and, after a time, a lapse into unconsciousness. When this happens, breathing may stop—a point at which first aid is essential otherwise death or brain damage could result. Remember, the brain cannot live long without a continuous supply of oxygenated blood (see Brain damage and disease).

1887

Sugars

Q Is it true that glucose tablets and drinks provide you with instant energy?

A No. Although glucose is the fuel that gives the body energy, it does not instantly give you energy. Glucose is absorbed into the body and stored in the liver and muscles as glycogen until it is required. The amount of glucose found in the blood is small (0.1 percent of the blood is glucose), and this is topped off from the glycogen store when blood sugar levels drop. All carbohydrates end up as glucose, so there is no advantage in eating pure glucose. In fact, extra glucose is like topping off the gas tank of an automobile—you may have more fuel, but the automobile doesn't go any faster.

Q Why do diabetics have to have a special diet that restricts their sugar intake?

A A special diabetic diet contains a controlled amount of all carbohydrates. Diabetes is caused by the inability of the body to control the amount of sugar in the blood, so the diet aims to provide the patient with the exact amount of carbohydrates needed.

Q My children eat lots of candy. Does this mean that they will get bad teeth?

A Yes. Sugary and starchy foods provide a breeding ground for bacteria. These bacteria tend to produce acid substances that attack the protective enamel of the teeth. Once the enamel barrier is breached, the problem gets worse. Encourage your children not to eat so much candy, and make sure they brush their teeth to get rid of the bacteria.

Q Is it true that brown sugar is better for you than ordinary white sugar?

A Basically, no. Brown sugar is virtually the same as white sugar, but it has not had all the impurities refined out of it. The basic constituent of sugar is sucrose. Brown sugar is almost pure sucrose.

The importance of sugar goes a long way beyond its use in sweetening our foods and drinks. In various forms, it plays a vital role in providing energy for the body.

The major part of our food intake consists of carbohydrates or, put more simply, sugars and starches. All carbohydrates contain atoms of carbon, hydrogen, and oxygen in varying configurations. It is the arrangements of these atoms that give the different carbohydrates their specific properties and names. The basic units are called simple sugars, such as glucose, and these consist of a single molecule; the next up the ladder are the disaccharides or double sugars, such as sucrose, lactose, and maltose, which are the sugars we normally encounter in our foods; the starches are chains of glucose molecules.

During digestion, all carbohydrates are broken down into simple sugars, especially glucose, which can be absorbed into our bodies, where they are used as fuel to provide energy for all our metabolic processes (see Digestive system).

The glucose absorbed into the body does not just pour into the bloodstream after being digested: a certain amount is diverted to the liver. Here it is captured and turned into glycogen, or animal starch (see Starch).

In effect, the liver acts as an energy store for the body (see Liver and liver diseases). When extra glucose is required, the liver converts some of the stored glycogen into glucose and releases it into the bloodstream. Thus, a high-glucose meal has no special energy-giving properties because the excess is simply stored. Even if there is a temporary lack of carbohydrate, the liver is able to synthesize glucose from fats and proteins (see Glucose).

Blood sugar

The blood contains about 0.1 percent glucose, and this is continuously supplying the energy needs of our various body tissues. It is particularly important to the brain, which has no means of storing fuel. It is therefore crucial that the body monitors and regulates the concentration of sugar in the blood.

Several hormones, of which insulin is the most important, are involved in the fine control necessary to strike the correct balance between the ready availability and storage of glucose (see Insulin). When the level of sugar in the blood rises, the pancreas releases insulin to the bloodstream and this enables glucose to be stored or used by the tissues. Too little insulin, or a total lack of it, leads to high concentrations of blood sugar; this condition is called diabetes mellitus, or sugar diabetes (see Diabetes).

White sugar is pure sucrose. Brown sugars are virtually the same. It is their impurities that give them their color.

Roger Payling

Aziz Khan

The simple sugars (monosaccharides) are commonly found in natural foods. Fructose, found in honey, is a prime example.

Obesity, and Teeth and Teething). In addition, sugar may be a contributory factor in hardening of the arteries.

There is a certain amount of evidence that an excess of sugar in the diet, along with smoking and a high fat intake, can contribute to atherosclerosis (see Fats, and Smoking). Also, sugar is a very potent source of calories, and people with a tendency to obesity should avoid pure sugar (see Obesity). Although all the starchy food we eat is converted to simple sugar in the body, it seems that the healthy way to eat is to take starchy foods in their highly complex forms, such as brown rice, grains, and other whole foods. By doing this, we may alter the body's way of handling fats, the other main source of

On the other hand, an overproduction of insulin leads to a condition called hypoglycemia, which results from too little sugar in the blood. This condition quickly impairs brain function, leading to such symptoms as hunger, uneasiness, and sweating; it may even lead to epileptic fits or unconsciousness. Generally speaking, people who suffer from hypoglycemia learn to recognize the symptoms and eat a sugar-rich food to arrest the problem (see Hypoglycemia).

Sugars and health

Although sugar contributes to providing energy for the body, an excess of sugar can also lead to harmful effects. These can include obesity and tooth decay (see

When two simple sugar molecules join together a disaccharide is formed. Ordinary table sugar (sucrose) is the best known.

calories. This helps to guard against atherosclerosis. In general, a healthy diet should contain more starch, less fat, and little refined sugar.

It is also thought that sugar and sweet things cause bad teeth. This is correct, but not the whole truth. All sugars can have an effect on dental health, but their action is indirect. Our mouths are a natural breeding ground for all sorts of bacteria, and these bacteria find the sugars just as good for them as we do. Bacteria in the mouth will feed off any sugars or starches left clinging to the teeth and produce waste products that, being acid, attack and etch the teeth, producing cavities.

When many sugar molecules join up, polysaccharides are formed. These are the starches found in vegetables.

Suicide

Q My sister is frequently depressed and is always threatening suicide. However, as far as I know she has never attempted it. Should I take her threats seriously?

A It is a common error to think that those who talk about suicide never do it. Her suicidal threats are an expression of her obvious distress, and treatment should be sought for her depression before it gets worse and she really does something drastic. Your doctor may suggest some professional help.

Q Is it true that the suicide rate is higher among artists and writers, or do they merely get more publicity?

A There is a high rate of suicide in all jobs that place a lot of pressure on the achievement of the individual. Nevertheless, the majority of suicides occur among people who receive little publicity: older people, the less well off, the unemployed, and the physically ill.

Q My neighbor's son committed suicide, and later it was learned that he was bullied in school. Could his suicide have been prevented?

A Possibly. Many suicides would not take place if the distressed person had been able to talk about problems that were troubling him. However, many factors usually contribute to drive an individual to suicide, and although the bullying may have been an important one, it may not have been the only cause.

Q Why do many women make repeated suicide attempts?

A It is thought that more women survive an attempt on their own life because of their tendency to use less violent methods than men (poisoning, for example), which leaves a chance of survival. It has also been suggested that women use the appeal effect of a suicide attempt more because other methods of exerting pressure or displaying aggression are not in their nature.

We all have moments of despair and self-hatred, but only a small number of us will actually attempt or commit suicide. What drives people to it, and what help is available for people who have reached the breaking point?

Rex Features

Many factors can contribute to causing the depression, despair, or low self-esteem that drive a person to suicide. Such individuals are now recognized as either being ill or in great distress, and should receive help and treatment before it is too late.

Who commits suicide?

More men commit suicide than women, but a far greater number of women make unsuccessful attempts to kill themselves. Studies show that virtually no children below the age of 15 commit suicide, but the rate tends to increase steadily as people get older. Divorced people and the widowed are far more likely to kill

Kurt Cobain's intense personality, his anxiety over his rising fame, his drug addiction, and a chronic stomach condition all contributed to his eventual suicide. As with many suicides, there was a clear warning of the approaching tragedy. Six weeks before he fatally shot himself in his Seattle home, Cobain went into a coma after overdosing on a cocktail of painkillers and champagne while in Rome on tour.

themselves than married or single people. Those with strong family, community, or religious ties are also less prone to suicide.

Suicide is more frequent among the professional classes (managers, executives, doctors, and businessmen) and among low-status unskilled workers than among the skilled workers who form the middle group of the population. Surprisingly, however, there seems to be no correlation between suicide rates and economic climate. People living in small country towns are among the least likely to kill themselves. Those living in big cities, especially in the city center rather than in the suburbs, are most at risk.

More people commit suicide in spring and early summer than at any other time of the year, and there are often more deaths during public holidays, when the lonely feel lonelier. The low rate of suicide in wartime has been explained by the closer involvement of the individual with the group, family, or community during that time.

Why?

Contrary to popular belief, suicide is not generally the result of a rational weighing of the pros and cons of living. Though an individual may have had suicidal thoughts, the final decision to kill him- or herself is usually made impulsively under severe emotional stress (see Stress).

Usually there is a combination of factors that drives an otherwise stable person over the edge into the desperate act of suicide. A major misfortune or life change, such as the end of a marriage or relationship, the death of a loved one, or the loss of a job, may trigger the despair that precedes suicide. Social factors have been found to contribute to suicide in two-thirds of cases; in one-third of suicides they were the principal cause.

Nearly a third of those who kill themselves are physically ill. It has been estimated that for one in five of all suicide cases poor physical health was the primary reason for the action. An unhappy love affair appears to be the motivation for suicide in only one out of twenty cases, and failed examinations or unmarried pregnancy are even less common as a cause.

Loneliness and alienation from the community are an important cause of suicide. The person who kills him- or herself is likely to experience a high degree of isolation and separation from the society he or she lives in. High rates of suicide are found where communities have disintegrated and are unstable, and where the needs of the individual are not satisfied.

The majority of those who kill themselves are severely depressed, and indeed a similar psychological state underlies depression and suicide. In both cases, the

Suicide is rarely a rational act. Often the final decision to take one's own life is made impulsively, when suffering from severe depression and emotional stress.

individual turns against him- or herself hostile impulses that were originally meant for other people. If he or she is unable to express angry or aggressive feelings externally, they may turn into self-aggression, which is expressed as self-criticism and self-hatred, or in the more extreme actions of self-injury and self-destruction in the case of a potential suicide.

Alongside the urge toward self-destruction, there is frequently a contrasting urge toward human contact and communication with other people. Suicides know their act will affect others, and usually they give warning before or during a suicide attempt. Sometimes an individual may use the act of suicide as a means of forcing others to express their love and concern for him or her.

The aged, the poor, and the physically sick make up a large proportion of those who kill themselves, and who are particularly vulnerable. Those living away from their family group are also more likely to commit suicide than others. The peak age for suicide is between 55 and 64 years.

Marriage and a big family have been linked with a lower rate of suicide but a higher rate of homicide, often a family crime. The impersonal life of the big city has been blamed for the large number of suicides, especially among immigrants and

those living alone. Poor areas with a highly mobile population show the highest rates of all worldwide.

The suicide rate among the unemployed is much higher than among the employed population. Heavy drinkers are also particularly vulnerable to attempts at suicide (see Alcoholism). Among people suffering depression (see Depression), those individuals most at risk are likely to be those undergoing prolonged bouts of insomnia (see Insomnia), those who come from a broken home, and those who have already made a previous suicide attempt. They are probably not receiving any psychiatric help.

Methods

Few suicides or attempted suicides are carefully planned. The method used depends on what is available to the individual. In the United States, where guns are quite easy to obtain, shooting is the most common means of suicide. In Great Britain, by contrast, where many kinds of gun are illegal, poisoning accounts for most deaths. Other common methods are hanging and drowning.

Those who survive a suicide attempt may suffer some lasting aftereffects, depending on the method used. Aspirin and acetaminophen can sometimes cause

Paul Windsor

Earl Young/Colorific!

permanent damage to the kidney and liver (see Kidneys and kidney diseases, and Liver and liver diseases). Some drugs taken in large quantities cause permanent brain damage (see Brain damage and disease). Survivors of more violent attempts may be left with a physical disability, or may spend some painful days or weeks in a hospital before dying from an indirectly caused ailment such as pneumonia (see Pneumonia).

Attempted suicide
For every one person who kills himself, there are at least 20 who attempt suicide and survive. Many more cases are never brought to the hospital, either because the injuries are small or because the individual or his or her family feels ashamed.

While the majority of actual suicides are older men, 65 percent of suicide attempts are made by women, and the rates are highest between 25 and 40 years of age. One-quarter of women who try to kill themselves are between the ages of 15 and 24, many of them taking an overdose of pills because they feel unable to cope or experience a sense of failure after separating from a boyfriend or husband.

In the past, those who attempted suicide were often branded as attention seekers who were making a gesture to manipulate others without any genuine intention of killing themselves. However, recent research has shown that apparently harmless acts of self-injury are often followed by more dangerous acts, and that 15 percent of those who attempt suicide afterward succeed in killing themselves. More than 10 percent of those who commit suicide had previously made several attempts. It is now

For every person who commits suicide there are 20 who attempt suicide but survive, either because the method chosen is not effective or they are rescued in time.

recognized that the cry for help of the attempted suicide generally represents a sincere statement of distress.

Treatment
Although many doctors will prescribe antidepressant drugs to tide an individual over a period of crisis, the only long-term cure is for the patient to receive some kind of psychotherapy (see Psychotherapy). This means that he or she will be able to discuss any problems and come to terms with painful or aggressive feelings whose suppression may be responsible for the self-injury.

The doctor or therapist may enlist the cooperation of sympathetic relatives or friends, who can very often contribute a great deal to the success of recovery, either providing insights into the patient's problems or giving the routine care and support that are vital if the patient is to feel secure, loved, and valued.

A suicide attempt sometimes reveals problems that can then be remedied. The impact that it creates may lead to an improvement in family relations or to the individual being moved from a socially

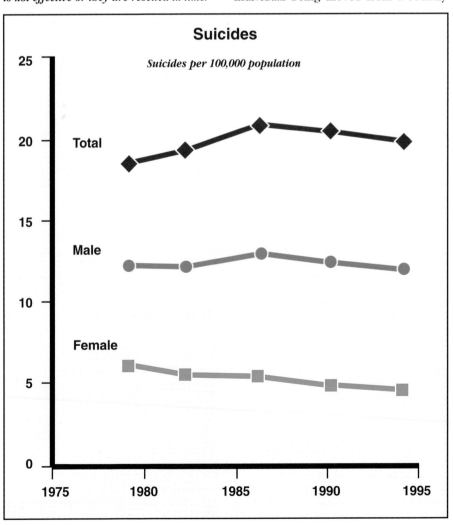

Q Someone I knew committed suicide last month after he lost his job. Is there really any link between unemployment and suicide?

A The change of life that occurs in a person who loses a job, and the consequent loss of self-esteem, disorientation, and isolation from the community, may trigger off a depression that leads to suicide. However, it is not possible to generalize from this and say that there is a close relationship between economic climate and levels of suicide. Many other factors will always come into play.

Q Why do some people make suicide pacts?

A Most people who make suicide pacts are not young unhappy lovers but older married couples, particularly where one may have a serious illness. Pacts, which are extremely rare, are illegal, and a survivor may be charged with the criminal offense of aiding and abetting the suicide of the other.

Q A friend recently took an overdose of pills, but it was not fatal. Will she do it again?

A Those who have attempted suicide are more at risk of suicide than any other members of the population, especially during the first four years after the attempt. The likelihood of a second attempt depends on whether the situation that caused the first attempt has been improved.

Q Does a person's religion or cultural background play any part in determining whether he or she might commit suicide?

A In some cultures suicide has been admired: for example, some Eastern religions have honored people choosing to free themselves from their bodies. In contrast, Jewish and Christian religions condemned suicide as sinful. However, modern attitudes in many countries have moved toward seeing suicide as a psychological and social problem.

John Greim/Science Photo Library

isolated situation. In many cases it highlights an emotional or physical illness which can be treated. Sometimes the social services of the community can give practical help and advice.

In recent years much valuable work in suicide prevention has been done by the Samaritans, Lifeline, and similar organizations. People in distress can call them at any time and speak in complete confidence to a sympathetic layperson. If appropriate, they may be referred to a doctor. In cities where these organizations operate, surveys have shown a reduction in the suicide rates.

Living wills and assisted suicides
For many people the right to die is an important part of human dignity. Some people who are terminally ill, for example, believe they have a right to end their own life if the quality of life sinks below what they consider bearable (see Euthanasia). Others argue, often from a religious viewpoint, that every life is sacred and that no one has the right to take it away. Doctors can sometimes find themselves caught between, on the one hand, their professional duty to preserve a patient's life and, on the other, their respect for a patient's right of self-determination and compassion for his or her suffering.

For many people who survive a suicide attempt, sympathetic counseling may be all they need to help them come to terms with their problems.

It is against this background that the phenomenon of the living will has developed. The living will is a document by which individuals let it be known what they would like to happen to them should they no longer be in a position to determine their future, for example, if they were to be permanently brain-damaged or in a coma. Those who have living wills elect not to be kept alive by artificial means if the chances of recovery seem very slight. Living wills have proved ethical and legal minefields, and in many states they are illegal. Before anyone makes a living will, it is important that they check with the district attorney's office to find out what position their state takes on this issue.

The related issue of assisted suicide (providing help to end the life of somebody who cannot end it himself or herself) is even more contentious. While under strictly defined circumstances it is legal in the Netherlands, it remains illegal throughout the United States. Any person who assists another to commit suicide can be indicted on a charge of homicide.

Sunburn

Q I am fair-skinned and my friend is dark. Why can she spend a long time in the sun without burning while I have to be very careful?

A Being fair-skinned means that you have little pigment in your skin. Your dark-skinned friend has more pigment, and in addition can also manufacture more than you when exposed to sunlight. Thus she not only has a natural barrier to the sun's harmful rays, but is capable of developing an even greater protection. You, on the other hand, will burn easily because your skin cannot produce enough protective pigment and no amount of sunbathing will alter this.

Q Can some drugs make you more sensitive to the sun?

A Certain drugs can cause an increased sensitivity to the sun in some individuals. Examples are the tranquilizer chlorpromazine and the antibiotic oxytetracycline. This abnormal reaction is called photosensitivity. A rash resembling sunburn develops on the areas exposed to the sun, but if the drug is stopped the rash will fade.

Q I have very sensitive skin. Is there any treatment I can have before going on vacation this year?

A You could have a course of ultraviolet ray therapy before you go on vacation, which will desensitize your skin to sunshine. However, it might be more convenient for you to use one of the sunscreen preparations which filter out the sun's stronger rays, allowing a slow tan to develop.

Q I have fair hair that becomes lighter in the sun while my skin becomes darker. Why is this?

A The pigment in hair is already present, while that in skin appears only when the pigment-producing cells are activated by sunlight. Fair hair has a different sort of pigment from dark hair and, unlike dark hair, becomes bleached on exposure to strong sunlight.

A depleted ozone layer means that exposure to the sun can be a risky thing. Common sense and forethought, however, will help prevent not only the discomfort of sunburn but also the danger of serious conditions such as skin cancer.

The sun has traditionally played a beneficent role in human civilization and has been seen above all as a life giver. Our attitudes are beginning to change, however. The discovery in the mid-1980s that the ozone layer—the part of the Earth's atmosphere that protects the planet from the sun's harmful ultraviolet radiation—was under assault from synthetic pollutants and that, as a consequence, we increasingly run the risk of developing skin cancer and cataracts from overexposure to the sun's rays, has colored our old worship with fear (see Ozone layer).

How sunburn occurs
Sunburn is the result of immediate sun damage to the skin. It is a form of radiation burn rather than heat burn. Unlike a burn caused by heat, sunburn is not felt until a few hours after it happens.

The sun is really a small star and its energy can be compared with a continuous and enormous atomic explosion. Some of its rays are deadly, but these are filtered out by the Earth's atmosphere and never reach the Earth itself. The rays that do pass through the atmosphere are part of the sun's spectrum. It contains visible rays that we see as light, infrared rays that we feel as heat, and the group that

Vacations and sunbathing seem to be made for each other; however, while we once unreservedly associated a deep golden tan with healthy good looks, we are now much more aware of the health implications of overexposure to the sun. If you do sunbathe, apply liberal amounts of sunscreen repeatedly, and try to avoid prolonged exposure during the middle of the day when the sun is at its zenith.

The epidermis also contains pigment-producing cells or melanocytes. These are stimulated by ultraviolet light to produce the pigment melanin, which acts as a very efficient filter of the ultraviolet rays (see Melanin). The new pigmentation (which is seen as a suntan) begins soon after exposure to the sun and builds gradually during continual exposure. After a period of exposure, the pigmentation will fade at varying rates, and is likely to disappear within nine months. Sunburn occurs when there is not enough pigment filter present.

There are two types of sun damage: immediate and delayed. The immediate type of damage is sunburn, but, like other radiation burns, its effects do not show for some hours. The first signs are redness and a sensation of burning caused by an increase in the blood supply to the skin. This may happen any time up to 24 hours after exposure. Later, small blisters may develop (see Blisters).

More severe damage produces larger blisters and can actually damage some of the cells in the epidermis. These damaged cells are called sunburn cells. The degree of sunburn depends on the strength of the ultraviolet rays.

causes sunburn—the ultraviolet rays. These are called ultraviolet because they are beyond the violet end of the visible spectrum.

The ultraviolet and infrared rays are both capable of damaging the human body. However, the infrared rays do not cause a problem, since they are registered as heat, and an exposed area can be withdrawn before any harm is done. It is the ultraviolet rays that cause sunburn because they can penetrate and damage the skin without giving an immediate feeling of warmth.

Ultraviolet rays produce their effect by transferring energy to molecules in the skin, causing a photochemical reaction. The amount of energy released depends

A tan does not prevent sunburn. Once the pigment-producing skin cells have been saturated with ultraviolet light, further exposure results in radiation burn.

on the wavelength of the rays. The shorter wavelengths carry and release more energy than the longer ones, but the latter have a greater ability to penetrate.

Effects on the skin

The skin is made up of two layers. In the outer layer (the epidermis), cells are continuously being shed from the surface and replaced by new ones, which are formed in the lowest level of the epidermis. It is in this outer layer that the effects of sunburn occur (see Skin and skin diseases).

Long-term sun damage

Sunburn itself is not as serious as the long-term damage to the skin. This is caused by repeated sun damage to the cells at the skin's surface and to the supporting tissues below. It takes years to develop, but once it has happened it is irreversible (see Wrinkles).

The changes are similar to those of aging (see Aging), and the obvious effects can be seen in the seaman's or land worker's face, where there is marked wrinkling and a leathery thickening of the skin. Other effects can be very localized, such as patchy increases in the pigmentation and a thickening of the horny covering of the skin. This can give rise to wartlike lumps, called solar keratoses,

which are common in the middle-aged and elderly. Widening of the blood vessels of the face and dryness and cracking of the skin are part of the aging process but are more marked in people who have spent their lives outdoors.

The most serious risk that can result from repeated overexposure to the sun is skin cancer (see Cancer). The high incidence in the 20th century of skin cancer among people of northern European descent can be directly related to the fact that for the first time they live in areas of bright sunshine. By contrast, skin cancer was very uncommon in the Victorian era, when there was little exposure of the skin. Today it occurs frequently in sun-

In the Victorian era (left) a pale skin was considered a sign of refinement and, in women, of beauty. This, and concealment of the body, almost certainly explains the low incidence of skin cancer over the general population. For much of the 20th century, by contrast, there was a mania for gaining a highly prized tan (below), often at the expense of health. We are now turning full circle: pale skin is becoming acceptable, even fashionable, again.

worshiping regions like California or Australia. Australia currently has the highest incidence of skin cancer in the world.

Fair-skinned people who can produce enough melanin pigment to get a good tan are still vulnerable to skin cancer. There is a limit to the number of harmful rays that can be absorbed by the pigment filter, and once this has been saturated these rays can then cause damage. It is therefore not impossible for a tanned person to develop sunburn from excessive exposure. Dark-skinned people suffer the same effects but to a much lesser degree.

Children are at particular risk from sunburn. Repeated sunburns during childhood increase the likelihood of skin cancer during adulthood (see Melanoma).

Treatment

Once sunburn has occurred, the most important factor in treatment is to prevent further damage by avoiding further exposure. In mild burns the redness and burning usually resolve in a few days, and are often followed by peeling. Soothing lotions such as calamine are most effective, and if sleep is disturbed antihistamines may be prescribed. These are

mildly sedative but have no effect on the skin. In more severe burns, the symptoms are usually most acute on the second day when blisters may form on the affected areas. Steroid ointments reduce the intensity and duration of the skin reaction.

Prevention
Most people quickly learn how much sun they can take without burning. The body's natural protection is, of course, a tan built up each day by gradually increasing the periods of exposure.

The intensity of the sun must also be taken into account. The most accurate way of gauging this is not by the degree of heat or light, but by the angle of the sun above the horizon. This determines the amount of ultraviolet light that reaches the skin. At midday, the sun is directly overhead and the rays pass through less of the Earth's atmosphere. When the sun is low, in the morning and evening, the strength of the ultraviolet rays is considerably reduced. You are therefore less likely to get sunburned in the early morning or after midafternoon. The danger period is thus roughly 10:00 A.M. to 3:00 P.M., when exposure should be kept to a minimum.

Particular care should be taken when swimming, sailing, or skiing. Water absorbs the heat rays but the ultraviolet rays are still being directed onto the skin, while snow gives a feeling of coolness but actually reflects the ultraviolet rays.

There are many sunscreen creams and lotions available that can help to prevent sunburn. Both the American Academy of Dermatology and the Skin Cancer Foundation advise that preparations should be applied frequently, and especially just before and after swimming.

They protect mainly against the sun's rays but, depending on their strength (sunscreen factor), will let through enough of the longer ultraviolet waves to produce a gradual tan. The tan is, however, no deeper than one obtained simply by gradual exposure without a sunscreen. Some sunscreens give almost total protection by stopping all the ultraviolet and visible rays, so that prolonged exposure without damage is possible.

Some parts of the body are more prone to sunburn than others because they are exposed the most. A bald head, the face, tops of the ears, forearms, and backs of the hands are particularly at risk. A hat should always be worn when the hair is thin, and this will also protect the nose and tops of the ears. Otherwise a sunscreen may be used on these small areas. Clothing is an efficient filter of the sun's harmful rays, if it is opaque.

Try to make sure that children always wear a hat out in the sun, and apply sunblock liberally and frequently to exposed areas of skin. If possible, don't allow children to stay out in the sun for prolonged periods between 10:00 A.M. and 3:00 P.M. However, sunscreen should not be used on babies of six months and under, who should be kept out of strong sunlight.

Outlook
In the future we will increasingly have to become more sun conscious and protect ourselves and our children against the possible negative effects of sunburn. However, it is important to remember that not all the effects of ultraviolet light are harmful. Sunlight is essential for health (see Vitamin C, and Vitamin D), good looks, and perhaps even emotional well-being (see Seasonal affective disorder).

> ## Recommendations of the American Academy of Dermatology and the Skin Cancer Foundation to help reduce the risk of skin cancer and sunburn
>
> - Keep exposure to the sun to a minimum at midday and between 10:00 A.M. and 3:00 P.M.
> - Apply sunscreen with at least a skin protection factor (SPF) 15, or higher, to all areas of the body that are exposed to the sun. Reapply the sunscreen every two hours, even on cloudy days, after swimming or perspiring.
> - Wear clothing that covers the body. Hats should have wide brims to shade both the face and the neck.
> - Avoid exposure to ultraviolet radiation from sunlamps.
> - Children should be protected from excessive exposure to the sun when radiation is strongest (10:00 A.M. to 3:00 P.M.). Sunscreen should be applied liberally and frequently to children aged six months or older. It should not, however, be used on babies under six months.
> - For those babies under six months, keep exposure to sunlight to an absolute minimum.

Sunstroke

Q If you go to a hot country, do you get acclimatized so that you are at less risk of sunstroke?

A Yes you do. However, it takes several weeks or even months for someone to get acclimatized to the heat. To a large extent, this depends on the amount of physical effort that is required in the heat. It is, after all, going to take much longer to be able to carry out strenuous work in the heat than it is if you are just going to take it easy. It is not clear exactly what changes are going on in the body during the period of acclimatization, although there is probably some increase in the efficiency of the sweat glands. Research suggests that a newcomer to the heat loses more salt in sweat than someone who has become used to the heat.

Q Is there any difference between sunstroke and heatstroke?

A No. Both terms describe the serious and potentially fatal condition that can occur if the body is excessively heated, resulting in the total breakdown of the body's temperature-regulating mechanism. Heatstroke, however, is a more accurate name because you can suffer from its effects at the bottom of a mine. In fact, in some South African mines heatstroke is a serious problem. It is important to realize that, if the temperature is high enough, you can suffer from heatstroke even if you stay out of the direct sun.

Q Does prickly heat make you more prone to sunstroke?

A Prickly heat occurs when the skin becomes so hot that the skin cells swell and block the sweat glands, resulting in an itchy rash of tiny, red blisters, at the same time as they are being asked to do more work. Prickly heat is actually very common, and doesn't really indicate any serious trouble. There is one form of heat exhaustion that is often preceded by an episode of prickly heat, but it is nowhere near as severe as heatstroke itself.

Sunstroke is a dangerous condition that occurs when the body's thermostat breaks down from overheating. Always take care in extreme heat since, even with treatment, sunstroke can be fatal or cause permanent damage.

We are all used to thinking of the extremely serious heat disorder called sunstroke as something that only happens to people who stay out too long in the hot sun. However, the real cause of the condition is not the sun's rays but the intense heat that the sun produces. For this reason, doctors prefer to talk about heatstroke rather than sunstroke.

Any environment that gets hot can be dangerous. For instance, people who find themselves in very hot places such as engine rooms and steelworks can suffer the severe effects of sunstroke without ever being near the sun (see Heat and heat disorders, and Travel and health).

The body's reaction to heat

The body has two main mechanisms for losing heat. First, the blood vessels to the skin are dilated so that more blood flows to the surface, allowing it to lose heat through the skin into the air. Second, the sweat glands pour out salty fluid onto the surface of the skin, where it evaporates and heat is lost as vapor (see Perspiration).

When temperatures soar to 106ºF (41ºC) the risk of heatstroke and other forms of heat disorder rises dramatically. Both the very young and the very old, who have inefficient temperature-regulating mechanisms, are at risk in these conditions.

Leslie Wong/Colorific!

Overheating

There are many ways in which the environment can intensify the effects of heat on the body. It isn't, therefore, just a question of reading the degrees on the thermometer. If the air is humid, then this reduces the ease with which the sweat evaporates so that it becomes more difficult to lose heat. Similarly, if the air is very still, then less heat is lost from the surface of the body by convection.

People doing hard physical work in a hot environment are, of course, producing a lot of heat of their own. They may be losing up to a quart of sweat every hour, compared with the one quart per day of the sedentary worker in a temperate climate. This loss of salt and water can contribute to a condition known as heat exhaustion, which, unless checked, can lead to the eventual breakdown of the body's temperature-regulating mechanisms. Fortunately, however, as the body gets used to working in a hot environment, it adapts and the loss of salts decreases, making the body less vulnerable to heat disorders.

Additional risk factors

The very young and the very aged are most at risk from heat disorders, and consequently from heatstroke. This is because their temperature-regulating mechanisms are not very efficient. And because of this deficiency, older people also tend to wear heavy clothes even on sunny days, thereby increasing the risk of overheating still further.

There are several other predisposing factors. People who are unused to heat, who are very overweight, who drink heavily, or who are suffering from a feverish illness may also be at a greater risk from heatstroke.

Symptoms and dangers

The three basic signs of heatstroke are: a high temperature (more than 106°F [41°C]); a total absence of sweating; and, most seriously, problems of the nervous system that may lead to coma (see Coma). Disturbances of mood, disorientation, and headache, often accompanied by dizziness and difficulty in walking, all happen in the early stages of heatstroke until consciousness is lost.

Unfortunately, fully developed heatstroke is an extremely dangerous condition and over 20 percent of sufferers may die, even with treatment. Even those who do recover may have persistent trouble in the nervous system and their balance and coordination may take months to return to normal. However, if treatment is prompt (at the first sign of symptoms and before consciousness is lost) then the chances of recovery are good.

On a hot, sticky day what could be nicer than being able to strip off and go for a paddle. Keeping cool in hot weather, whether at home or abroad on vacation, is a priority. Swimming is an effective and fun way to help the body's cooling systems.

To guard against sunstroke, troops serving in the tropics wear uniforms specifically designed for the intense heat.

Treatment and prevention

As soon as any of the symptoms of heatstroke appear it is essential to call a doctor immediately. Meanwhile, cool the patient down as quickly as possible. The temperature needs to be brought down to about 102°F (39°C), but no lower as the patient's circulation may go into shock (see Shock). Remove the patient's clothes and cover him or her with a thin cotton blanket, which should be continually doused in cold water. If possible, the best way to cool the patient down is in a tub of cold water. In a hospital, special slatted beds on which sufferers can be doused with water and cooled by fans are used.

The most sensible and effective way to fight sunstroke is, of course, prevention. This can be done quite simply by insuring that the body is not overheated. This means not staying out too long in the sun; wearing cool, loose clothing in the heat; and taking salt tablets and drinking plenty of liquids when doing physical work in very hot environments.

Suppositories

Q Can all medicines be taken in suppository form?

A No. Some drugs consisting of large complex molecules, such as vaccines and tissue extracts, cannot be given by mouth. They have to be given by injection instead since they will not go through the wall of the intestine into the bloodstream. The same principle applies in the rectum, and these types of drugs are useless if they are given by suppository. However, most drugs that we are used to taking by mouth in tablet or capsule form could be taken rectally in suppository form.

Q Are there any advantages in taking medication in suppository form?

A Yes, in certain circumstances there can be. A person who has an illness that involves vomiting may not be able to keep down drugs given by mouth, so an alternative route of administration must be found. Giving the drug rectally by means of suppository may prove a satisfactory solution. Similarly, there are drugs that irritate the stomach, with dyspepsia and even vomiting. Here, too, the suppository form may prove to be the best alternative.

Q Are there any dangers in using suppositories?

A In general, no. Many people find their use distasteful, but it is rarely dangerous. There are two points, however, that need to be borne in mind. The first is to remember not to insert the suppository until you are sure that you are not going to want to go to the bathroom for some time. The second point is to avoid getting into the habit (as happens to some people with hemorrhoids) of using proprietary suppositories on an almost continuous basis. They may only be completely safe if used for a short course. Prolonged use can damage the tissues that line the rectum. In any case, hemorrhoids should not be allowed to go on for more than a week or two before you visit your doctor. He or she will advise the best course of action.

Frank Kennard

Taking medicine by mouth or injection can sometimes be inappropriate. Introducing a drug rectally by means of suppositories is a safe and effective alternative.

The term *suppository* describes a particular pellet-shaped object used as a means of introducing a drug or medicine into the body, the suppository being inserted into the rectum. This method offers an alternative to more traditional methods of taking medicines, such as by mouth (in the form of tablets, capsules, or liquid mixtures), by inhalation (in the form of gases or sprays), or by injection. Suppositories may also be inserted into the vagina when used in the treatment of vaginal infection, in which instance they are termed *pessaries*.

How a suppository is inserted

With the patient in a comfortable position, here standing, the person inserting the suppository takes it in a gloved hand and gently pushes it into the rectum with one

finger until the sphincter muscles grip on the finger's second joint. The suppository must be retained in the rectum as long as possible for it to be effective.

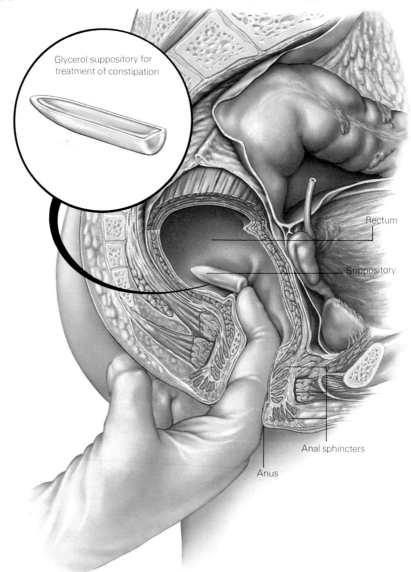

Glycerol suppository for treatment of constipation

Rectum

Suppository

Anal sphincters

Anus

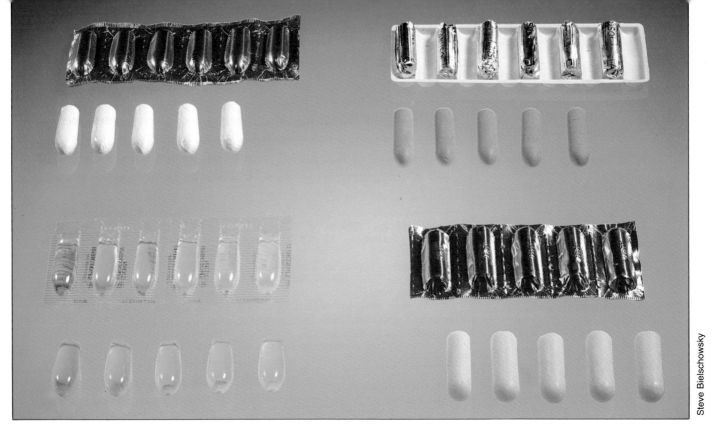

Steve Bielschowsky

Because of the way it is used, the suppository has certain physical characteristics that enable it to be used without undue discomfort. First, it is cone-shaped so that it can be pushed easily through the anus. Second, it is constructed from an oily or greasy base material so that it can be inserted without any difficulty or pain. The suppository slowly melts and the drug is gradually released, to be absorbed through the rectal tissues.

Why use suppositories?

There are often special reasons why a drug should be administered by suppository rather than orally (tablets or liquid) or by injection. The most obvious need for taking a medicine in suppository form is when the area that the doctor wishes to treat (the target site) is in the rectum or anus itself. Speedy and direct contact between the drug and an infection in this area can best be achieved by this method.

The use of suppositories may be preferred by both doctor and patient when a drug prescribed by the doctor is found to cause stomach irritation. In addition, an unacceptable amount of indigestion may arise if the drug is taken by tablet. Taking the drug by suppository avoids these unpleasant side effects (see Side effects).

Some drugs are broken down by gastric juices during their passage through the stomach and become useless. The suppository method will prevent this happening since the drug is absorbed into the blood without having to go through the digestive process.

Drugs taken in suppository form are absorbed into the circulation more slowly than if taken by mouth, and sometimes this can be of positive benefit in treating some conditions. The release of the drug can be sustained over longer periods, perhaps lasting as long as 12 hours from a single dose. This method of drug administration also avoids the need to take tablets at frequent intervals, or having to wake up during the night to take important medication.

Where vomiting is a feature of an illness, it is not possible to give medicines by mouth since they are not likely to get past the stomach before being vomited back. Taking drugs by suppository through the anal canal is ideal (see Vomiting).

Conditions treated

Suppositories are most commonly used in the treatment of hemorrhoids, and a great variety of suppositories are suitable for this purpose (see Hemorrhoids). Some contain astringents such as hamelis or bismuth subgallate, which have the effect of shrinking the hemorrhoids; some are local anesthetics to diminish soreness; others contain mild antiseptics to prevent infection.

Suppositories are also widely used in the treatment of constipation (see Constipation), especially in older people, because they go straight to the site where treatment is required. Glycerol suppositories (which generally contain 70 percent glycerol) both soften and lubricate the feces, and are particularly useful if evacuation is painful. Bisacodyl and danthron suppositories are more powerful than glycerol and act by irritating the rectum into action.

Suppositories all share the same pellet-shaped form and are used to treat an extremely diverse range of conditions, from hemorrhoids to rheumatism.

Hydrocortisone suppositories are used on local inflammatory conditions of the anus and rectum (see Anus, and Rectum), and nystatin suppositories are used for the treatment of thrush (see Thrush). Some rheumatic (see Rheumatism) and arthritic (see Arthritis) conditions can also be treated with suppositories, usually where the drugs used (such as indomethacin and phenylbutazone) may cause side effects in the stomach if taken by mouth. The drug is absorbed just as effectively in the rectum as in the stomach but the side effects are avoided.

In some cases, respiratory disorders (see Breathing), pain (see Pain management), and even vertigo (see Vertigo) are treated with drugs given by suppository. This is because some of the drugs used are most effective when absorbed slowly into the bloodstream, having the necessary action over a longer period of time.

Safe use

Young children should not be given suppositories unless recommended by your doctor, although doctors sometimes give suppositories to babies, who may be unwilling to swallow tablets. Long-term or habitual use of suppositories (because sometimes happens with hemorrhoid sufferers) should also be avoided, as constant exposure to the chemicals in the suppositories could damage the tissues lining the rectum.

Suppuration

Suppuration *is the medical term used to describe any inflammatory process where there is a formation of pus—the mixture of bacteria, water, protein, and white blood cells that is produced in response to infection.*

Q Is it dangerous for a wound to fester for a long time?

A It could be. In the normal course of events, if an individual is healthy and is able to resist infection, then the suppurating (festering) wound should eventually heal, providing that the pus can escape and does not get trapped, forming an abscess. However, if the patient is undergoing any degree of general illness, the suppuration may continue for a long time and could have lasting effects such as general ill health, loss of weight, and anemia.

Q My husband had a boil on his leg, which, when it burst, continued to produce pus for a long time. Is this usual?

A All abscesses have to burst eventually. As the pus escapes the cavity, the abscess gradually gets smaller and finally disappears. In your husband's case, the hole through which the pus drained from the boil was probably not big enough, so that there was a buildup inside. This would delay the healing process considerably. If an abscess is drained, it should have a large opening to allow all the pus to escape.

Q Can you get infected by being contaminated by pus from a wound?

A It's unlikely. The organisms present in the pus are normally found on the skin and on things around the house. You would only get an infection if you were very sick yourself and your resistance was low, or if you had a recent wound through which the organisms could gain access.

Q Why do some infections lead to the formation of pus and others only cause the tissue to become red and swollen?

A Whether or not suppuration occurs depends on the particular organism involved. Viral infections do not cause suppuration, and only some bacterial infections are capable of causing it.

Inflammation is the body's natural reaction to damage. When the damage is caused by infection, the inflammation may be accompanied by suppuration (the formation of pus; see Pus), which is our main defense mechanism against invading bacteria.

There are also particular types of bacterium (see Bacteria) that provoke suppuration, and they are the organisms that normally live on the skin and in the large intestine.

Common causes

When people get colds, they sometimes develop a sore throat and dry nose, which lasts for a few days (see Common cold). The symptoms may progress to the formation of a yellow discharge from the nose, perhaps with some pain around the eyes and a high fever. Initially a virus causes inflammation of the lining membranes. A bacterial infection causes suppuration, gaining access to the body through the membrane that has been damaged by the virus. It is at the stage of suppuration that antibiotics are needed to clear up the infection (see Antibiotics).

Suppuration will also occur if a wound becomes infected, and this is something that surgeons, in particular, try to guard against. Sometimes, however, there is already infection present when surgery is performed and, in spite of the use of antibiotics, the wound becomes infected. When this happens, the formation of pus usually takes place after about a week, although it can occur several months after surgery. Sometimes the pus has to be let out by means of a small operation; sometimes the wound ruptures spontaneously (see Wounds).

Possible side effects

As well as the local effects of the formation of pus, the constant presence of suppuration somewhere in the body may in time lead to other more remote effects (see Side effects).

A patient may feel generally unwell and may lose his or her appetite and consequently lose weight. Suppuration can eventually lead to anemia, which is caused by a problem in the bone marrow where red blood cells are manufactured (see Anemia).

The risk of surgical wounds suppurating is kept to a minimum by the sterile conditions in operating rooms.

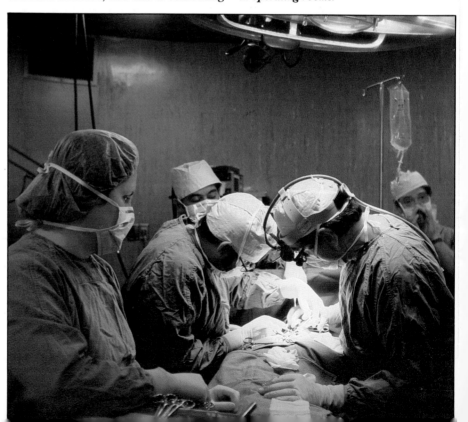

Surgery

Q I have heard of surgery lasting for many hours at a time. What is the average length of an operation?

A Operations can last from a few minutes to many hours, sometimes as many as 10 or 12. On average, abdominal surgery, such as a removal of the gallbladder, can take between one and three hours, depending on how straightforward the procedure is.

Q My father is due to have surgery on his bladder, but because his chest is bad they are going to give him spinal anesthesia. Does this mean that surgery will be painful?

A No. Spinal anesthesia should take away all painful sensation from the lower half of the body, and lasts for a few hours after surgery. During surgery, even though he will be awake he will be given a tranquilizing injection.

Q How many years does it take to become a fully qualified surgeon?

A All surgeons have to go through the basic training to become a doctor, and this usually takes a minimum of four years. They then have to do a year as an intern, after which they have to begin specialist jobs while working for their examinations for the American Board of Surgery. This usually takes a further four or five years, after which the surgeon in training carries on as a resident for five to seven years.

Q Why do some patients have to have a tube inserted through their nose when they have just undergone surgery?

A This type of tube, which is known as a nasogastric tube, passes through the nose into the stomach. It is used to remove the secretions from the stomach before they have built up, and is commonly used after surgery on the abdomen. The tube is left in place for two or three days until the intestines are able to work normally again.

Medical knowledge and techniques are continually advancing, and nowhere with more dramatic effect than in surgery. Today's surgeon is a highly skilled specialist capable of hitherto impossible feats.

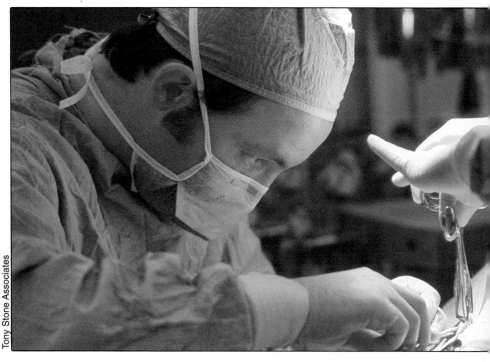

Tony Stone Associates

It is difficult to realize how much the practice of surgery has evolved in the past 100 years or so when one sees how often operations are performed today, with seemingly very little fuss.

Until about a century ago, surgery was performed with no anesthesia (see Anesthetics) and with little regard for the problems of infection. As a result some patients died directly as a result of the surgery rather than of the condition for which they were being treated.

Four major advances have revolutionized surgical procedures: anesthesia, asepsis, microsurgery, and minimally invasive (keyhole) surgery.

Anesthesia

In modern surgery, operations can be performed under local, regional, spinal, or general anesthesia. In local anesthesia, a solution of a drug (usually lignocaine) is injected into the tissues to be operated on. The effect is almost instantaneous and should provide complete anesthesia so that the patient cannot feel any pain at all. If pain is felt, this means that the drug was not injected into the right place.

The effect of the anesthesia usually lasts for a few hours after the injection has been administered.

It is not surprising that it takes a long time to become a surgeon: not only does it require expert medical and technical knowledge, but also remarkable manual dexterity, concentration, and stamina.

Regional anesthesia involves the use of the same drug, lignocaine, but in such a way that a whole region of the body is anesthetized. This can be achieved by injecting into or around a large nerve, or by putting a tourniquet around a limb and injecting the drug into a vein in the limb, thus filling up the blood vessels of the limb with the local anesthetic. Many operations can be performed using this type of anesthesia.

Spinal anesthesia is a method of blocking the pain impulses as they pass up the nerve column of the spine to the brain. This can be done in one of two ways, both of which involve passing a needle or fine tube between two of the bones of the spine (the vertebrae). The local anesthetic drug can be injected into the fluid that surrounds the spinal cord (the cerebrospinal fluid), or it can be injected into the potential space outside the outer membrane, the dura mater, that sheaths the cord. The latter is a difficult technique known as epidural anesthesia, and calls

Q My mother has just had surgery to have a tumor removed from her large intestine. How long will it be before we know whether the operation has been successful?

A Assuming she makes an uncomplicated recovery from the surgery, it will be one or two years before you will know whether the operation has been a success. The surgeon who has performed the operation may be able to tell you about the likelihood of a complete cure when he or she has the report on the specimen from the pathologist. In any case, your mother will have to continue to be seen by the surgeon for several years to come.

Q What are the risks involved in having any type of major surgery today?

A This is very difficult to gauge since there are so many factors involved. The age of the patient, the disease for which the surgery is being performed, as well as any other illnesses that the patient might have, all play a part. In general, however, major surgery is only undertaken when the risks of not having the operation outweigh the risks of having it.

Q I underwent surgery about a month ago and the scar is still very red and prominent, in spite of my being told by the doctor that it would not be noticeable. How long does it usually take before a surgical scar becomes less unsightly?

A Most surgical scars become red at about this stage, and do look ugly. However, given time, the redness disappears and by the end of a year the scar should be pale and fine. It may even continue to improve after a year, and so you shouldn't worry about it unless it is still prominent 18 months after surgery, in which case you should go back to your doctor. Unfortunately there is really nothing that can be done to speed up this natural healing process. Try to be patient, and in time your scar should disappear or at least fade significantly.

Hank Morgan/Science Photo Library

for great skill and care. Spinal anesthetics do not involve loss of consciousness and are extensively used for surgery on the lower part of the body in patients in whom general anesthesia might involve some risk.

General anesthesia, where the patient is put to sleep, involves the administration of drugs by injection and the inhalation of anesthetic gases. Using this method, the patient is both insensitive to pain and also immobile. If necessary the patient can be paralyzed, so that the muscles throughout the body become lax, and this can make operating on the abdomen much easier. With the development of safer anesthetics, and safer anesthetic techniques, surgery need no longer be a rush job as it used to be, and the surgeon can perform the operation without feeling that he or she has to hurry through it. Part of this improvement in anesthetic technique was the realization, only about 50 years ago, that the transfusion of blood and saline during and after surgery greatly improves the patient's progress toward recovery.

Aseptic techniques
In the 19th century, the discovery by French medical pioneer Louis Pasteur that disease could be transmitted by organisms called bacteria (see Bacteria) paved the way for the development by

A nurse will check the patient's identity an hour or two prior to surgery, and will then administer the premedication, which prepares the patient for anesthesia.

Although gloves are worn, a surgeon's skin must be scrupulously clean. He or she first scrubs with soap and water and then with an antiseptic such as iodine.

spraying carbolic acid on and around the wound at the time of surgery decreased the incidence of infection. This technique, which was really an antiseptic technique, then led to aseptic techniques, where bacteria were not allowed near the wound.

In modern surgery everything is sterilized, from the surgical instruments and suture materials to the surgeon's gloves and gown. Thus the open wound is contaminated very little by extraneous bacteria. This technique has led to a near-zero rate of infection in so-called clean surgery such as hernia repairs (see Hernia). There is still a significant infection rate in dirty surgery, where there is contamination with bacteria from within the patient.

Examples of this would be removal of the appendix, or operations on the intestine. However, even with these operations, the use of modern antibiotics (see Antibiotics) is bringing down the infection rate significantly.

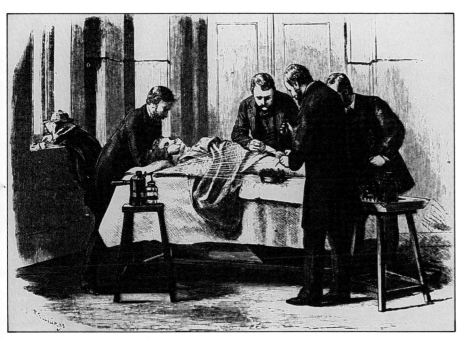

An operation in the early days of antiseptic surgery. The anesthetic used was chloroform, and the steam-operated carbolic spray, invented by Joseph Lister, produced an antiseptic atmosphere.

Today's anesthesiologist has a wealth of equipment at hand. During surgery, he or she monitors the patient's heartbeat, measures blood pressure, and administers the anesthetic gases.

British surgeon Joseph Lister of aseptic techniques. Before this, surgery was performed in a large room before an audience (hence the British term *operating theater*) by a surgeon who often took off his frock coat and put on another one covered with old blood. He did not wear rubber gloves, and the instruments were only superficially clean, but not sterilized. Not surprisingly, all surgical wounds became infected. Joseph Lister found that

Surgical stitches

There are various types of suture material in use today, each with its own special properties (see Stitch). Stitches can be divided into those that dissolve in the body tissues and those that stay permanently in the tissues, or are removed some time after the operation. In the first category come catgut, collagen, and Dexon. Catgut is not, as the name suggests, made from cats' intestines, but is in

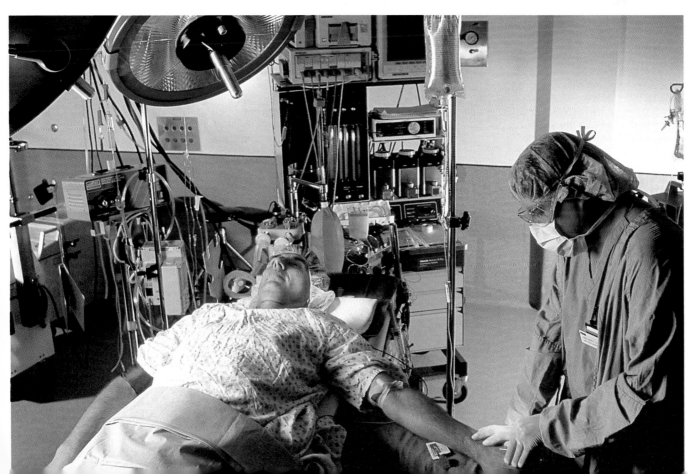

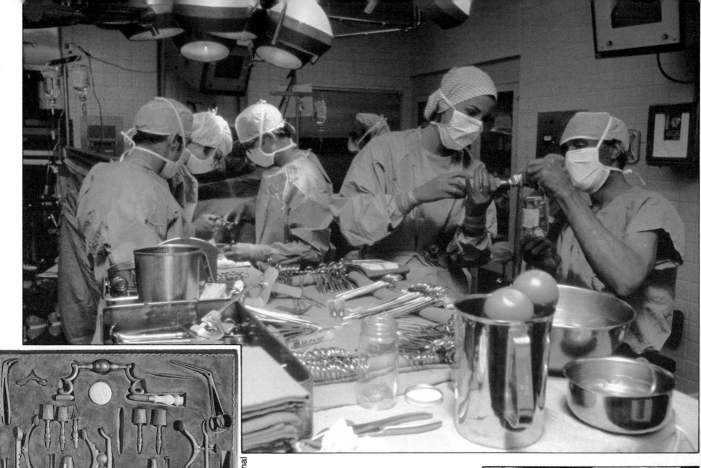

Sterilized surgical instruments are systematically laid out before an operation. Having the right instrument close at hand saves precious time. These rather forbidding instruments (left) were once used to make holes in the head, thereby letting out "evil humors"!

Scala/Vision International

fact made from the lining of sheep's intestines. The material is dried and twisted, and may be subject to a process akin to tanning to make it last longer in the tissues. It is then sterilized and packed in hermetically sealed tinfoil packs in alcohol. Dexon is a synthetic material that also dissolves in the tissues, but is not as pliable or as easy to knot during the stitching process as catgut.

Among the stitches that are nonabsorbable are silk and linen thread, monofilament nylon, braided nylon, and wire. All these materials are used for specific purposes and are left in the body. They may weaken over the years, but it is possible to find traces of these materials in a patient many years later.

All these substances are used both for tying around structures, when they are known as ligatures, and for stitching tissues together, when they are known as sutures (see Sutures). Nowadays, when sutures are used, the thread is fixed to the needle by the manufacturer by a process known as swaging. This means that the blunt end of the needle does not have an eye, like a dressmaker's needle, but instead has a hollow end. The thread is

pushed into the hollow end and the metal of the needle is pinched onto the thread. This means that when the needle is pulled through the tissue there is no injury caused by the knot of thread. Needles are made straight, to be handheld, or curved, to be held in a special needle holder. The point may be conical, or it may be triangular in cross section so that it cuts through the tissue. This type of needle is used for sewing up the skin.

Surgical instruments

With aseptic techniques and general anesthesia there was a large advance in the techniques of operating, and many of the instruments used today were developed as far back as the end of the last century. There have been, of course, many modifications and new developments since, but the basic types of instrument have changed very little.

Scalpels: A modern surgical scalpel consists of a solid metal handle onto which can be clipped stainless steel blades of varying sizes. The blades are only used once, and several different blades may be used during the course of an operation. The essential of good surgi-

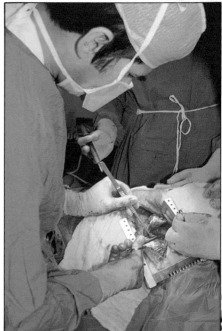

Although simple in design, the retractor (above) is an essential piece of surgical equipment. This metal frame, which can be handheld or self-retaining, keeps the wound open during surgery.

Advanced technology now means that the most intricate microsurgery can be performed. With the aid of a laryngoscope, the surgeon (right) can see into the patient's throat to remove a cyst.

cal dissection is that the tissues should be cut cleanly, and so it is necessary to have a sharp scalpel blade at all times. As well as differing in size, they also differ in shape to suit varying kinds of surgery.

Scissors: There are many different designs of scissors, some long, some short, some curved, and some straight. They are always of the finest quality steel, and they are kept in excellent working order. Many surgeons have their own favorite design of scissors.

Artery forceps: If an artery or a vein is cut during the course of surgery, it is first clipped with artery forceps in two places, and the vessel is cut between the two forceps. Artery forceps look a little like scissors at first glance, but are really a pair of tiny pincers, with a ratchet mechanism on the handle so that they stay shut at a particular tension. There are dozens of different designs of artery forceps, differing only slightly in size and shape.

Retractors: These are specially shaped pieces of metal that are used to hold the edges of the wound open during an operation. They can be held by an assistant, or are designed to be self-retaining, that is, they are attached to a frame so that they can be fixed into the wound at a predetermined distance apart. Surgery on the abdomen would be impossible without adequate retraction.

As well as all these instruments, there are countless others that are used for various specialist procedures. In the

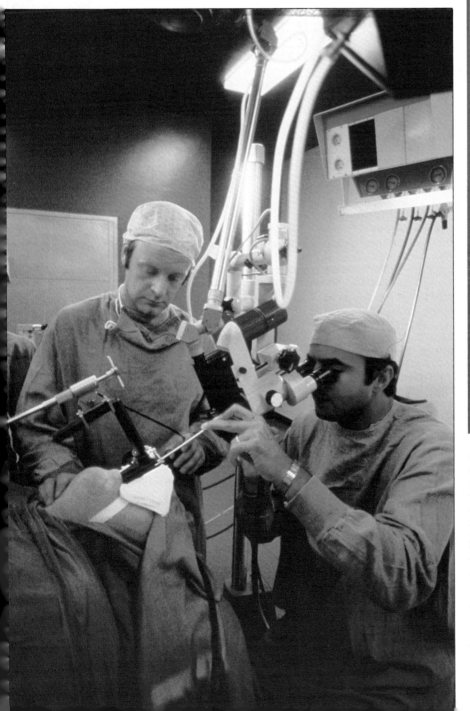

Surgeons: who they are	
Title of specialty	**What they do**
Neurological surgeon	Brain and spinal cord
Ear, nose, and throat surgeon	Nose, tonsils, adenoids, tongue, face, ears, larynx, thyroid gland, upper part of esophagus, floor of mouth
Ophthalmic surgeon	Eyes
Orthopedic surgeon	Bones (except the bones of the skull)
Obstetrician & Gynecologist	Uterus, ovaries, vagina, and cesarian births
Thoracic surgeon	Heart, lungs, esophagus, diaphragm, chest wall
Pediatric surgeon	Babies and small children
Urologist	Kidneys, ureters, bladder, urethra, prostate gland
General surgeon	Stomach, gallbladder, liver, intestines, appendix, breasts, thyroid, glands in face (salivary glands), main arteries and veins, lumps under the skin, hernias, and hemorrhoids

operating room of today, there are various packs made up containing all the instruments that might be needed for a particular operation. The pack is labeled on the outside, and always has the same numbers and types of instrument for a particular procedure. This does not mean that some instruments are repeatedly sterilized and are not used, but the system does insure that time is not wasted during surgery. If an unexpected surgical procedure has to be undertaken during the course of another operation, then extra instruments can be brought in. At the end of surgery, all the instruments

Q How does the surgeon decide if and when surgery is the best form of treatment?

A This varies according to the particular condition that requires treatment. Some conditions, such as cancer of the colon, are best treated by surgery, and this would be performed unless the patient is otherwise unfit for surgery. Other conditions, such as a duodenal ulcer, could be treated either by surgery or by medication, and then the decision whether or not to operate is governed by such things as the patient's response to medical treatment or the likelihood of complications from the ulcer if surgery were not performed.

Q I am very frightened of needles, and am wondering how likely it is that I will have to have an IV after I have my appendix removed. Is it possible to do without an IV?

A Most patients have an IV after any surgery on the abdomen. This prevents the patient becoming dehydrated during the postoperative period when he or she is unable to drink adequately. There is nothing unusual today about having an IV.

Q A few days ago my husband had surgery on his stomach and is terribly worried that he might burst the stitches by coughing or moving about. Is this possible?

A No, the materials used to stitch the abdominal wall are extremely strong, and it is very unlikely that coughing would cause them to break.

Q Is the catgut that surgeons use for stitches really made from cats' intestines?

A No, it is not real catgut. It is made from the lining of sheep's intestines, and is the same material used for the strings of musical instruments. However, the surgical variety is treated so that it is free from bacteria. Surgical catgut usually takes about two weeks to dissolve completely.

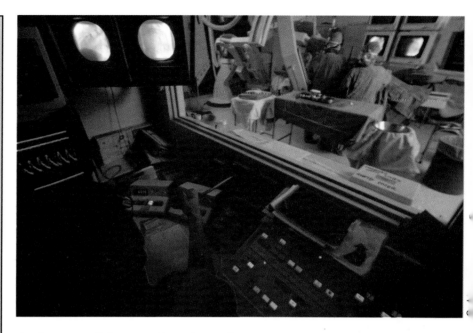

that have actually been used are cleansed and put back in the tray with the unused instruments. The whole tray is then checked carefully before being wrapped up, labeled, and sterilized ready for the next time. A large modern hospital has many duplicate sets of instruments so that several operations can be performed on the same day without having to wait for the instruments to be resterilized.

Microsurgery

The use of the operating microscope, from the 1960s onward, was the third major revolution in surgery. These binocular instruments were introduced first by ophthalmic (eye) surgeons and were then taken up by otologists (ear surgeons). They allowed a remarkable degree of delicacy and precision so that operations previously impossible soon became routine (see Microsurgery).

Microsurgery rapidly highlighted the relative crudeness of current operating instruments, and a succession of generations of ever more delicate, miniaturized, and refined tools were developed specially for use under the microscope. Soon surgeons in other disciplines exploited microsurgery and it gradually extended its scope. Vascular surgeons, concerned with repair to small blood vessels, neurologic surgeons joining cut nerves, and gynecologists working on fallopian tubes and suspected cancer of the cervix, all found that the scope of their practice could be greatly extended by microsurgery.

One of the most spectacular advances allowed by this technique is the successful reattachment of whole limbs that have been severed in accidents. This involves rejoining arteries, veins, nerves, tendons, and muscles.

Operating rooms in many major hospitals are built with observation rooms, which enable doctors and students to watch surgical procedures being performed.

Minimally invasive surgery

Experience has shown that the factor mainly responsible for the length of the recovery period after surgery is the time taken for a long incision to heal. Surgical incisions involve not only skin, but also muscle and various tissue planes under the skin. The development of fiberoptic and other forms of internal viewing instruments (endoscopes) made it possible for the interior of the body to be examined either through natural orifices or through a tiny surgical opening. Surgeons then found that it was easy to take small samples (biopsies) for pathological examination through the endoscopes. The next step was the introduction of endoscopic instruments that could perform surgical procedures other than cutting.

When it became apparent that a range of surgical operations could be done through two or three ports—short metal or plastic tubes less than half an inch across—the fourth surgical revolution was under way. Ports involve tiny incisions and small splits in the muscle layers. Often these require only one or two stitches. Gases are blown in to make space, then miniaturized, closed-circuit television cameras can be used via fiberoptic channels. Instruments can be operated by remote control while the surgeon sits comfortably watching his or her progress on a TV monitor. It is even possible for a surgeon in New York to perform an operation on a patient in London. After this kind of surgery, patients can often return to full activity the following day.

The surgeon

The person who performs operations is known as a surgeon. He or she is a qualified doctor who then goes on for further specialist training, but this was not always so. At one time, surgeons were members of the Worshipful Company of Barber-surgeons, that is, they were barbers who also dabbled in a bit of surgery. The barber's pole, with its red and white stripes, is supposed to be a symbol of a bandage and blood.

After qualifying as a doctor, a person who wants to become a surgeon has to pass further exams to become a fully qualified surgeon. He or she takes these examinations in separate parts over a period of about five years after qualifying, and while he or she is working as an apprentice surgeon. During this time the surgeon learns to perform operations himself or herself, being taught by an experienced senior surgeon.

People often wonder how a training surgeon gets to do his first operation. In fact, it is a gradual process, starting with very small surgical procedures under strict supervision, and building up to more major surgery. By the time a trainee surgeon performs a major operation, he or she has probably helped the senior surgeon with the same type of operation many times.

What the job entails

A surgeon's job entails seeing patients, examining them, diagnosing the cause of their symptoms, and then deciding whether or not the condition is best treated with medication, or by surgery. If the surgeon decides to treat the patient with medication, the surgeon may undertake this task, or may ask a physician (a medical specialist who treats illnesses with drugs) to see the patient and take over the case. If he or she decides that surgery is appropriate, then the relevant procedure will be performed.

It may be that at the time of the operation there are several options open and the surgeon will have to decide which is the most suitable operation to perform in light of what he or she knows about that patient and his or her illness.

After the operation, the surgeon will see the patient on the floor and deal with any complications, should they arise. He or she will also be responsible for seeing the patient on follow-up visits until he or she feels that the patient is well enough to be discharged back into the care of

All the equipment used in surgery must be accounted for after the operation—even the swabs. These absorbent pads, which are used to keep the operating site free from blood, are hung up and counted.

their own physician. The contemporary surgeon, therefore, may be considerably involved in the care of the patient, both before and after the operation. In fact, he or she probably spends only about one-third of the work time actually operating.

Different types of surgery

It would be difficult to give a list of all the different operations that are done on the human body, as it would run into hundreds, but in general they fall into eight broad groups. They are: repair operations on hernias, fractured bones, or parts of the body that have suffered injury; removal of tumors, ulcers, limbs, and overactive glands; division of strictures, such as releasing tight fibrous bands pressing on a nerve; transplantation of organs; insertion of prostheses such as breast implants, and heart valves; bypassing blocked arteries; correction of congenital deformities; and skin grafts.

Obviously things can go wrong with surgical operations (for example, damage to other structures near the operative site, bleeding, infection, or poor wound healing) but, fortunately, with improved skills and technology these risks have been greatly reduced.

Surgeons are divided into groups of specialists such as neurologic, ear, nose, and throat, opthalmic, orthopedic, obstetric, thoracic, pediatric, and urologic. Each surgeon has his or her own territory, except for the general surgeon, who is trained to do a wide range of operations. Most general surgeons, however, also tend to be specialists within one smaller field.

The vast majority of hospitals have at least one general surgeon, but not every hospital has the other specialists, and so the general surgeon may often be called on to perform a wide range of operations in an emergency.

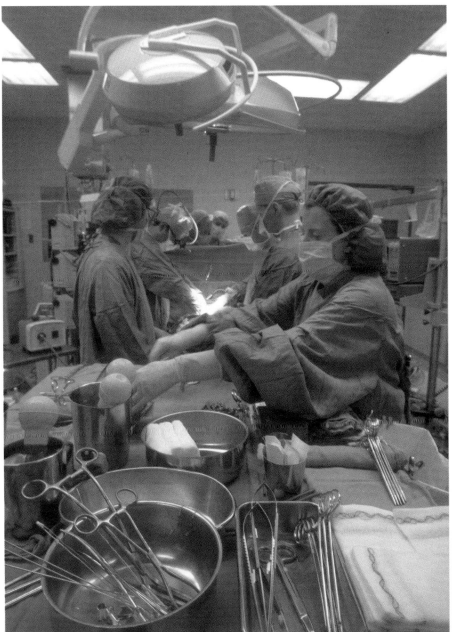

Corbis

Surrogacy

Q How much does a couple usually have to pay to arrange to have a child by a surrogate mother?

A If the couple arranges for a surrogate mother through an agency, which has become the normal route, they can expect to pay around $25,000; $10,000 of that typically goes to the surrogate mother. The agency gets the remaining $15,000. Part of that goes to pay the surrogate's medical expenses, and part goes to pay health and legal professionals.

Q What are some of the features of a typical surrogate contract?

A A typical surrogate contract requires the surrogate to agree to be inseminated with sperm provided by the man whose wife is sterile, to carry the child conceived to term, and to surrender the child to the couple for adoption immediately after delivery. The contract would require the couple to pay the surrogate's medical bills, and a specified fee for her services, and to take the child whether or not it has any mental or physical defects. Some contracts require the surrogate mother to undergo amniocentesis, and then to abort the fetus if the results of the test show any abnormality.

Q Why would a woman want to go through pregnancy and the pain of labor to have a baby for someone else?

A According to some surrogate mothers, they enjoy being pregnant. Some have already had children and look forward to being pregnant without the responsibility of raising another child. Others have had an abortion or a miscarriage, or have experienced loss in their lives and feel a need to resolve it by bearing a child, even if it is for someone else. Some women do it out of a sincere desire to help a couple have the baby they could not have by themselves. But some women may have done it just for the money. This last motive is the one that has given the most concern.

The controversy surrounding surrogate motherhood is made all the more difficult by the sadly ironic fact that most of those on both sides of the issue say they are driven by the same noble motive—the love of children.

Surrogate motherhood is fast becoming one of the thorniest controversies of modern family law. The technical aspects of maternal surrogacy involve major arguments between those who favor this arrangement and those who do not.

The types of surrogacy

The term *surrogate mother* was first used in connection with a very sophisticated medical procedure called in vitro fertilization (IVF) and embryo transfer (see In vitro fertilization). This technique was first employed in the late 1970s in situations where both prospective parents were fertile but an abnormality affecting the woman, such as blocked or missing fallopian tubes, prevented conception (see Conception). In this procedure, an ovum is surgically removed from the woman, fertilized outside her body with her husband's sperm, and then transferred into the woman's uterus.

But some women are not able to bear a child. One out of every 1,000 women, for example, is born without a uterus—and a variation of the IVF/embryo transfer procedure is used to overcome the problem. The fertilized egg is transferred into the uterus of another woman, who then carries the pregnancy to term. In a most unusual surrogacy arrangement of this type, a 48-year-old woman gave birth to triplets in 1987. She was acting as a surrogate for her daughter, so the children she gave birth to were her genetic grandchildren (see Genetics).

The term *surrogate mother* is also applied to a different sort of maternal surrogacy arrangement known as artificial insemination (see Artificial insemination). This procedure involves injecting semen into the vagina when an anatomic abnormality in the male prevents direct fertilization, or when the male is infertile (see Infertility). In the latter case, the sperm is usually provided by an anonymous donor. The child that is conceived is genetically linked to the inseminated woman but not to her husband.

The newest use of artificial insemination resulted in 65 births in 1986, and gave rise to the latest meaning of the term *surrogate mother*. This method involves introducing the sperm of a man whose wife is infertile into a woman who has contracted to bear the child conceived as a result of the insemination, which is then given to the couple after the birth. The genetic father of the child

An ultrasound scan shows a clear profile of the developed head of a human fetus at 22 weeks' gestation.

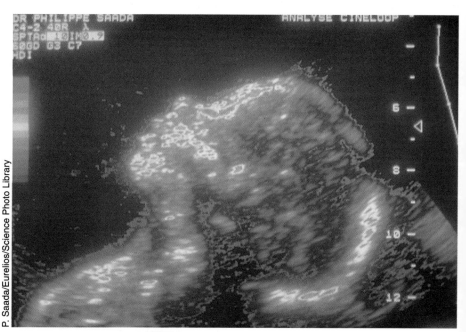

P. Saada/Eurelios/Science Photo Library

is obviously the husband. There is no biological link, however, between the child and the wife.

The whole issue of surrogate motherhood received national attention in 1986, when a surrogate mother, Mary Beth Whitehead, refused to surrender the daughter she had borne for Elizabeth Stern and her husband, William, with whose sperm she had been artificially inseminated. Mrs. Whitehead and the Sterns had been brought together by a private agency specializing in surrogate parenting arrangements. After a long and widely publicized trial, a judge ruled that the contract between Mrs. Whitehead and the Sterns was valid and assigned sole custody of the child to Mr. Stern. Mrs. Whitehead later won on appeal.

Another distressing case occurred in Britain in 1997. A nurse, age 31, had agreed with a Dutch married couple to undergo artificial insemination with the husband's semen and to hand over the resulting baby at birth. The couple had paid her $18,000. The nurse had become pregnant, but in May 1997 informed the couple that she had aborted the baby. A few days later, however, she confessed that this was untrue and that she had lied because she wanted to keep the baby.

The case received wide publicity and acted as a focus for the expression of public opinion on the matter of surrogacy. As is inevitable in such matters, emotions were aroused and views were strongly polarized. One view expressed abhorrence at the idea of treating babies as commodities to be traded; the other was the view that women have the right to have children, whatever the means.

This case also prompted an editorial in the prestigious British medical journal, the *Lancet*. In this, attention was drawn to Article 16 of the Universal Declaration of Human Rights issued by the General Assembly of the United Nations in 1948. The article states that: "Men and women of full age, without any limitation due to race, nationality or religion, have the right to marry and to found a family."

Medical advances since 1948 have brought possibilities that could never have been considered by those who drafted this Article, and the declaration has been interpreted as justifying all kinds of procreative methods. One of the consequences of such methods is, of course, surrogacy, with all its accompanying social and ethical problems.

The *Lancet* editorial makes the point strongly that "the rampant marketization of reproductive medicine demands urgent reassessment." There is criticism of the lack of leadership shown by the medical profession in calling for serious study of the reasons for these ethical shifts and

Colin Ramsey

evaluation of their likely consequences. "This shameful silence," it concludes, "leaves the market as the only voice to be heard, a voice that threatens to drown out those who raise even the most reasoned of objections."

The arguments involved

The Catholic Church, which opposes all forms of intervention that it feels sever procreation from the marital union, has stated that surrogate motherhood "offends the dignity and the right of the child to be conceived, carried in the womb, brought into the world and brought up by its parents."

Other institutions and individuals object to any form of parental surrogacy on a variety of moral, ethical, and philosophical grounds.

However, it is surrogate motherhood arrangements like the one entered into by Mary Beth Whitehead and the Sterns that have galvanized surrogacy advocates and opponents.

The advocates have argued that for many couples a surrogacy arrangement is their only hope of ever having a baby, and that a woman donating her ovum is really not all that different from the widely accepted practice of a man donating his sperm to a sperm bank.

Those who are opposed to surrogacy argue that anonymously donating sperm is a far cry from the woman's role of being artificially inseminated, bringing a

There are more than a dozen privately operated (and unregulated) surrogacy centers in major US cities. Careful screening of both prospective parents and the surrogate mothers, proponents argue, may help prevent problems such as those in the Mary Beth Whitehead case. Some 85 percent of applicants to be surrogate mothers are rejected by some agencies as psychologically or physically unsuitable.

pregnancy to term, giving birth, and then having to surrender the baby.

Some people worry about the long-term effects of surrogacy on the surrogate mother. How many surrogate mothers will come to regret their decision the way Mary Beth Whitehead did? But champions of surrogate parenting contend that the great majority of surrogate mothers actually experience a sense of fulfillment from having helped a couple in need. They also suggest that women like Mary Beth Whitehead, who found she could not part with the child, would probably not become surrogate mothers in the first place if they were given better psychological counseling initially.

The antisurrogacy camp wonders about the adverse reactions children might have when they learn that their genetic mothers brought them into the world, probably for a fee, and then surrendered them. They question also if these children will experience profound feelings of rejection and how their own

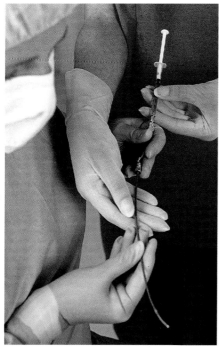

Hank Morgan/Science Photo Library

Following in vitro fertilization, a catheter is used to transfer the healthy embryo into the mother's uterus via the cervix.

tice is essential. Under normal circumstances, the woman who bears the child is legally the mother, and her husband, if any, is legally the father. Surrogacy legislation cannot entirely ignore this principle, which is based on more than purely historical principles. It is also based on the recognition, or at least the strong presumption, that the woman who bears and delivers the child, even if it is genetically unrelated to her, has a greater psychological and legal claim on the child than anyone else.

Surrogacy disputes have given rise to several custody cases and, in these, this principle has usually been upheld. It is not, however, universally held. Some research has shown that at least 40 percent of people may dispute it and opt for the genetic relationship. Many women take this view, although the view is more prevalent among men.

The question of the rights of embryos to achieve existence as humans may also have to be considered by legislators. This has been held to be grounds for allowing surrogacy in cases in which a frozen embryo would otherwise be destroyed.

In the 1989 frozen embryo case, Judge Young found for the potential mother, Mary Sue Davies, holding that such an embryo should be defined as a "human being waiting to be born."

The argument against surrogate parenting arrangements that seems to have raised the most concern is that surrogate motherhood is little more than a formalized form of baby selling. No state, of course, permits a couple to sell a baby,

and most states have statutes that forbid compensating a woman who offers her child for adoption.

The antisurrogacy forces say that states should pass bills that at least prohibit the payment of a fee that goes above and beyond medical expenses to any surrogate mother. They would also make illegal the fees paid to the agencies that make surrogacy arrangements.

Those in favor of surrogate parenting counter that it is not baby selling, because the father is genetically related to the child. Many women, they claim, would still be willing to act as surrogates even if fees were made illegal.

Many state legislatures are now considering bills that would either strictly regulate surrogate parenting arrangements or would make them entirely illegal. Some would permit the practice, but limit or prohibit the payment of fees to the surrogate mother or to any intermediaries. Most would require psychological counseling for the prospective surrogate mother, legal representation for all parties, and court approval of the conditions set down in the contract.

While some pending legislation would require a surrogate mother to surrender the child to the father at the time of birth, other bills propose allowing the surrogate a specified period of time following the birth to decide if she still wants to give the child up.

Whatever laws are passed they are sure to be tested in the courts, and the debate over surrogate motherhood will no doubt be with us for some time to come.

After the birth, the surrogate mother fulfills her part of the contract and hands over the child for adoption.

future attitudes about having and raising children will be influenced. The prosurrogacy camp responds that these children would not exist were it not for the arrangement between the surrogate mother and the sperm donor, and that bringing children into the world in this way will soon be so common that surrogate-born children will not feel unusual.

In the light of these conflicting arguments, it would seem to be almost impossible to arrive at an ethical arrangement for surrogacy that does not simultaneously offend some people and interfere with the liberties or rights of others.

Attempts to establish guidelines are apt to end in paradox. This is inevitable since the central fact in surrogacy is the separation of gestation, with its emotional and emotive elements, from nurturing, rearing, and upbringing, which has its own emotional concomitants. This consequence of surrogacy, incidentally, highlights the extraordinary level of compassion shown by voluntary surrogate mothers in carrying and then donating the child, usually to a relative, without thought of personal gain. It is in striking contrast to the blatant consumerism of women who think they can use surrogacy as an easy way to earn a large sum of money. The experience of such women is apt to be a painful reminder to them that there are more important things than money.

The need for legislation

The issues of human rights that are raised by surrogacy are so pressing that effective legislation to control the prac-

Rex Features

Sutures

Q Does it hurt to have skin stitches removed after some kinds of surgery?

A No, not really. Today the materials used for skin stitches are much smoother than the old materials and slide easily through the tissues. It's really only the thought of having stitches out that makes it hurt. If you are worried about it, ask the surgeon to put in absorbable stitches.

Q After major surgery do the internal stitches last a long period of time?

A Yes. Some of the stitch material used will last for a lifetime. Monofilament nylon, for instance, is virtually inert and does not provoke any reaction from the tissues. It will still be there in 30 years' time, although it may be weaker than it was when it was originally inserted.

Q I have recently had surgery on my stomach. How long will the stitches have to stay in before they are removed?

A Usually between 7 and 10 days. If they are taken out before this time the skin may come apart; if they are left in longer the wound may develop an inflammation around the area where the stitches have been put in.

Q After surgery on the abdomen, is it possible to burst the stitches by coughing or straining?

A Nowadays it is extremely unusual for this to happen. It is the internal stitches that determine the strength of an abdominal wound closure, not the stitches in the skin. Most surgeons therefore use a nonabsorbable material, such as nylon, to repair the muscle layers. Previously, catgut was used, but this lost its strength so quickly that it was possible to burst the wound. Now, however, if the abdominal muscles have been stitched up satisfactorily with the kind of thread that lasts indefinitely, the stitches should easily be able to bear the strain of repeated coughing.

What we call stitches, surgeons call sutures. They are one and the same thing—a simple way of keeping a wound closed while the tissues heal.

When a surgeon is stitching tissues back together he or she may, surprisingly enough, use stitches that are very like those used by a tailor or dressmaker (see Surgery). The materials used can be divided into two basic types: those that dissolve over a period of time, and those that last for a lifetime. The former includes catgut and Dexon, a synthetic substance, while the latter includes nylon, silk, linen, and wire.

Methods and materials

The two edges of a wound may be stitched together in different ways. A continuous stitch may be used with a knot at each end, or the same effect can be obtained by inserting a row of separate stitches, each with its own knot. The latter method (interrupted sutures) insures that if one knot comes undone, or the material used breaks, then the whole seam will not come apart.

The decision whether or not to use absorbable stitches depends on many factors, the most important being the speed at which the tissues are likely to heal. Dissolvable sutures lose their strength early and so are used when healing occurs quickly, such as in stomach repair surgery, when the wound will heal in a few days (see Healing). On the other hand, for a hernia repair, most surgeons use nylon stitches, which remain strong for many years, and especially until scar tissue has formed. If absorbable sutures were used, the hernia would be more likely to recur.

Skin stitches

There are many ways of joining the skin together. Continuous or interrupted stitches may be used, with absorbable or nonabsorbable materials. Metal clips or staples may be used, or butterflies made of adhesive tape. Where nonabsorbable sutures are chosen, they are usually nylon or silk, and are left in the skin for about a week, until healing is far enough advanced for the wound not to reopen.

Sutures on the face are usually removed after a few days because the skin heals quickly, and also because, if left too long, the stitches will leave puncture marks. Absorbable sutures, usually inserted as one continuous thread just beneath the skin, cannot be seen from the outside.

The interrupted vertical mattress and subcuticular stitches are those most commonly used. The latter eliminates any scarring from holes made by the needles. Deep sutures are used with other stitches when there would be a gap, or dead space, beneath the surface. With all three kinds, however, each stitch is individually tied, so that if one gives way, the others remain secure, unlike in continuous stitching. The actual choice is dictated by the surgeon's preference, and by practicalities such as tissue type, location, and final cosmetic appearance.

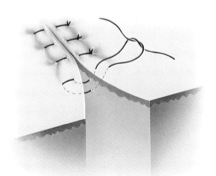

Interrupted vertical mattress sutures

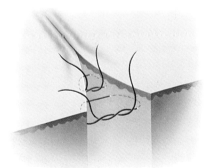

Interrupted subcuticular sutures

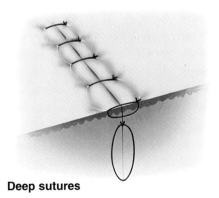

Deep sutures

Mike Courteney

Swellings

Q My four-year-old son seems to have swollen neck glands all the time. Why is this?

A Children have large lymph glands and tonsils to deal with new virus infections with which they are in contact. The glands swell in response to various infections such as tonsillitis and return to their normal size when the infection has been overcome, but may still remain fairly large.

Q Why does the ankle swell so much if it is sprained?

A When standing still, half your body weight is supported by each leg. When you walk, all your weight is transferred from one foot to the other. A minor twist of the ankle when it is bearing a whole body's weight can result in severe damage to the ligaments that support it. Fluid leaks from the tiny damaged blood vessels into the tissues around the ankle. You may or may not see obvious bruising. The best way to decrease the painful swelling is to use ice to constrict the blood vessels, then elevation, compression (with an elasticized bandage), and NSAIDs.

Q Why do some people's feet swell on long air journeys?

A Normally, blood is helped on its journey back to the heart from the feet by muscles that squeeze the veins when a person is walking. Sitting for long periods with the feet down does not improve the return of blood to the heart. The atmospheric pressure in an airplane is usually a bit low, and all these factors allow fluid to escape from the veins into the tissues of the feet. This is called edema, and the feet swell.

Q Why do my face and tongue swell dramatically when I eat shellfish?

A You are allergic to the shellfish. This condition of swelling caused by allergy is known as angioneurotic edema. You should never eat shellfish—always ask what is in food that you have not prepared yourself.

A swelling is usually just a simple and passing reaction to infection or injury. But even so, it should not be ignored, since it can also be a symptom of an underlying condition that may require prompt medical treatment.

Swellings can be found in any part of the body, in the skin or in the structures that lie beneath it. There are many causes of swellings, ranging from a boil beneath the skin to the hugely enlarged abdomen caused by pregnancy!

Infections and injuries

Swellings are caused by many different conditions. Infected areas become filled with blood to try to get rid of the invading bacteria or viruses. This is obvious in an infected finger, for example, which becomes swollen, red, hot, and painful.

Swelling also occurs as a result of injury, and is nature's way of cushioning the injured part and protecting it until it has had time to heal. This is often seen in a joint, such as the knee or ankle joint. The whole joint becomes filled with fluid in a bad injury. This fluid is made up of an increase in the normal synovial fluid found inside every joint, and fluid that leaks from torn capillary blood vessels and lymphatic vessels.

Edema

Many people have swollen ankles at some time in their lives. The swelling is caused by fluid that leaks from the small blood vessels of the lower legs and is not

Puffiness of the legs and ankles is a very common form of swelling, known as edema. Women are particularly vulnerable, especially those who are overweight or have varicose veins.

returned efficiently into the blood system to be pumped around the body. If the swelling is pressed firmly with the thumb, then the fluid is squeezed out from under the thumb, leaving a depression in the tissues. This swelling is called edema (see Edema).

Mild edema is very common. People who are overweight are more prone to ankle swelling. Women frequently notice that their ankles swell just before a period. Contraceptive pills may make this condition worse (see Contraception).

The ankles also have a tendency to swell during pregnancy, partly because of the increased pressure of the baby on the large veins in the pelvis. Very swollen ankles, however, may be a sign of toxemia of pregnancy and, therefore, should not be ignored. Some pregnant women may also find that their hands and faces swell a little (see Pregnancy).

Puffiness of the face, especially around the eyes, is also a very common form of minor swelling that frequently occurs on waking. The precise cause is not known, but the swelling can be reduced by lying on the back instead of on the face, avoiding heavy night creams, and splashing the face with very cold water.

More persistent edema is often a symptom of some underlying condition. For example, many forms of heart disease produce ankle swelling. If the swelling is severe, medical advice should be sought, especially if there is chest pain or shortness of breath (see Heart disease).

Varicose veins are also a common cause of swollen ankles (see Varicose veins). Thrombosis in a vein in the calf can cause a swollen ankle and a swollen painful calf because of the obstruction of the blood flow by a clot. Wearing elastic support hose will help to reduce an ankle swelling, and the sufferer should put his or her feet up as often as possible. Diuretic tablets may be prescribed to reduce the edema (see Diuretics).

Fluid also builds up in the body in a certain type of kidney disease (nephrotic edema), liver disease, and malnutrition. In all these cases there is a lack of protein in the blood, and water escapes into the tissues, producing swelling.

Long air journeys where travelers don't have the opportunity to move about often result in swollen feet and ankles. Always wear comfortable shoes or slippers and, if possible, keep your feet up.

Allergies

Sometimes people will swell up in just a few minutes if they are in contact with something they are allergic to, or if they have eaten something to which they are allergic. This can be alarming. Often the face is affected and the eyelids swell with fluid and may completely close the eyes. This condition of acute swelling caused by fluid in response to an allergic substance is called angioneurotic edema. The most common cause of this is probably an insect bite or sting (see Allergies).

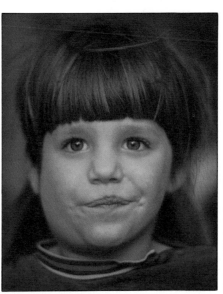

If you have ever suffered from this allergic condition, you should ask your doctor for advice. He or she will probably suggest you carry antihistamine tablets in the event of such an allergic reaction.

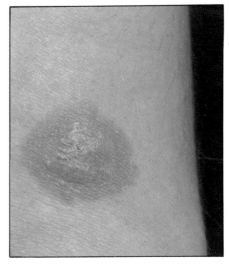

Institute of Dermatology

The body's reaction to an insect bite (above) or sting varies from person to person, and can range from simple inflammation to a dramatic swelling.

The characteristic swollen glands of mumps (left). This viral infection is common among children and causes inflammation of the salivary glands.

Sally and Richard Greenhill

Quantas

Anthea Sieveking/Vision International

Skin swellings

Urticaria is a skin condition where hard, white, itchy swellings quickly appear in the skin as a result of skin contact with an allergic substance.

The skin is often the site for swellings, either from sebaceous cysts or from fatty lumps, known as lipomas. Both conditions are benign.

Sebaceous cysts are often seen in young men, on the neck or upper chest or scalp. They cause few problems unless they become infected, but are often removed for cosmetic reasons. Lipomas may range in size from being just noticeable to being the size of an orange. They are very common and are not painful.

Lumps or cysts in the skin are removed for three reasons: first, to improve the person's appearance and for his or her comfort; second, to make a diagnosis by looking at the tissue under a microscope; third, to remove any lump that is obviously malignant (see Cancer).

Glands

The glands in the neck often swell with a sore throat, or with a fever in a flulike illness. Most of these viral illnesses disappear in two to three days, and the best thing to do is to go to bed, drink plenty of

Ankles often swell during pregnancy. Resting with the legs raised will help keep discomfort to a minimum (above).

fluid, and take soluble aspirin or acetaminophen to reduce the temperature and ease headache, sore throat, and general aches and pains.

Sometimes the swollen glands persist, together with a sore throat, and then infectious mononucleosis (see Infectious mononucleosis) may be suspected, especially if the patient is a teenager or a young adult.

In mononucleosis all the body's lymphatic glands and the spleen may be enlarged (see Spleen). It may take some time to recover completely from this condition, as it often leaves the sufferer feeling lethargic and debilitated.

Breasts

The breasts should be examined regularly for swellings. They sometimes vary in size and texture during the menstrual cycle and will also enlarge during pregnancy. The best time to examine them is just after a period (see Breasts).

If, on examination, you should find any lump or swelling, you should always see your doctor. Many breast lumps are not

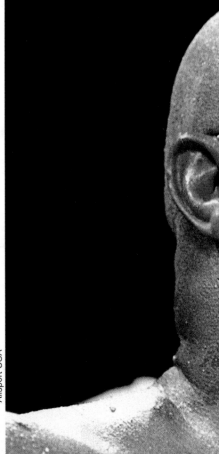

Allsport USA

serious, but cancer in a breast should be treated without delay, as the chances of a cure are high if it is diagnosed and treated quickly (see Mammography).

Abdomen

Swelling of the abdomen has many causes. Constipation caused by too little fiber in the diet is common. Many women find their abdomens distend before a period and return to normal afterward. This is caused by hormonal changes.

Painful sudden swelling of the abdomen may be due to intestinal obstruction or some other acute cause, and medical attention should be sought. Abdominal swelling without any pain may also be caused by the enlargement of one or more of the organs within the abdomen, or by fluid, and should be reported to your doctor immediately.

Ruptures

A hernia, or rupture, is a swelling that contains intestine that has pressed through a weak point of the muscular wall of the

Wisdom teeth trying to break through can lead to infection. The affected area then becomes swollen in an attempt to fight off the invading bacteria (above). A pilar cyst (right) sometimes appears as a swelling in the area of the eyebrow.

Swollen features are an occupational hazard in the world of boxing, as George Foreman displays (below).

abdomen so that a loop of intestine lies just under the skin.

In babies and young children the two most common hernias are an umbilical hernia at the navel and an inguinal hernia in the groin. An inguinal hernia is a lump in the groin that enlarges or appears on coughing, and may pass into the scrotum in a boy. Umbilical hernias normally disappear spontaneously by the age of five. Inguinal hernias can appear at any age and usually need surgery because of the risk of trapping the intestine and causing obstruction and gangrene. If the hernia is large, then the intestine is unlikely to get trapped and a truss may be offered instead of surgery. This is a device which presses on the weakness in the muscular abdominal wall to prevent the intestine from emerging (see Hernia).

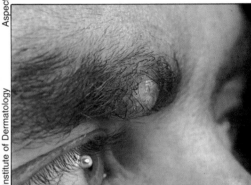

See your doctor...

- if you have a new ankle swelling and symptoms such as shortness of breath, chest pain, or fatigue
- if you have a very swollen, painful joint. If you know you have injured the joint, apply a firm elasticized bandage and take painkillers and rest it as much as possible. The swelling should disappear in a few days. If it doesn't, see your doctor
- if you would like a skin lump removed for cosmetic reasons, or if you are worried about it
- if you have an infection in the skin that is more than a small boil
- if you swell up in response to an allergic substance
- if you have a growing swelling and you don't know what it is
- if you have a swollen abdomen that you don't think is due to being overweight or being constipated, or having poor muscle strength
- if you notice a breast lump
- if you have a hernia